California Central District

Bankruptcy

COURT AND CHAMBERS PRACTICE MANUAL

BANKRUPTCY COURT
Selected General Orders

INDIVIDUAL JUDGES
Procedures and Practices
Case Management Orders and Forms
Chambers and Biographical Information

Mid-2012 Edition

Compiled by Practicing Attorneys
Meliora Law

Printed and bound in the United States of America.
ISBN: 978-0-9838302-1-4

Comments and corrections may be sent to comments@melioralaw.com. Although the publisher has made every effort to ensure the accuracy of information contained in this publication, it cannot assume liability for inadvertent errors.

Meliora Law LLC
19250 Stevens Creek Boulevard, Suite 100
Cupertino, CA 94015
www.melioralaw.com

PUBLISHER'S PREFACE

The information contained herein are current as received through March 2012.

THE PUBLISHER

March 2012

TABLE OF CONTENTS

This page intentionally left blank.

This page intentionally left blank.

PART I

Bankruptcy Court

Selected General Orders

I. General Orders

A. *General Order No. 96-06 – Order Grantable as a Matter of Course by the Clerk of the Bankruptcy Court*

IN THE UNITED STATES BANKRUPTCY COURT
FOR THE CENTRAL DISTRICT OF CALIFORNIA

In re	
	GENERAL ORDER 96-06
ORDER GRANTABLE AS A MATTER OF COURSE BY THE CLERK OF THE BANKRUPTCY COURT	

WHEREAS, the Court may issue any order, process, or judgment that is necessary or appropriate to carry out provisions of the Bankruptcy Code pursuant to Section 105(a) of the Bankruptcy Code,

IT IS HEREBY ORDERED that the following orders may be entered by the Clerk of the Bankruptcy Court without further direction from the Court as a matter of course:

1. ORDER FIXING TIME TO FILE CLAIMS (FOR POSSIBLE DIVIDENDS)
2. ORDER FIXING TIME TO FILE CLAIMS (FOR SURPLUS OF FUNDS)
3. ORDER FOR CREDITORS TO FILE CLAIMS INCURRED AFTER THE COMMENCEMENT OF THE CHAPTER 11 PROCEEDINGS
4. ORDER TO COMPLY WITH FRBP 1007 AND 3015(b) AND NOTICE OF INTENT TO DISMISS CASE UNDER 11 U.S.C. SECTION 109(g)(1)
5. ORDER OF DISMISSAL FOR FAILURE TO FILE COMPLETE CASE COMMENCEMENT DOCUMENTATION
6. ORDER OF DISMISSAL FOR FAILURE TO FILE COMPLETE CASE COMMENCEMENT DOCUMENTATION WITH 180-DAY RESTRICTION
7. ORDER OF DISMISSAL FOR FAILURE TO FILE SCHEDULES, STATEMENTS, OR PLAN WITH 180-DAY RESTRICTION
8. ORDER OF DISMISSAL FOR FAILURE TO FILE SCHEDULES, STATEMENTS, OR PLAN
9. ORDER OF DISMISSAL FOR FAILURE TO APPEAR AT 341(a) MEETING OF CREDITORS WITH 180-DAY RESTRICTION
10. ORDER OF DISMISSAL FOR FAILURE TO APPEAR AT 341(a) MEETING OF CREDITORS (BUSINESS ONLY)
11. ORDER DISMISSING PROCEEDING FOR FAILURE TO PAY CLERK'S FILING FEES

12. ORDER OF DISMISSAL FOR FAILURE TO COMPLY WITH INSTALLMENT PAYMENT SCHEDULE
13. ORDER OF DISMISSAL FOR FAILURE TO COMPLY WITH LOCAL RULE 105(6)(c) – FILING OF DISKETTE FOR CASES WITH MORE THAN 100 CREDITORS OR EQUITY HOLDERS
14. ORDER TO SHOW CAUSE RE: DISMISSAL FOR FAILURE TO PAY CONVERSION FEE
15. ORDER OF DISMISSAL FOR FAILURE TO PAY CONVERSION FEE
16. ORDER CLOSING A DISMISSED CASE
17. ORDER DISCHARGING DEBTOR
18. ORDER DISCHARGING DEBTOR AFTER COMPLETION OF CHAPTER 12 PLAN
19. ORDER DISCHARGING DEBTOR AFTER COMPLETION OF CHAPTER 13 PLAN
20. ORDER TO SHOW CAUSE RE: DISMISSAL FOR FAILURE TO REPAY FILING FEES FOR INSUFFICIENTLY FUNDED CHECK
21. ORDER TO SHOW CAUSE RE: DISMISSAL FOR FAILURE TO COMPLY WITH LOCAL RULE 105(6)(c) – FILING OF DISKETTE FOR CASES WITH MORE THAN 100 CREDITORS OR EQUITY HOLDERS
22. ORDER TO SHOW CAUSE RE: DISMISSAL FOR NONPAYMENT OF FILING FEES PURSUANT TO FRBP 1006(a) or (b)
23. ORDER VACATING THE ORDER OF CONVERSION (DUE TO CLERICAL ERROR)
24. ORDER VACATING DISCHARGE (DUE TO CLERICAL ERROR)
25. ORDER VACATING ORDER OF DISMISSAL (DUE TO CLERICAL ERROR)
26. ORDER FOR RELIEF AND ORDER TO FILE SCHEDULES, STATEMENTS, AND LISTS
27. ORDER TO FILE FINAL REPORT AND ACCOUNT AND SCHEDULE OF UNPAID DEBTS INCURRED AFTER COMMENCEMENT OF THE CHAPTER 11, 12, OR 13 PETITION PURSUANT TO FRBP 1019(5)
28. ORDER DISCHARGING TRUSTEE AND CLOSING CASE.

DATED: August 12, 1996

____

CALVIN K. ASHLAND
Chief Judge
United States Bankruptcy Court

B. *General Order No. 96-02 – Judicial Workload Equalization Pilot Program*

IN THE UNITED STATES BANKRUPTCY COURT
FOR THE CENTRAL DISTRICT OF CALIFORNIA

In re	)	
	)	**GENERAL ORDER 96-02**
JUDICIAL WORKLOAD	)	
EQUALIZATION PILOT	)	
PROGRAM	)	
______________________	)	

The Ninth Circuit has established a Workload Equalization Pilot Program that allows for the hearing and determination of all issues through trial in certain adversary proceedings by designated judges from other districts within the Ninth Circuit.

IT IS HEREBY ORDERED that, effective immediately, the United States Bankruptcy Court for the Central District of California implement the Judicial Workload Equalization Pilot Program.

For adversary complaints which have been selected for this program, the procedure for filing papers with the Court is as follows:

(a) The parties shall continue to file the original and one copy of the adversary complaint with the Clerk of the United States Bankruptcy Court, Central District of California. The Clerk will transmit a copy of the complaint to the designated judge of the other participating court;

(b) Except in those instances where a judge's signature is required, the parties shall continue to file the original and one copy of all subsequent pleadings with the Clerk of the United States Bankruptcy Court, Central District of California. In addition, the parties shall mail a separate copy of all subsequent pleadings directly to the chambers of the judge of the other participating court;

(c) Where a judge's signature is required, such as on a default judgment, summary judgment or pre-trial order, the original and one copy shall be mailed directly to the chambers of the judge of the other participating court and a copy filed with the Central District of California Bankruptcy Court.

Proceedings requiring physical appearances will continue to be held in Los Angeles. It is the intent of the program that issues be resolved via teleconferencing whenever possible; however, it will be at the discretion of the judge hearing the matter whether an in-court appearance will be required or whether teleconferencing will be utilized.

DATED: March 27, 1996

____
CALVIN K. ASHLAND
Chief Judge
United States Bankruptcy Court

C. *General Order No. 95-01 (Third Amended) – Adoption of Mediation Program for Bankruptcy Cases and Adversary Proceedings*

IN THE UNITED STATES BANKRUPTCY COURT
FOR THE CENTRAL DISTRICT OF CALIFORNIA

In re)
)
ADOPTION OF MEDIATION PROGRAM FOR BANKRUPTCY CASES AND ADVERSARY PROCEEDINGS)

THIRD AMENDED GENERAL ORDER 95-01

1.0 PURPOSE AND SCOPE

The United States Bankruptcy Court for the Central District of California (the "Court") recognizes that formal litigation of disputes in bankruptcy cases and adversary proceedings frequently imposes significant economic burdens on parties and often delays resolution of those disputes. The procedures established herein are intended primarily to provide litigants with the means to resolve their disputes more quickly, at less cost, and often without the stress and pressure of litigation.

The Court also notes that the volume of cases, contested matters and adversary proceedings filed in this district has placed substantial burdens upon counsel, litigants and the Court, all of which contribute to the delay in the resolution of disputed matters. A Court-authorized mediation program, in which litigants and counsel meet with a mediator, offers an opportunity for parties to settle legal disputes promptly, less expensively, and to their mutual satisfaction. The judges of the Court hereby adopt the Mediation Program for Bankruptcy Cases and Adversary Proceedings (the "Mediation Program") for these purposes.

It is the Court's intention that the Mediation Program shall operate in such a way as to allow the participants to take advantage of and utilize a wide variety of alternative dispute resolution methods. These methods may include, but are not limited to, mediation, negotiation, early neutral evaluation and settlement facilitation. The specific method or methods employed will be those that are appropriate and applicable as determined by the mediators and the parties, and will vary from matter to matter.

Nothing contained herein is intended to preclude other forms of dispute resolution with the consent of the parties.

2.0 CASES ELIGIBLE FOR ASSIGNMENT TO THE MEDIATION PROGRAM

Unless otherwise ordered by the judge handling the particular matter (the "Judge"), all controversies arising in an adversary proceeding, contested matter, or other dispute in a bankruptcy case are eligible for referral to the Mediation Program.

3.0 PANEL OF MEDIATORS

3.1 Selection.

a. The Court shall establish and maintain a panel ("Panel") of qualified professionals who have volunteered and been chosen to serve as a mediator ("Mediator") for the possible resolution of matters referred to the Mediation Program. The Panel shall be comprised of both attorneys and non-attorneys.

b. Applicants shall submit an Application (in the form attached) (the "Application") to the judge appointed as the administrator of the Mediation Program (the "Mediation Program Administrator"), setting forth their qualifications as described in Paragraph 3.3 below.

c. The judges of the Court will select the Panel from the applications submitted to the Mediation Program Administrator. The judges will consider each applicant's training and experience in mediation or other alternative dispute resolution, if any, as well as the applicant's professional experience and location. Appointments may be limited to keep the Panel at an appropriate size and to ensure that the Panel is comprised of individuals who have broadbased experience, superior skills, and qualifications from a variety of legal specialties and other professions.

3.2 Term. Mediators shall serve as members of the Panel for a term of 3 years unless the Mediator is advised otherwise by the Court or submits a written request to withdraw from the Panel to the Mediation Program Administrator. Reappointment will occur at the judges' discretion, and an application for reappointment is not required.

3.3 Qualifications.

a. Attorney Applicants. An attorney applicant shall certify to the Court in the Application that the applicant:

1. Is, and has been, a member in good standing of the bar of any state or of the District of Columbia for at least 5 years;

2. Is a member in good standing of the federal courts for the Central District of California;

3. Has served as a principal attorney of record in at least 3 bankruptcy cases (without regard to the party represented) from case commencement to conclusion or, if the case is still pending, to the date of the Application, or has served as the principal attorney of record for a party in interest in at least 3 adversary proceedings or contested matters from commencement to conclusion or, if the case is still pending, to the date of the Application; and

4. Is willing to undertake to evaluate or mediate at least one matter each quarter of each year, subject only to unavailability due to conflicts, personal or professional commitments, or other matters which would make such service inappropriate.

b. Non-Attorney Applicants. A non-attorney applicant shall certify to the Court in the Application that the applicant has been a member in good standing of the applicant's particular profession for at least 5 years, and shall submit a statement of professional qualifications, experience, training and other information demonstrating, in the applicant's opinion, why the applicant should be appointed to the Panel. Non-attorney applicants shall make the same certification required of attorney applicants contained in Paragraph 3.3.a.4.

3.4 **Geographic Areas of Service.** Applicants shall indicate on the Application all counties within the Central District in which they are willing to serve. Applicants must be willing to travel to all such counties to conduct Mediation Conferences.

4.0 ADMINISTRATION OF THE MEDIATION PROGRAM

The Chief Judge will appoint a judge of the Court to serve as the Mediation Program Administrator. The Mediation Program Administrator will be aided by assigned staff members of the Court, who will maintain and collect applications, maintain the roster of the Panel, track and compile results of the Mediation Program, and handle such other administrative duties as are necessary.

5.0 ASSIGNMENT OF MATTERS TO THE MEDIATION PROGRAM

5.1 **Assignment by Request of Parties.** A contested matter in a case, adversary proceeding, or other dispute (hereinafter collectively referred to as "Matter" or "Matters") may be assigned to the Mediation Program if requested in writing by the parties in the form attached as Official Forms 701 and 702.

5.2 **Assignment by Judge.** Matters may also be assigned by order of the Judge at a status conference or other hearing. While participation by the parties in the Mediation Program is generally intended to be voluntary, the Judge, acting *sua sponte* or on the request of a party, may designate specific Matters for inclusion in the Mediation Program. The Judge may do so over the objections of the parties. If a Matter is assigned to the Mediation Program by the Judge at a status conference or other hearing, the parties will be presented with an order assigning the Matter to the Mediation Program, and with a current roster of the Panel. The parties shall normally be given the opportunity to confer and to select a mutually acceptable Mediator and an Alternate Mediator from the Panel. If the parties cannot agree, or if the Judge deems selection by the Judge to be appropriate and necessary, the Judge shall select a Mediator and an Alternate Mediator from the Panel.

5.3 **Assignment of Non-Panel Mediators.** The Judge may, in his or her sole discretion, appoint individuals who are not members of the Panel as the Mediator and Alternate Mediator at the request of the parties and for good cause shown.

5.4 **Use of Official Court Order Assigning Matter to Mediation Program.** The order appointing the Mediator and Alternate Mediator and assigning a Matter to the Mediation Program shall be in the form attached as Official Form 702 ("Mediation Order"). The original Mediation Order shall be docketed and retained in the case or adversary proceeding file and copies shall be mailed, by the party so designated by the Judge, to the Mediator, the Alternate Mediator, the Mediation Program Administrator, and to all other parties to the dispute.

5.5 **Existing Case Deadlines Not Affected by Assignment to Mediation.** Assignment to the Mediation Program shall not alter or affect any time limits, deadlines, scheduling matters or orders in the case, any adversary proceeding, contested matter or other proceeding, unless specifically ordered by the Judge.

5.6 Disclosure of Conflicts of Interest. No Mediator may serve in any Matter in violation of the standards regarding judicial disqualification set forth in 28 U.S.C. § 455.

a. Disclosure by Attorney Mediators. An attorney Mediator shall promptly determine all conflicts or potential conflicts in the manner prescribed by the California Rules of Professional Conduct and disclose same to all parties in writing. If the attorney Mediator's firm has represented one or more of the parties, the Mediator shall promptly disclose that circumstance to all parties in writing.

b. Disclosure by Non-Attorney Mediators. A non-attorney Mediator shall promptly determine all conflicts or potential conflicts in the same manner as a non-attorney would under the applicable rules pertaining to the non-attorney Mediator's profession and disclose same to all parties in writing. If the Mediator's firm has represented one or more of the parties, the Mediator shall promptly disclose that circumstance to all parties in writing.

c. Report of Conflict Issue by Parties. A party who believes that the assigned Mediator and/or the Alternate Mediator has a conflict of interest shall promptly bring the issue to the attention of the Mediator and/or the Alternate Mediator, as applicable, and shall disclose same to all parties in writing.

d. Resolution of Conflict Issue by Judge. If the Mediator and/or the Alternate Mediator does not withdraw from the assignment, the issue shall be brought to the attention of the Judge in writing by the Mediator, the Alternate Mediator, or any of the parties in the form attached as Official Form 704. The notice shall be filed with the Court, and copies of the notice shall be mailed to the Judge, all of the parties to the dispute, their counsel, if any, the Mediator, the Alternate Mediator, and the Mediation Program Administrator. The Judge will then take whatever action(s) he or she deems necessary and appropriate under the circumstances to resolve the conflict of interest issue.

6.0 CONFIDENTIALITY

6.1 In General. No written or oral communication made, or any document presented, by any party, attorney, Mediator, Alternate Mediator or other participant in connection with or during any Mediation Conference, including the written Mediation Conference statements referred to in Paragraph 7.8 below, may be disclosed to anyone not involved in the Mediation, nor may any such communication be used in any pending or future proceeding in this Court or any other court. All such communications and documents shall be subject to all of the protections afforded by FRBP 7068. Such communication(s) may be disclosed, however, if all participants in the Mediation, including the Mediator, agree in writing to such disclosure. In addition, nothing contained herein shall be construed to prohibit parties from entering into written agreements resolving some or all of the Matter(s), or entering into or filing procedural or factual stipulations based on suggestions or agreements made in connection with a Mediation Program conference ("Mediation Conference").

6.2 Non-Confidentiality of Otherwise Discoverable Evidence. Notwithstanding the foregoing, nothing herein shall require the exclusion of any evidence otherwise discoverable merely because it is presented in the course of a Mediation Conference.

6.3 Written Confidentiality Agreement Required. The parties and the Mediator shall enter into a written confidentiality agreement in the form attached as Official Form 708.

6.4 Effect of Recorded Settlement Agreement on Confidentiality. An oral agreement reached in the course of a Mediation Conference is not made inadmissible or protected from disclosure if all of the following conditions are satisfied:

a. The oral agreement is recorded by a court reporter, tape recorder, or other reliable means of sound recording;

b. The terms of the oral agreement are recited on the record in the presence of the parties and the Mediator, and the parties express on the record that they agree to the terms recited;

c. The parties to the oral agreement expressly state on the record that the agreement is enforceable or binding or words to that effect; and

d. The recording is reduced to writing and the writing is signed by the parties and their counsel, if any, within 3 days after it is recorded.

6.5 Effect of Written Settlement Agreement on Confidentiality. A written settlement agreement prepared in the course of a Mediation Conference is not made inadmissible or protected from disclosure if the agreement is signed by the settling parties and their counsel, if any, and either of the following conditions are satisfied:

a. The agreement provides that it is admissible or subject to disclosure, or words to that effect; or

b. The agreement provides that it is enforceable or binding or words to that effect.

6.6 Court Evaluation of Mediation Program Not Precluded by Confidentiality Provisions. Nothing contained herein shall be construed to prevent Mediators, parties, and their counsel, if any, from responding in absolute confidentiality to inquiries or surveys by persons authorized by the Court to evaluate the Mediation Program.

6.7 Confidentiality of Suggestions and Recommendations of Mediator. The Mediator shall have no obligation to make any written suggestions or recommendations but may, as a matter of discretion, provide counsel for the parties (or the parties, where proceeding in *pro per*), with a written settlement recommendation memorandum. No copy of any such memorandum shall be filed with the Court or made available, in whole or in part, directly or indirectly, to the Judge.

7.0 MEDIATION PROCEDURES

7.1 Selection of Mediator. Counsel for the parties (or the parties, where proceeding in *pro per*), are encouraged to contact the proposed Mediator and Alternate Mediator as soon as practicable (preferably before submitting the Mediation Order to the judge for approval, if possible) to determine the availability of the Mediator and Alternate Mediator to serve in the Matter.

7.2 Availability of Mediator. If the Mediator is not available to serve in the Matter, the Mediator shall notify the parties, the Alternate Mediator, and the Mediation Program Administrator of that unavailability by mail in the form attached as Official Form 703 as soon as possible, but no later than 7 days from the date of receipt of notification of appointment. **Upon notification of the Mediator's unavailability to serve, the Alternate Mediator shall automatically serve as the Mediator without the necessity for further court order.**

7.3 Availability of Alternate Mediator. If the Alternate Mediator is not available to serve in the Matter, the Alternate Mediator shall notify the parties and the Mediation Program Administrator of that unavailability by mail in the form attached as Official Form 703 as soon as possible, but no later than 7 days from the receipt of notification by the Mediator, pursuant to Paragraph 7.1 above, of the Mediator's unavailability to serve.

7.4 Selection of Successor Mediator.

a. By Parties. Within 7 days of receipt of the Alternate Mediator's notification of unavailability, the parties shall choose a mutually acceptable Successor Mediator and Successor Alternate Mediator by mail in the form attached as Official Form 702. (This is the same Official Form which is used to appoint the original Mediator and Alternate Mediator, as described in Paragraph 5.4 above. However, the word "Successor" **must** be inserted in the caption of the Mediation Order in front of the words "Mediator" and "Alternate Mediator"). The parties shall file such form with the Court and provide a courtesy copy to the Judge and the Mediation Program Administrator.

b. By Judge. If the parties are unable to agree on a choice of Successor Mediator and Successor Alternate Mediator, they shall notify the Judge and the Mediation Program Administrator of their inability to do so by mail in the form attached as Official Form 704. In that event, the Judge shall appoint the Successor Mediator and Successor Alternate Mediator.

c. Use of Official Court Order Assigning Successor Mediator. When the Successor Mediator and Successor Alternate Mediator have been chosen by the parties and/or appointed by the Judge, the Judge shall execute an order appointing the Successor Mediator and Successor Alternate Mediator in the form attached as Official Form 702. (This is the same Official Form which is used to appoint the original Mediator and Alternate Mediator, as described in Paragraph 5.4 above. However, the word "Successor" **must** be inserted in the caption of the Mediation Order in front of the words "Mediator" and "Alternate Mediator").

7.5 Initial Telephonic Conference. Promptly, but no later than 14 days of receipt of notification of appointment, the Mediator shall conduct a telephonic conference with counsel for the parties (or the parties, where appearing in *pro per*) to discuss (a) fixing a convenient date and place for the Mediation Conference, (b) the procedures that will be followed during the Mediation Conference, (c) who shall attend the Mediation Conference on behalf of each party, (d) what material or exhibits should be provided to the Mediator before the Mediation Conference, and (e) any issues or maters that it would be especially helpful to have the parties address in their written Mediation Conference Statements.

7.6 Mediation Conference Scheduling. Also within 14 days of receipt of notification of appointment, the Mediator shall give notice to the parties of the date, time and place for the Mediation Conference. The Mediation Conference shall commence no later than 30 days following the receipt of notification by the Mediator, and shall be held in a suitable neutral setting such as the office of the Mediator, or at a location convenient and agreeable to the parties and the Mediator.

a. Continuance of Mediation Conference. The date for the Mediation Conference may be continued for a period not to exceed 30 days upon written stipulation between the Mediator and the parties. The stipulation need not be filed with the Court but the parties must mail a copy of it to the Judge and the Mediation Program Administrator.

b. Additional Continuance. At the written request of the parties and for good cause shown, the Judge may, in his or her sole discretion, approve an additional continuance of the Mediation Conference beyond the period specified in Paragraph 7.6.a.

7.7 Mandatory Service of Mediation Order Prior to Mediation Conference. Prior to the Mediation Conference, the parties' counsel shall serve a copy of the Mediation Order on the Mediator, Alternate Mediator, Mediation Program Administrator, and all parties to the dispute.

7.8 Mediation Conference Statements. Each party shall submit a written Mediation Conference statement ("Mediation Statement") directly to the Mediator and to the parties to the Mediation Conference no less than 7 days prior to the date of the initial Mediation Conference, unless modified by the Mediator.

a. Format. Mediation Statements shall not exceed 10 pages, excluding exhibits and attachments. Mediation Statements shall comply with all of the requirements of Court Manual Section 2-5, unless such compliance is excused by the Mediator.

b. Confidentiality. Mediation Statements shall be subject to all of the protections afforded by the confidentiality provisions contained herein and by FRBP 7068.

c. Statements Not Filed with Court. The Mediation Statements shall not be filed with the Court, and the Judge shall not have access to them. In addition, the phrase **"CONFIDENTIAL – NOT TO BE FILED WITH THE COURT"** shall be typed on the first page of the Mediation Statements.

d. Mandatory Contents. Mediation Statements must:

1. Identify the person(s), in addition to counsel, who will attend the Mediation Conference as representative(s) of the party, who have authority to make decisions;

2. Describe briefly the substance of the dispute;

3. Address any legal or factual issue(s) that might appreciably reduce the scope of the dispute or contribute significantly to settlement;

4. Identify the discovery that could contribute most to preparing the parties for meaningful discussions;

5. Set forth the history of past settlement discussions, including disclosure of any prior and any presently outstanding offers and demands;

6. Make an estimate of the cost and time to be expended for further discovery, pretrial motions, expert witnesses and trial;

7. Indicate presently scheduled dates for further status conferences, pretrial conferences, trial, or otherwise; and

8. Attach copies of the document(s) from which the dispute has arisen (*e.g.*, contracts), or the document(s) whose availability would materially advance the purposes of the Mediation Conference.

e. Recommended Additional Contents. Parties may identify in the Mediation Statements the person(s) connected to a party opponent (including a representative of a party opponent's insurance carrier) whose presence at the Mediation Conference would substantially improve the prospects for making the session productive. The fact that a person has been so identified shall not, by itself, result in an order compelling that person to attend the Mediation Conference.

f. Additional Mediation Statements for Mediator Only. Each party may submit directly to the Mediator, for his or her eyes only, a separate confidential Mediation Statement describing any additional interests, considerations, or matters that the party would like the Mediator to understand before the Mediation Conference begins. Such Mediation Statements shall not exceed 10 pages, excluding exhibits and attachments, and shall comply with all of the requirements of Court Manual Section 2-5, unless such compliance is excused by the Mediator.

7.9 Mandatory Attendance at Mediation Conference.

a. By Counsel. Counsel for each party who is primarily responsible for the Matter (or the party, where proceeding in *pro per*) shall personally attend the Mediation Conference and any adjourned session(s) of that conference, unless excused by the Mediator for cause. Counsel for each party shall come prepared to discuss all liability issues, all damage issues, and the position of the party relative to settlement, in detail and in good faith.

b. By Parties. All individual parties, and representatives with authority to negotiate and to settle the Matter on behalf of parties other than individuals, shall personally attend the Mediation Conference and any adjourned session(s) of that conference, unless excused by the Mediator for cause. Each party shall come prepared to discuss all liability issues, all damage issues, and the position of the party relative to settlement, in detail and in good faith.

c. **By Governmental Agencies.** A unit or an agency of government satisfies this attendance requirement if represented by a person who has, to the greatest extent feasible, authority to settle, and who is knowledgeable about the facts of the case, the governmental unit's position, and the procedures and policies under which the governmental unit decides whether to accept proposed settlements.

d. **Telephonic Appearance.** Any party or lawyer who is excused by the Mediator from appearing in person at the Mediation Conference may be required by the Mediator to participate by telephone. This decision is within the Mediator's sole discretion.

7.10 Consequences of Failure to Attend Mediation Conference and Other Violations of Mediation Program Procedures. Willful failure to attend the Mediation Conference and/or other violations of the Mediation Program procedures shall be reported to the Judge by the Mediator by written notice in the form attached as Official Form 705, and may result in the imposition of sanctions by the Judge. The Mediator's notice shall be filed with the Court and copies of the notice shall be mailed to the Judge, all of the parties to the dispute, their counsel, if any, and the Mediation Program Administrator. The Judge will then take whatever action(s) he or she deems necessary and appropriate under the circumstances to resolve the issue of such willful failure to attend the Mediation Conference and/or other violations of the Mediation Program procedures.

7.11 Conduct at the Mediation Conference. The Mediation Conference shall proceed informally. Rules of evidence shall not apply. There shall be no formal examination or cross-examination of witnesses. The Mediator may conduct continued Mediation Conferences after the initial session where necessary. As appropriate, the Mediator may:

a. Permit each party (through counsel or otherwise) to make an oral presentation of its position;

b. Help the parties identify areas of agreement and, where feasible, enter into stipulations;

c. Assess the relative strengths and weaknesses of the parties' contentions and evidence, and explain as carefully as possible the reasoning of the Mediator that supports these assessments;

d. Assist the parties, through separate consultation or otherwise, in settling the dispute;

e. Estimate, where feasible, the likelihood of liability and the dollar range of damages;

f. Help the parties devise a plan for sharing the important information and/or conducting the key discovery that will assist them as expeditiously as possible to participate in meaningful settlement discussions or to posture the case for disposition by other means; and

g. Determine whether some form of follow up to the Mediation Conference would contribute to the case development process or to settlement.

7.12 Suggestions and Recommendations of Mediator. If the Mediator makes any oral or written suggestions as to the advisability of a change in any party's position with respect to settlement, the attorney for that party shall promptly transmit that suggestion to the client. The Mediator shall have no obligation to make an written comments or recommendations, but may, as a matter of discretion, provide the parties with a written settlement recommendation memorandum. No copy of any such memorandum shall be filed with the Court or made available in whole or in part directly or indirectly, to the Judge.

8.0 PROCEDURE UPON COMPLETION OF MEDIATION CONFERENCE

8.1 Upon the conclusion of the Mediation Conference, the following procedures shall be followed:

a. If Matter Settled. If the parties have reached an agreement regarding the disposition of the Matter, the parties, with the advice of the Mediator, shall determine who shall prepare the writing to dispose of the Matter. If necessary, the parties may, with the Mediator's consent, continue the Mediation Conference to a date convenient for all parties and the Mediator. Where required, they shall promptly submit a fully executed settlement stipulation to the Judge for approval, and shall mail a copy to the Mediation Program Administrator. The Judge will accommodate parties who desire to place any resolution of a Matter on the record during or following the Mediation Conference.

b. Mediator's Certificate of Completion of Conference. Within 14 days of the Mediation Conference, the Mediator shall file with the Court and serve on the parties and the Mediation Program Administrator a certificate in the form attached as Official Form 706, which shows whether there has been compliance with the Mediation Conference requirements and whether or not a settlement has been reached. Regardless of the outcome of the Mediation Conference, the Mediator will not provide the Judge with any details of the substance of the Mediation Conference.

c. Confidential Evaluation. In order to assist the Mediation Program Administrator in compiling useful data to evaluate the Mediation Program and aid the Court in assessing the efforts of the members of the Panel, the Mediator shall provide a Mediation Conference Report to the Mediation Program Administrator in the form attached as Official Form 709. The Mediation Conference Report shall not be filed with the Court and the Judge shall **not** have access to it. In addition, the phrase **"CONFIDENTIAL – NOT TO BE FILED WITH THE COURT"** shall be typed on the first page of the Mediation Conference Report.

9.0 *PRO BONO* AND COMPENSATED SERVICE OF MEDIATORS

9.1 Mandatory *Pro Bono* Service. The Mediator shall serve on a *pro bono* basis and shall not require compensation or reimbursement of expenses for the first full day of at least one Mediation Conference per quarter per year. If, at the conclusion of the first full day of the Mediation Conference, it is determined by the parties that additional time will be both necessary and productive in order to complete the Mediation Conference, then:

> **a.** If the Mediator consents to continue to serve on a *pro bono* basis, the parties may agree to continue the Mediation Conference; or
>
> **b.** If the Mediator does not consent to continue to serve on a *pro bono* basis, the Mediator's compensation shall be on such terms as are satisfactory to the Mediator and the parties, and shall be subject to the prior approval of the Judge if the estate is to be charged with such expense.

9.2 Compensated Service Upon Completion of Mandatory *Pro Bono* Service. After a Mediator has concluded at least one *pro bono* mediation for the particular quarter, nothing herein shall prohibit the Mediator and the parties from agreeing that the Mediator may be compensated for services rendered by the Mediator. The amount of such compensation and the terms governing the amount and payment shall be as agreed upon among the parties. If applicable, any party or parties to the mediation may apply to the Judge for authorization to compensate the Mediator from property of the estate. Nothing in this provision, however, shall require any party to compensate a Mediator other than as may be mutually agreed upon among the parties and the Mediator.

10.0 IMPLEMENTATION

10.1 The Mediation Program became effective on July 1, 1995.

10.2 Judge Barry Russell is appointed the Mediation Program Administrator.

DATED: January 5, 2010

VINCENT P. ZURZOLO
Chief Judge,
United States Bankruptcy Court

This page intentionally left blank.

This page intentionally left blank.

PART II

Individual Judges

Procedures and Practices
Case Management Orders and Forms
Chambers and Biographical Information

Hon. Alan M. Ahart

Bankruptcy Judge

Contact Information

U.S. Bankruptcy Court, Central District of California
Courtroom 303
21041 Burbank Boulevard, Suite 342
Woodland Hills, CA 91367
Courtroom Deputy: (818) 587-2853

Biographical Information

Appointment(s):

- Appointed 04/04/88 by the United States Court of Appeals for the Ninth Circuit;
- Reappointed 04/04/02 by the United States Court of Appeals for the Ninth Circuit. (Current term expires 04/03/16.)

Education:

- University of California at Berkeley, 1970, A.B.;
- State University of New York, 1975, J.D.;
- University of Pennsylvania School of Law, Philadelphia, Pennsylvania, 1979, LL.M.

Career Record:

- Represented financial institutions before appointment to the bench in 1988.

Professional Memberships:

- Federal Bar Association

I. Judge Ahart's Procedures and Practices

A. *Procedure for Approval of Disclosure Statement and Confirmation of Chapter 11 Plan*

PROCEDURE FOR APPROVAL OF DISCLOSURE STATEMENT AND CONFIRMATION OF CHAPTER 11 PLAN FOR CASES ASSIGNED TO JUDGE ALAN M. AHART

A. Requests for orders approving disclosure statements pursuant to 11 U.S.C. § 1125 and for orders confirming a plan of reorganization pursuant to 11 U.S.C. § 1129 are motions within the meaning of Federal Rules of Bankruptcy Procedure 9013 and 9014. All motions must be supported by evidence admissible under the Federal Rules of Evidence.

B. Unless the Court orders otherwise upon request, and except as provided below, the proponent of any plan must use the form combined "Disclosure Statement and Plan of Reorganization for____________," which is available on the Court's website, www.cacb.uscourts.gov.

Please note: The combined "Disclosure Statement and Plan of Reorganization" utilized by Judge Alan M. Ahart is different from the separate Chapter 11 Disclosure Statement and Chapter 11 Plan adopted by the Central District of California as forms F3017-1 and F3018-1, respectively. However, while the procedures outlined herein differ somewhat from the procedures followed by the Honorable Vincent P. Zurzolo, the combined "Disclosure Statement and Plan of Reorganization" is the same.

An individual Chapter 11 debtor must use either 1) the combined "Disclosure Statement and Plan of Reorganization for " described above or 2) the separate Individual Debtor's Disclosure Statement in Support of Plan of Reorganization and Individual Debtor's Chapter 11 Plan of Reorganization, adopted by the Central District of California as forms F 2081-1.DISCLSR.STMT and F 2081-1.PLAN, respectively.

C. Hearings on approval of disclosure statements shall be set on at least 36 days notice, unless the Court prescribes a shorter period. The plan proponent must serve with the disclosure statement a notice of the disclosure statement hearing date and of the requirement that objections to disclosure statements must be filed and served on the proponent at least 14 days before hearing.

D. An amended disclosure statement shall not be filed before the initial hearing on the adequacy of the original disclosure statement. The Court strongly encourages all plan proponents to submit a copy of the disclosure statement to creditors, the United States trustee, and any committee prior to filing the disclosure statement with the Court, to permit changes pursuant to comments made by these parties in interest.

If a hearing on approval of the disclosure statement is continued to permit revision of the disclosure statement, the plan proponent shall make all necessary changes and prepare, in anticipation of the next hearing, "red-lined" copies of the amended disclosure statement. A "red-lined" copy and a "clean" copy should be filed with the Court and served on all other parties who appeared at the previous hearing.

E. After granting a disclosure statement motion, the Court shall:

(1) Set a deadline for filing of claims and for objecting to claims, if not already set; and

(2) Set a deadline for creditors and equity security holders to transmit ballots.
The disclosure statement should contain the hearing date for the Motion to Confirm the Plan.

F. A Confirmation Motion shall be prepared, filed and served in accordance with Local Bankruptcy Rule 9013-1 and therefore must meet at least the following criteria:

(1) The Confirmation Motion must be supported by evidence establishing that the plan is confirmable under 11 U.S.C. § 1129.

(2) The Confirmation Motion ordinarily must be served at least 21 days before the confirmation hearing on the United States Trustee, any official committee, and all impaired creditors and equity security holders who rejected the plan.

(3) If the disclosure statement does not specify the date for the confirmation hearing, the plan proponent must serve with the Confirmation Motion a notice of the confirmation hearing date and of the requirement that any party opposing the Confirmation Motion must file and serve, at least 14 days before the confirmation hearing date, its written opposition supported by evidence.

NOTE: Because the Confirmation Motion ordinarily must be served at least 21 days before the confirmation hearing, the proponent should select the confirmation hearing date so that sufficient time is given for ballots to be returned and for the preparation of the Motion.

G. Unless otherwise ordered, every order confirming a chapter 11 plan must contain the language required by Local Bankruptcy Rule 3020-1(b). The proposed order shall be accompanied by proof of payment of any special charges due the Clerk's Office as described in Local Bankruptcy Rule 3020-1(a).

B. Telephonic Appearance Guidelines

TELEPHONIC APPEARANCE GUIDELINES

Policy Governing Telephonic Appearances

Telephonic appearances before Judge Alan M. Ahart in courtroom 303 are allowed only due to extenuating circumstances as to why a party(ies) cannot appear in person. In order to appear telephonically counsel must strictly adhere to the following procedure:

I. Standard Procedure

At least 72 hours prior to the hearing, counsel must call the Courtroom Deputy for Judge Ahart to arrange their telephonic appearance. Counsel may reach the Courtroom Deputy at 818.587.2853.

II. Emergency Procedure (Approval requested without 72 hours notice)

If an unexpected emergency arises that prevents counsel from following the standard procedure detailed above, counsel must telephone the courtroom deputy to obtain approval to appear telephonically. The courtroom deputy will only approve tardy requests for legitimate and unanticipated emergencies.

III. Procedure for Telephonic Appearance

Telephonic appearances are connected directly with the courtroom's public address system and electronic recording equipment so that a normal record is produced. To ensure the quality of the record, the use of car phones, cellular phones, speaker phones, public telephone booths, or phones in other public places is prohibited except in the most extreme emergencies. Participants should be able to hear all parties without difficulty or echo. At the time your matter is scheduled for hearing, the court clerk will call and connect you to the court's public address system.

After your call is connected to the courtroom, the Judge will call the case, request appearances, and direct the manner in which the hearing proceeds. Each time you speak, you should identify yourself for the record. When the Judge informs participants that the hearing is completed, you may disconnect.

Before the hearing you should check Judge Ahart's Calendar on the website, www.cacb.uscourts.gov, and review any Tentative Ruling concerning the matter on calendar. If the court has issued a Tentative Ruling prior to the hearing, each individual who appears telephonically should have reviewed the Tentative Ruling prior to the hearing.

If an individual schedules a telephonic appearance and then fails to respond to the call of a matter on calendar, the court may pass the matter or treat the failure to respond as a failure to appear. Furthermore, in deciding to appear telephonically, counsel is agreeing to waive any prejudice attributable to quality or irregularities of the record that may result.

Hon. Theodor C. Albert

Bankruptcy Judge

Contact Information

U.S. Bankruptcy Court, Central District of California
Courtroom 5B
411 West Fourth Street, Suite 5085
Santa Ana, CA 92701
Courtroom Deputy: (714) 338-5383

Biographical Information

Appointment(s):

- Appointed 06/01/05 by the United States Court of Appeals for the Ninth Circuit. (Current term expires 06/01/19.)

Education:

- Stanford University (California), 1971-75, B.A.;
- University of California, Los Angeles School of Law 1975-78, J.D.

Career Record:

- 1983-1995, Law office of Buchalter, Nemer, Fields & Younger, Newport Beach, California
- 1995, co-founded law practice Albert, Weiland & Golden, Costa Mesa, California
- 1978, admitted to California Bar

Professional Memberships:

- Orange County Bankruptcy Forum
- Orange County Bar Association
- State Bar of California

Awards:

- 2000, Peter M. Elliott Award for highest standard of ethics and scholarship.

I. Judge Albert's Procedures and Practices

A. *Early Meeting of Counsel and Joint Status Conference Instructions*

EARLY MEETING OF COUNSEL, JOINT STATUS CONFERENCE INSTRUCTIONS FOR JUDGE THEODOR C. ALBERT

1. A COPY OF THESE INSTRUCTIONS MUST BE ATTACHED TO THE COPY OF THE COMPLAINT SERVED UPON EACH PARTY, AND THE PROOF OF SERVICE OF THE SUMMONS AND COMPLAINT MUST INDICATE THAT SUCH COPY WAS SERVED THEREWITH.

2. These instructions apply only to parties represented by counsel. If you do not have an attorney, you must appear at the status conference in person.

3. The appearance at the status conference hearing may be made **by telephone** if arranged by calling **Court Call** at **(866) 582-6878** not later than **3:00 p.m.** the day prior to the court hearing date. Any request for telephonic appearance made after the 3:00 p.m. deadline is disfavored, and must be court approved by contacting Judge Albert's Calendar Clerk, Kim Ngo at (714) 338-5383 and be accompanied by a suitable explanation for the lateness.

4. If the proceeding involves money or property exceeding $10,000 or if the plaintiff believes trial time will be 4 hours or more, plaintiff must serve, with the summons and complaint, a notice in compliance with **Local Rule 7026-1**. Plaintiff must also file proof of service of the notice with proof of service of the summons and complaint.

5. If **Local Rule 7026-1** applies, counsel for the parties **MUST TIMELY MEET TO DISCUSS SETTLEMENT AND TO EXCHANGE DOCUMENTS, OTHER EVIDENCE, AND LISTS OF WITNESSES AND PRELIMINARY DISCOVERY SCHEDULES AS PROVIDED IN THE RULE**.

6. Unless all defendants have defaulted, the parties shall file a Joint Status Report pursuant to **Local Rule 7016-1(a)(2)** at least **fourteen (14) days** before the date of the status conference in a form substantially similar to **Local Form No. 7016-1.1**. If **Local Rule 7026-1** applies, the parties must include in the Joint Status Report a statement that they have met to discuss settlement and have exchanged documents, other evidence, lists of witnesses and preliminary discovery schedules. If cooperation in the filing of a Joint Status Report cannot reasonably be obtained, a Unilateral Status Report is expected from each appearing party with an explanation of the reasons why a Joint Status Report was not filed.

7. If no response to the complaint is timely filed, plaintiff may request entry of default by the Clerk or by the Court.

8. If the parties dispute whether the adversary proceeding is "**core**" or "**non-core**," they shall file points and authorities in support of their positions. Any party that contends the proceeding is "**non-core**" shall file and serve its points and authorities at least **fourteen (14) days** before the status conference. Any response must be filed and served at least **seven (7) days** before the status conference.

9. Failure to comply with these instructions may subject the responsible party to **sanctions**.

10. Failure of counsel for any party to appear at a status conference or pre-trial

conference may be considered an abandonment or failure to prosecute or defend diligently and the proceeding may be dismissed or judgment entered against the defaulting party.

11. Any demand for jury trial on any issue must be filed by either the plaintiff or defendant(s) within 10 days of the filing of the first pleading contesting the issue(s). Such demand must also contain a statement that the party does or does not consent to a jury trial conducted by the Bankruptcy Court. Within 10 days of the service of the demand and statement of consent or non-consent, all other parties shall file and serve a statement of consent or non-consent to a jury trial conducted by the Bankruptcy Court. *See McCarthy v. Bronson*, 906 F.2d 835 (2d Cir. 1990), *certiorari granted in part*, 11 S. Ct. 578, 498 U.S. 1011, 112 L. Ed. 584, *affirmed on other grounds*, 111 S. Ct. 1737, 500 U.S. 136, 114 L. Ed. 2D 194. *See also* LBR 9015-2 (a) and (b). Failure to abide by this instruction shall be deemed a waiver of the right to a jury.

B. Emergency Motions Procedures

EMERGENCY MOTIONS PROCEDURES FOR JUDGE THEODOR C. ALBERT

To obtain a hearing date for a motion on an emergency basis, the movant must file the following documents with the Clerk's Office:

1. Application for an order setting the hearing date for a motion on an emergency basis and a proposed order thereon;

2. Supporting declaration(s) justifying the setting of a hearing on an emergency basis; and

3. Motion, including all supporting papers, for which the movant seeks an emergency hearing.

To expedite the process of obtaining an emergency motion hearing date, when the movant files the documents with the Bankruptcy Court Clerk's Office, they should also place courtesy copies of all the pleadings in the courtesy copy box outside of Judge Albert's Chambers' door on 5th floor of the Santa Ana Divisional office, The Ronald Reagan Building, 411 West Fourth Street, Santa Ana, CA 92701-4593.

Judge Albert's Law Clerk will prepare an order (applicants are invited to submit Court-approved form orders) within 48 hours of the documents being filed. If the movant is not contacted by the Law Clerk within 48 hours of filing the emergency motion, the movant may call Amna Chaudhary, Judge Albert's Law Clerk, at (714) 338-5432.

C. Mandatory Use of L.O.U. for Section 362 Orders

MANDATORY USE OF L.O.U. FOR Section 362 Orders

Effective January 1, 2009

These guidelines apply to orders on motions: (1) for relief from the automatic stay; (2) to impose the stay; or (3) to continue the stay (collectively "Section 362 Orders").

The guidelines will add certainty to the process and minimize costs/delay by:

1) Utilizing electronic processes of filing documents ("CM/ECF"), Lodged Order Upload ("LOU"), and service by Notice of Electronic Filing ("NEF");

2) Clarifying the "Service List for Entered Order"; and

3) Eliminating the need to provide envelopes and copies of orders.

A. Check Tentative Rulings

Judge Albert posts tentative rulings one court day prior to hearings. Check to see if relief will be granted without a hearing, and if so, what relief. Go to www.cacb.uscourts.gov. The Tentative Rulings link is on the bottom left-hand corner of page one.

B. Lodge Proposed Orders via LOU

All CM/ECF users must lodge Section 362 Orders via LOU. NO exceptions.

C. When Should a Proposed Order be Lodged?

Lodged via LOU – Proposed orders may be lodged via LOU after tentative rulings are posted; if a tentative ruling is not posted, lodge the proposed order after the hearing.

Lodged at Intake Window – Non CM/ECF users may only lodge proposed orders after the hearing.

D. Are F 4001-1 Form Orders Mandatory?

MANDATORY FORMS – All Section 362 Orders must be prepared using a mandatory F-4001-1 order available at www.cacb.uscourts.gov under Local Bankruptcy Rules ("LBR") and Forms.

E. Preparing Proof of Service of Proposed Order

1. **Proposed Orders on Unopposed Motions** – There is no obligation to serve a proposed form of order on any person, entity, or attorney ***who did not file an opposition to the motion. This includes a case trustee or the United States trustee.***

2. **Proposed Orders on Opposed Motions** – Pursuant to LBR 9021-1(b)(4) and 9021-1(b)(3)(A), a proposed order must be served only upon any person, entity, or attorney who filed an opposition to the motion. ***There is no obligation to serve the proposed order on any other person or entity.***

F. Prepare Service List for Entered Order

Parties who will be served by the Court:

- Debtor
- Debtor's Counsel (if any)
- Case Trustee
- U.S. Trustee

- Movant
- Any person, entity, or attorney who filed an opposition to the motion

METHOD OF SERVICE

1. **Served Electronically by the Court** – List the names and email addresses *only* of attorneys who are listed in CM/ECF on the Electronic Mail Notice List to receive an email notice. ***The U.S. trustee and case trustee will always be in this category.*** (*See* the Court Manual for help in determining who receives electronic service.)

2. **Served via U.S. Mail by the Court** – list the names and mailing addresses of persons, entities, and/or attorneys listed in CM/ECF under Manual Notice List. ***The debtor will always be in this category.*** **DO NOT** list any of the same people being served electronically. **DO NOT** list anyone who is not one of the **Parties who will be served by the Court**. (*See* the Court Manual for help in determining who receives manual – U.S. Mail – service.)

3. **Service by Movant** – If Movant desires to serve a copy of the entered order on persons or entities not listed in **Parties who will be served by the Court**, movant may do so. Movant must then file a Declaration re proof of service listing the parties' names addresses and method of service. Under this category, Movant can list other lien holders, co-borrowers, or persons/entities they want to serve.

G. Copies of Proposed Order; Envelopes

All Section 362 Orders are served electronically by the Court via NEF to case trustees, the United States trustee, and to attorneys who are on the Electronic Mail Notice List for the particular bankruptcy case.

All Section 362 Orders are served by the Bankruptcy Noticing Center ("BNC") in Herndon, Virginia via U.S. Mail to debtor and to persons or entities that are on the Manual Notice List for the particular bankruptcy case.

1. Copies of All Proposed Orders, Regardless of How Lodged

DO NOT provide any copies of the proposed order for mailing, because copies will be printed either by the BNC (for all relevant addresses on the Manual Notice List) or by the court (in the rare, unique case).

ONLY SEND ONE COPY to the court along with the LOU receipt per the LOU procedures, and do so the same day that the proposed order is lodged.

2. Stamped, Addressed Envelopes, Regardless of How Proposed Order is Lodged

DO NOT provide envelopes for the debtor or other Manual Notice parties, as the BNC will prepare envelopes for them.

DO NOT provide envelopes for the case trustee or U.S. trustee or other Electronic Mail Notice parties, as they will be served electronically via NEF.

DO NOT provide envelopes for any other person or entity as it is the responsibility of the Movant to serve the entered order and provide the Court with a Declaration re proof of service.

D. Notice to Practitioners Regarding LBR 7016-1(a)(2)

NOTICE TO PRACTITIONERS – SANTA ANA DIVISION REGARDING REQUIREMENT FOR TIMELY FILING OF STATUS CONFERENCE REPORTS IN ADVERSARY PROCEEDINGS AND IMPOSITION OF SANCTIONS

The Judges of the Santa Ana Division have noticed a steady increase in the number of parties failing to file either timely or at all the status conference reports required under Local Bankruptcy Rule 7016-1(a)(2). The Rule requires a filing of the status conference report *at least 14 days* before the status conference and provides for imposition of sanctions under Local Rule 7016-1(f) for noncompliance. Until now the Judges have merely exhorted practitioners to remember the Rule and have threatened imposition of sanctions for noncompliance, but have rarely actually imposed sanctions. However, these measures appear to have been ineffective. Failure to abide by the Rule severely interferes with the processes of the Court and last-minute filing of status conference reports imposes an undue burden on the Court and its staff. **Therefore, please take notice that commencing January 2009 sanctions will be imposed** as the rule rather than the exception for failure to comply with Local Rule 7016-1.

E. Suggestions for Filing Objections to Multiple Claims

SUGGESTIONS FOR FILING OBJECTIONS TO MULTIPLE CLAIMS IN CHAMBERS OF JUDGE THEODOR C. ALBERT

The following is required when filing multiple objections to claims:

1. A complete copy of each objected-to proof of claim must be attached to the motion.

2. Each attached copy of a proof of claim must be authenticated by declaration.

3. Exhibit tabs must be numbered to correspond to the claim(s) docket numbers.

4. When the same type of objection is made to several claims, those claims must be grouped together.

Please see the NOTICE TO ATTORNEYS AND TRUSTEES RE: MULTIPLE OBJECTIONS TO CLAIMS CALENDAR procedures under Court Forms in the Court's website at <www.cacb.uscourts.gov>. For additional guidance, please call Judge Albert's Law Clerk, Amna Chaudhary at (714) 338-5432 or Kim Ngo, Courtroom Deputy at (714) 338-5383.

F. Telephonic Appearance Procedures

TELEPHONIC APPEARANCE PROCEDURES

I. POLICY GOVERNING TELEPHONIC APPEARANCES

Telephonic appearances are allowed in all matters before Judge Albert in Courtroom 5B except the following:

1. Trials and Evidentiary hearings (all counsel and all witnesses must appear in person).

2. Contested Chapter 11 Confirmation Hearings (debtor, debtor's counsel, and all objecting creditors must appear in person). All other parties in interest may appear telephonically.

3. Hearings on Reaffirmation Agreements (debtor must appear in person).

4. Any matter designated by the Court as one requiring a personal appearance.

No telephonic appearance will be allowed unless it is made through CourtCall, an independent conference call company, pursuant to the procedures set forth in Section II.

Before requesting a telephonic appearance, you should check Judge Albert's Calendar on the Court's website (www.cacb.uscourts.gov) and review any Tentative Ruling concerning the matter on calendar. (Click on Tentative Ruling Box on bottom left corner of homepage) If the court has issued a Tentative Ruling prior to the hearing, each individual who appears telephonically should have reviewed the Tentative Ruling prior to the hearing.

If an individual schedules a telephonic appearance and then fails to respond to the call of a matter on calendar, the court may pass the matter, treat the failure to respond as an intent to accept the tentative ruling, or treat the failure to respond as a failure to appear. Scheduling simultaneous telephonic appearances in multiple courts does not excuse a failure to appear.

The 3:00 p.m. deadline for scheduling telephonic appearances noted below is independent of the Tentative Ruling process. Late scheduling of a telephonic appearance is not justified by the fact that Tentative Rulings have not been posted on the court's website by 3:00 p.m. the day before the hearing.

Individuals making use of the conference call service are cautioned that they do so at their own risk. Hearings generally will not be rescheduled due to missed connections.

Parties are also cautioned to consider whether their cases are ones suitable to telephonic appearance. On closer, contested matters, there is no doubt that personal presence adds weight to the presentation of the case.

II. SCHEDULING A TELEPHONIC APPEARANCE

By telephone: Telephone appearances may be arranged by calling **CourtCall** at **(866) 582-6878** not later than **5:00 p.m.** the day prior to the court hearing date.

III. PROCEDURE FOR TELEPHONIC APPEARANCE

CourtCall will provide counsel with written confirmation of a telephonic appearance and give counsel a number to call to make the telephonic appearance. It is counsel's responsibility to dial into the call not later than 10 minutes prior to the scheduled hearing. **CourtCall does not place a call to counsel.** The initial charge per participant for a CourtCall appearance is $25 for the first 45 minutes, $6.50 for each additional 15 minutes. These rates are subject to change without prior notice; please confirm current rates with CourtCall.

Telephonic appearances are connected directly with the courtroom's public address system and electronic recording equipment so that a normal record is produced. To ensure the quality of the record:

- No car phones
- No cellular phones
- No speaker phones
- No public telephone booths, or phones in other public places

Exceptions to these restrictions may be permitted only in the most extreme circumstances.

At the time of your hearing you may initially be in the listening mode, in which case you will be able to hear the case before yours, just as if you were in the courtroom. After your call is connected to the courtroom, the Judge will call the case, request appearances, and direct the manner in which the hearing proceeds. Each time you speak you should identify yourself for the record. The court's teleconferencing system allows more than one speaker to be heard, so the Judge can interrupt a speaker to ask a question or redirect the discussion. When the Judge informs the participants that the hearing is completed, you may disconnect and the next case will be called.

Telephonic appearances by multiple participants are only possible when there is compliance with every procedural requirement. Sanctions may be imposed when there is any deviation from the required procedures or the Court determines that a person's conduct makes telephonic appearances inappropriate. Sanctions may include dropping a matter from calendar, continuing the hearing, proceeding in the absence of an unavailable participant, a monetary sanction, and/or a permanent prohibition against a person appearing telephonically.

G. Tentative Ruling Procedures

TENTATIVE RULING PROCEDURES FOR JUDGE THEODOR C. ALBERT

Tentatives are available via the Court's webPACER service. The Judge issues tentative rulings whenever possible and appropriate prior to the scheduled hearing date. Usually the tentatives are published by 4:00 p.m. the day prior to the scheduled hearings. Please do not call chambers to inquire if no tentative has been posted if it is before 4:00 p.m.

In most situations where tentative rulings are issued, an appearance is usually not required unless otherwise indicated in the tentative ruling. Please check the tentative for any appearance instructions.

If a tentative ruling is issued, a party may submit on the tentative by telephoning Judge Albert's Calendar Clerk/Courtroom Deputy, Kim Ngo, at (714) 338-5383 the **night before the hearing**. If she does not answer, please leave Kim a message that you will submit on the tentative. Kim will post this information the next morning under "Courtroom Deputy Notes" which the Judge will have on the bench. If you call the **day of the hearing**, and you cannot reach Kim directly, please call chambers at (714) 338-5430 to advise that you will submit on the tentative. If the Judge issues a tentative ruling in an uncontested matter and excuses the movant's appearance, or a party submits on the tentative, but a party appears in Court to contest the motion, the Judge will listen briefly and either allow the tentative ruling to stand or continue the hearing to allow the absent parties to be heard. The parties should check the Court's docket to verify the outcome of the hearing.

The moving party must lodge a proposed order that conforms to the Judge's tentative ruling, accompanied by a notice of entry, a service list, self-addressed, stamped envelopes bearing the names and addresses of those who are to receive a copy of the signed, entered order, along with the appropriate number of copies of the proposed order to go in those envelopes. The Court will prepare any e-filed orders.

You may deposit the proposed order and notice of entry, along with all the copies and envelopes, in the "order box" in the Courtroom (not in the Judge's courtesy copy box located outside of chambers) the day of the hearing. All proposed orders submitted after the hearing date must be lodged at the filing window.

H. Trial Procedures Supplemental to Local Rules

TRIAL PROCEDURES SUPPLEMENTAL TO LOCAL RULES

Trial Briefs: Unless otherwise ordered by the Court, trial briefs are required. Trial briefs shall be filed seven (7) calendar days prior to trial. Courtesy copies of the trial briefs should be delivered to Chambers 5085 on the same date. The parties are encouraged to include a brief statement of the pertinent facts in their briefs, with citation to exhibits.

Testimony: All direct testimony shall be by declaration unless:

i) the witness is adverse or refuses to give testimony by declaration; or

ii) the testimony is offered to impeach or rebut.

The parties may request permission to offer oral testimony supplementing matters covered in the declarations or present portions of the testimony in the declaration orally, and the Court may grant such a request in the interest of justice.

Witnesses whose declarations are offered shall be present for cross-examination when the declarations are offered into evidence (unless the parties agree otherwise).

Plaintiff(s) shall file and serve its/their declarations on counsel for the defendant(s) thirty (30) days before the trial date. Defendant(s) shall serve its/their declarations on counsel for the plaintiff(s) twenty-one (21) days before the trial date.

Evidentiary objections to any declaration must be served and filed at least seven (7) calendar days before the trial date.

Unless the parties stipulate in the pre-trial order to the admission of an exhibit, foundation for admission of exhibits (other than for impeachment or rebuttal purposes) shall be established in the declarations, although the Court may allow oral testimony for this purpose. Exhibits referenced in any declaration shall be offered into evidence when the declaration is offered into evidence.

Exhibits: On or before trial, the Court shall be given a bench copy of exhibits to be offered into evidence (other than exhibits offered for impeachment or rebuttal purposes). Counsel shall have sufficient conformed sets of exhibits for opposing counsel's witnesses and for each party in the proceeding. Counsel shall also have copies of exhibits used for impeachment or rebuttal for opposing counsel, witnesses and the Court. If the number of exhibits exceeds five (5), or if they are more than 10 pages in length, they shall be placed in a binder properly indexed, numbered, tabbed and consecutively bates stamped in the lower right corner of each page. An exhibit register shall be provided with each set of exhibits.

Continuance/Postponement of Trial: As a general rule, scheduled trials will not be continued prior to or at trial, except for compelling reasons and in the interest of justice. Motions/stipulations for continuance of the trial must be submitted in writing at least two (2) court days prior to the scheduled trial date with any explanatory declarations or other evidence supporting the continuance. Convenience of the parties or counsel alone ordinarily is **not** a sufficient reason for continuance. The parties will be contacted by the Judge's Law Clerk or Judicial Assistant as to whether the continuance has been granted or denied.

Settlement: In the event that the adversary matter is settled prior to trial, the parties shall immediately contact and advise the Judge's law clerk Amna Chaudhary, at (714) 338-5432.

Hon. William V. Altenberger

Bankruptcy Judge

Contact Information
U.S. Bankruptcy Court, Central District of California
Courtroom 1639
255 E. Temple Street, Suite 1634
Los Angeles, CA 90012
Courtroom Deputy: (213) 894-1485

Biographical Information

Appointment(s):

- Appointed to Recalled Bankruptcy Judge by the Seventh Circuit Court of Appeals, 2000
- Chief Bankruptcy Judge, Central District of Illinois, 1993-2000
- Bankruptcy Judge, Central District of Illinois, 1985-1993

Education:

- University of Illinois, 1957
- University of Illinois, J.D., 1963

Career Record:

- Partner, Kavanagh, Scully, Sudow, White & Frederick, P.C.

I. Judge Altenberger's Procedures and Practices

A. *Trial and Evidentiary Hearing Procedures*

TRIAL AND EVIDENTIARY HEARING PROCEDURES

Honorable William Altenberger
Courtroom #1545

During the week prior to a trial or evidentiary hearing, Judge Altenberger may move the starting date and time of a particular matter. Judge Altenberger's Courtroom Deputy, Sonny Milano, will advise parties of any such change by telephone. Parties are cautioned to be prepared to adjust their schedules accordingly. The first trial or evidentiary hearing of the week will begin promptly on Monday morning. Judge Altenberger will expect counsel and witnesses to be available on 2-3 hours telephonic notice for the remainder of the week.

BRIEFS

LBR Reference: Please comply with LBR 9013-2

Judge's Copy: Please comply with LBR 5005-2(d)
Please comply with Court Manual Sections 2-5(d), 3-5(b) and Appendix F

EXHIBITS

LBR Reference: Please comply with LBR 9070-1

Identification: Per LBR 9070-1(a)(2):
Numbers: plaintiff/movant exhibits must be marked with numbers in increasing order.
Letters: defendant/respondent exhibits must be marked with letters in alphabetical order.

Tags All parties presenting exhibits are responsible for tagging their own exhibits prior to the start of trial. Exhibit tags may be obtained from the Courtroom Deputy, Sonny Milano, in Room 940 or the court recorder prior to the trial.

# of Copies Please bring one original set for the court recorder and 4 sets of copies (1/each counsel, 1/judge, 1/witness)

Exhibit Register All parties presenting exhibits must prepare an exhibit register on Form B 3024 "EXHIBIT REGISTER AND NOTICE RE DISPOSITION OF EXHIBITS" available on the court's website at www.cacb.uscourts.gov., under "Court Forms."

Continuance /Settlement Motions for continuance or stipulation for settlement must be filed and a proposed order lodged with the assigned judge at least five (5) **court** days prior to the scheduled trial or evidentiary hearing date with courtesy copies delivered to Judge Altenberger's Courtroom Deputy, Sonny Milano at Room 940. He will contact the parties as to whether the continuance/settlement agreement has been granted or denied.

Lodging Orders Orders that are capable of being lodged electronically shall be lodged with the original assigned judge via the Court's electronic Lodge Order Upload (LOU) system.

If you have further questions regarding Judge Altenberger's procedures please contact **Sonny Milano @ 213.894.1485**.

Hon. Neil W. Bason

Bankruptcy Judge

Contact Information

U.S. Bankruptcy Court, Central District of California
Courtroom 1545
255 E. Temple Street, Suite 1552
Los Angeles, CA 90012
Courtroom Deputy: (213) 894-4085

Biographical Information

Appointment(s):

- Appointed 10/24/11 by the United States Court of Appeals for the Ninth Circuit. (Current term expires 10/23/25.)

Education:

- Johns Hopkins University, B.A. 1984
- Boston University School of Law, J.D. Magna Cum Laude 1988; Law Review

Career Record:

- 1988-89, Law Clerk, Chief Justice Paul J. Liacos, Massachusetts Supreme Judicial Court
- 1989-92, Associate, Palmer & Dodge; Edwards & Angell, Massachusetts
- 1992-00, Private practice; Hovis, Smith, Stewart, Lipscomb & Cross etc., San Francisco, California
- 2000-08, Law Clerk, Hon. Dennis Montali (U.S. Bankruptcy Court, Northern District of California, and Bankruptcy Appellate Panel of the Ninth Circuit)
- 2008-09, Special Counsel, Howard Rice Nemerovski Canady Falk & Rabkin, P.C., San Francisco, California
- 2009-11, Special Counsel, Duane Morris, LLP, San Francisco and Los Angeles, California

Private Practice Specializations:

- Commercial bankruptcy and insolvency practice, including a focus on secured creditor representation and substantial representation of trustees, receivers, debtors/borrowers, guarantors, unsecured creditors, prospective purchasers of assets out of bankruptcy, parties to executory contracts and unexpired leases, equity holders, and other parties in interest.

I. Judge Bason's Procedures and Practices

A. *Procedures*

JUDGE BASON'S PROCEDURES

The following procedures may be modified at any time without prior notice.

I. **Urgent matters.**

A. **Shortened time.** First, file the motion papers. Second, deliver a judge's_copy of the motion papers to chambers and ring the bell to notify chambers of such delivery. Third, call the judge's law clerk to obtain a hearing date, and ask the law clerk if the judge will require witnesses to be present. Be sure to follow LBR 9075-1.

B. **Shortened time for certain automatic stay matters.** Notwithstanding the above procedures, parties can self calendar the following motions to be heard on shortened time (minimum 14 days notice) without prior approval:

1. motions for relief from the automatic stay involving:
   a) residential unlawful detainer actions;
   b) two or more bankruptcy filings affecting the subject property within six months before the present case was filed;
   c) postpetition transfers of real property to the debtor; or
   d) prepetition transfers to the debtor that:
      i. were within 90 days of the debtor's petition date; or
      ii. that involve a fractionalized interest in real property; or
2. motions to continue or impose the automatic stay under Section 362 (c)(3) or (4). To self calendar any motion listed above on shortened time, the moving party must self-calendar a hearing date (see Judge Bason's posted Self-Calendar Procedures) and then file and serve all moving papers on the following persons by overnight mail, facsimile or personal service at least 14 days before the date scheduled for a hearing: (w) the debtor, (x) the debtor's attorney, (y) any trustee, and (z) any creditor who may be affected. The moving party must amend the local notice form to indicate that oppositions must be filed at least seven (7) days before the hearing. – Exception: a motion to continue or impose the automatic stay affects all creditors, but unsecured creditors who are not among the 20 largest can be served via U.S. mail rather than the expedited service described above. Caution: Be sure your service is adequate – see below under "Common Issues, Service." A declaration regarding service must be filed at least 7 days before the scheduled hearing.

C. **Discovery disputes.** The judge generally will hold a telephonic conference to resolve discovery disputes in lieu of formal motions to compel or quash discovery. Call the judge's law clerk to arrange the telephonic conference and related procedures (*e.g.*, the judge typically (1) requires an email summary of the issues in dispute, copied to opposing counsel, and (2) may permit or require copies of relevant documents, such as discovery requests or responses). Any request for sanctions relating to a discovery dispute must be made by separate noticed motion.

D. "First day" matters. Please pay special attention to Rules 4001(b)-(d), 6003 & 6004 and LBR 2014-1, 2081-1 & 4001-2(e), 5075-1 & 6004-1. Caution: Please also pay special attention to providing sufficient notice to all interested parties, and be sure your service is adequate – see below under "Common Issues, Service." In addition, declaration(s) should provide sufficient information to gauge the impact on general unsecured creditors and other parties in interest, such as: (1) the current cash situation; (2) asset/debt information to the extent that the bankruptcy schedules and Statement of Financial Affairs ("SOFA") either have not been filed or do not reflect actual values or require explanation; (3) connections between the debtor and any prospective purchaser or person providing financing; and (4) unless unknown, the Chapter 11 exit strategy of the debtor (e.g., sale as a going concern, liquidation of assets, continuation of business with infusion of capital, etc.).

II. Contacting the Court's staff. You may not communicate with court staff regarding any cases (see Rule 9003(a) and Rule 5-300(C) of Cal. R. Prof. Conduct) except to inform the court:

A. that an emergency pleading or application for order shortening time ("OST") is being submitted;

B. that a party will file an opposition to an emergency pleading, OST application, *ex parte* matter, or proposed form of order, or will submit an alternative form of proposed order (do not discuss the contents of the opposition/alternative proposed order);

C. that a proposed order has been pending for more than 14 days, or is required before that time;

D. that a Chapter 11 plan proponent intends to go forward with a disclosure statement or confirmation hearing; or for E. calendaring.

III. Motion practice.

A. Calendaring. Except for (a) urgent matters (see special procedures under "Urgent Matters" above), (b) matters that are eligible for self-calendaring (see Judge Bason's posted Self-Calendar Procedures), and (c) initial status conferences (which are set by the court), all matters must be calendared by calling the judge's courtroom deputy.

B. Calendar changes. If a motion is settled or will be voluntarily dismissed (withdrawn), please inform the judge's courtroom deputy as soon as possible and file and serve an appropriate notice.

C. Tentative rulings. It is counsel's responsibility to check the judge's posted calendar for tentative rulings.

1. When to check for tentatives. Starting approximately 48 hours before the scheduled time of the hearing, the court will post tentative rulings on the judge's calendar (or will post an alternative notice, such as a notice that

there is no tentative ruling or that the court is determining whether to accept late-filed papers). If nothing is posted under the "tentative ruling" for your matter then you should continue checking periodically until a tentative ruling or other notice is posted under your matter. Exception: No tentative rulings are posted for (a) the Chapter 13 confirmation calendar or (b) motions brought by the Chapter 13 trustee (generally motions to dismiss).

2. **Parties' options in response to tentatives.** No appearance is required unless a party in interest disagrees with the tentative ruling. That party may request to be heard at the scheduled time by doing the following no later than 24 hours (counting only business days) before the hearing: (a) telephoning the judge's courtroom deputy and (b) notifying all other interested parties of that party's intent to appear at the hearing. If a party does not follow these procedures, but nevertheless appears in court to contest the motion, the judge generally will allow the tentative ruling to stand but may, upon a sufficient showing, continue the matter so that absent parties can be afforded an opportunity to be heard. Exception: If the tentative ruling is not posted in time to provide 24 hours' notice of intent to dispute the tentative, and if the party seeking to be heard shows sufficient efforts to provide notice, then the judge may excuse compliance with the foregoing procedures.

D. **Telephonic appearances.** Permission to appear telephonically generally will not be given for the following matters:

1. Trials and evidentiary hearings (all counsel and all witnesses must appear in person);

2. Chapter 9 & 11 status conferences (debtor and debtor's counsel must appear in person at the initial conference; other parties in interest may appear telephonically);

3. Chapter 9, 11, 12 & 13 disclosure statement or confirmation hearings (debtor, debtor's counsel, and all objecting creditors must appear in person, but for Chapter 13 confirmation hearings that are uncontested or continued by consent no appearance is required except by counsel for the Chapter 13 trustee);

4. Reaffirmation hearings (debtor must appear in person; other parties in interest may appear telephonically); or

5. Any matter designated by the court as requiring a personal appearance. For other matters, you may request permission to appear by telephone by calling the judge's law clerk at least 24 hours before the hearing. The judge does not use Court Call, Tele-Court or other third-party providers – if permission is given to appear by telephone then follow the law clerk's instructions (which generally will involve calling chambers at a designated time and then being transferred to the courtroom sound system). Please note: (a) use your mute button to avoid interfering with other hearings in progress, (b) no speaker phones allowed ever, (c) no cell phones allowed

without a very good reason, and (d) please identify yourself for the record every time you speak.

E. **Priority.** Attorneys may request priority when they check in with the judge's court recorder just before the calendar call. Within reason, such requests usually are granted, especially if the matter can be dealt with very briefly. A priority matter should not take longer than fifteen minutes.

F. **Second call.** Attorneys may request that their matter be heard toward the end of the calendar ("second call") by either (1) calling the judge's law clerk or (2) making the request personally to the court recorder before the calendar call. The judge normally will honor reasonable requests, subject to balancing the reason for the request against the inconvenience to other parties.

G. **Testimony.** Declarants normally are not required to be present at hearings on motions. Oral testimony seldom is required or allowed unless the judge has agreed in advance to hear oral testimony. If live testimony is essential (either on direct or cross-examination), be sure first to notify opposing counsel and second to call the judge's law clerk to obtain permission.

IV. **Trial practice (includes not only trials in adversary proceedings but also any contested matter that will include live witnesses).**

A. **Status & pretrial conferences.** *See* LBR 7016-1.

B. **Calendar changes.** Requests for continuances, even by stipulation, will rarely be granted. The judge normally will schedule several cases for trial one week per month, starting at 10 a.m. on Monday of the trial week (or Tuesday if Monday is a holiday). The court will contact counsel the week before the scheduled trial date to determine counsels' current trial time estimates. The court will then determine the sequence in which the scheduled trials will be held. If you reach a settlement, please call the judge's chambers promptly and, on or before the first date set for trial, either confirm in writing that the settlement has been reduced to a writing signed by all parties or their counsel or alternatively put the settlement on the record.

C. **Trial.** Opening statements are welcome (but usually are not necessary). Counsel should be prepared to complete closing argument as soon as the parties have rested.

V. **Common matters.**

A. **Service:** Please double-check who needs to be served, remember that initial motion papers are treated like a complaint for purposes of service (*see* Rules 9014 & 7004), and remember that there are special rules for service on some types of persons. For example: (1) Entities generally must be served "to the attention of an officer, a managing or general agent, or to any other agent authorized by appointment or by law to receive service of process …." Rule 7004(b)(3). Addresses often can be found on the California Secretary of State website. (2) Insured Depository Institutions. Many lienholders are FDIC-insured institutions and must be served in accordance with Rule 7004(h). The FDIC website has a feature to search for institutions and their main office:

http://www2.fdic.gov/idasp/main.asp. **Note:** Do not rely on the court's limited resources to double-check that your service was adequate. If a party in interest was not properly served and was deprived of an opportunity to object to your motion, then relief may include reduction in allowed fees, sanctions, voiding any order granting the motion, ruling that such order was always void, etc.

B. **Automatic stay (Section 362).** (1) Stipulations. Generally, the judge will not approve a stipulation for relief from stay that purports to be effective in any subsequent case filed by the debtor. (2) Extraordinary Relief. The judge's policy is *not* to grant the relief set forth in the Extraordinary Relief Attachment in local form F 4001-1.ORDER.RP (concerning real property) except for the following, upon a sufficient showing: (a) the relief for two years authorized in Section 362(d)(4) (order binding in certain subsequent cases)), and (b) relief for 180 days under sections 1, 2 and 3 of the Extraordinary Relief Attachment (because (i) it is a form of alternative and lesser relief under Section 362(d)(4)) and (ii) it permits the movant to use any similar non-bankruptcy laws, subject to compliance with the recording and/or notice provisions of any such laws). In rare instances comparable additional relief may be appropriate, such as a scheme involving transfers of personal property analogous to the schemes involving real property described in Section 362(d)(4)(A) and (B). (3) Relief as to co-debtors and non-debtors. If you want the order to bind co-debtors and non-debtors, be sure to serve your motion on those persons (if known). (4) Motions to continue the automatic stay (Section 362(c)(3)). Judge Bason follows *In re Reswick*, 446 B.R. 362 (9th Cir. BAP 2011). Please see section VI below for more information.

C. **Lien avoidance (Section 506(d)).** Required forms: The judge requires use of Local Form 4003-2.4-MOTION, entitled "Debtor's Motion to Avoid Junior Lien on Principal Residence [11 U.S.C. § 506(d)]" and Local Form 4003-2.4.ORDER. Calendaring: Your Chapter 13 plan will not be confirmed until after (1) any Motions to Avoid Lien(s) have been adjudicated AND (2) the orders on all such motions have been signed and entered by the Court, so please calendar all such motions as soon as possible. Admissible evidence with appropriate declaration(s) should address: (1) value of the property as of the petition date, such as an appraisal, or a broker's opinion of price/value, or a debtor's opinion of value – a debtor's declaration should contain more than, e.g., "I believe that my residence is worth $xxx,xxx," and should state the basis for the debtor's opinion such as familiarity with the residence, the neighborhood, and recent sales (note that hearsay such as a valuation from zillow.com is generally inadmissible and, even for expert opinions, may be of little weight), and (2) current principal balance owed on all senior liens (*e.g.*, bank statements for mortgage liens, and tax statements for tax liens).

D. **Chapter 13 confirmation hearings.** As noted in LBR 3015-1(d), "[t]he judges of this district do not have a uniform policy governing calendaring and appearance at a [Chapter 13] confirmation hearing." Judge Bason has adopted the following generally applicable procedures. Any party in interest can seek alternative procedures for good cause shown, either by proper motion/application or by appropriate oral request at the confirmation hearing.

1. Trustee. The Chapter 13 Trustee assigned to administer Judge Bason's Chapter 13 cases is Kathy A. Dockery. The contact information for the Trustee's office is (a) website: www.latrustee.com and (b) telephone: (213) 996-4400.

2. Calendaring. Attorneys for debtors and debtors without counsel should contact the Chapter 13 Trustee to set a hearing to confirm their plan (the available hearing dates are noted on the posted calendar entitled "Judge Bason's Hearing Dates" included in the posted instructions for Self-Calendaring). Note: All motions to value and avoid liens should be scheduled for hearing and the order(s) on the motion(s) should be entered ***before*** the hearing on confirmation of the Chapter 13 plan (see above under "Lien avoidance (Section 506(d))").

3. Payments. All required pre-confirmation payments must be current or else the case may be dismissed at the confirmation hearing.

4. Check-in procedure. If an appearance by debtor or debtor's attorney is required (see below), then the Chapter 13 Trustee generally conducts an informal meet-and-confer style "check-in" with parties approximately one hour prior to the confirmation hearing. Parties in interest are strongly advised to use this check-in procedure and should contact the Trustee's office for further information.

5. Appearances – when required. Attorneys for debtors and debtors without counsel must appear at the confirmation hearing, except that the Chapter 13 Trustee may excuse that appearance in two situations:

   a. Continuances. (i) Written stipulation. If debtor(s) and creditor(s) wish to submit a written stipulation to request a continuance of a confirmation hearing, the written stipulation must also be forwarded to the Chapter 13 Trustee for the Trustee's agreement and signature as a party in interest. (ii) Oral stipulation. If there is an oral agreement to a continuance by all debtor(s) and all creditor(s) who have either checked in with the Chapter 13 Trustee or filed and served a written objection, then only the Chapter 13 Trustee is required to appear. The Trustee will notify the Court of the proposed continued hearing date. If the Court orders any alternative disposition (*e.g.*, continuance to a different date) then the Trustee (or such other person as the Court may designate) will provide any appropriate notice to any persons entitled to notice.

   b. No opposition to confirmation. If the Chapter 13 Trustee recommends confirmation of the plan proposed by the debtor(s), and no party in interest has either filed a written objection or checked in with the Trustee to note their opposition to confirmation, then only the Chapter 13 Trustee is required to appear. The Trustee will recommend to the Court that the plan be confirmed. If the Court orders any alternative disposition (e.g., continuance to address the Court's own concerns) then the Trustee (or such other person as the Court may designate) will provide any appropriate notice to any persons entitled to notice.

E. **Individual Chapter 11 Cases.** Please see Local Forms F 2081-1 *et seq.*

F. **Temporary Restraining Orders ("TROs").** Serve opposing parties at least 72 hours prior to any TRO hearing (absent truly exceptional circumstances). Any request for a TRO or other injunctive relief requires an adversary proceeding, so a complaint must be filed prior to the hearing. *See* Rule 7001(7).

G. **Settlements (Rule 9019).** Declaration(s) should support each of the four factors in *In re A & C Properties*, 784 F.2d 1377, 1381 (9th Cir. 1986). In routine settlements, the factors can be addressed briefly. Motions to approve settlements generally must be filed in the main bankruptcy case, and after a settlement is approved please follow up promptly with a separate motion or application for dismissal in the adversary proceeding.

H. **Default Judgments (Rule 7055).** When requesting a default judgment in an adversary proceeding, the moving party must submit a proof of service showing that the request was served on the non-responding defendant. Except in certain matters (*e.g.*, trustee avoiding actions, Section 523(a)(2)(C) claims, and others as determined on a case-by-case basis by telephoning the judge's law clerk), a plaintiff seeking a default judgment must schedule a "prove-up" hearing (*see* Rules 55(b)(2) and 7055) and serve notice of the hearing on the defendant at least 14 days prior to the hearing. In the event that the judge requires live testimony by witnesses for the plaintiff, the defaulting defendant will be entitled to cross-examine the witness but is not permitted to present its own evidence or witnesses.

I. **Status conference reports.** A thorough, written status report, filed 14 days in advance, is required before each Chapter 11 status conference and 14 days in advance before each adversary status conference. In adversary proceedings, use of court-approved status conference report forms is strongly recommended.

J. **Employment and compensation of professionals.** The judge will not allow auctioneers to charge a buyers' premium or real estate brokers representing the estate (as seller) to represent buyers. See 11 U.S.C. § 327(a) (trustee may employ "professional persons, that do not hold or represent an interest adverse to the estate"). Any application to employ such professionals should reflect their agreement with these limitations. <u>Conflicts Checks/Ethical Walls:</u> Time spent identifying, clearing and avoiding conflicts generally is not compensable. The judge does not expect counsel to run every creditor and party in interest through a conflicts check, but at a minimum counsel should include in their conflicts check any party who has a major interest in the case (*e.g.*, major unsecured creditors, secured creditors, major equity security holders / owners, officers and directors, landlords / lessors, and other professionals retained in the case). Counsel should disclose potential conflicts with any such party, including anticipated future conflicts.

K. **Section 363(m) "good faith" findings.** Supporting declaration(s) should address: (1) the bidder's prepetition and postpetition relationship with other bidders, the debtor, major creditors or equity security holders in the case, or any of the debtor's officers, directors, agents, or employees, (2) the bidder's expected relationship after the sale with the debtor's present or former officers, directors, agents, or employees (including whether any offers of employment or compensation have been made or will be offered to debtor's present or former officers, directors, agents, or employees), (3) whether any consideration is contemplated to be transferred or has been transferred by bidder in connection with the sale to any person other than the debtor (or the trustee of the debtor's estate), and (4) the absence of fraud or collusion between the bidder and any other bidders or the debtor's officers, directors, agents or employees, or any attempt to take unfair advantage of other bidders. *See generally In re M Capital Corp.*, 290 B.R. 743, 748-49 (9th Cir. BAP 2003). As used in this paragraph, a "bidder" includes all known prospective bidders.

VI. Judge Bason's Rulings of Common Interest.

A. **Section 362(c)(3) (termination of automatic stay 30 days after filing 2d bankruptcy case in one year):** Judge Bason follows *In re Reswick*, 446 B.R. 362 (9th Cir. BAP 2011) (if automatic stay is not continued beyond 30 days then it terminates in all respects, not just for limited purposes). See *In re Hernandez*, case no. 2:11-bk-53730-NB, docket #40 (Memorandum Decision). Judge Bason recognizes that termination of the automatic stay may harm creditors, or otherwise undermine important bankruptcy policies, and therefore one of two remedies may be appropriate: (1) if it appears that a plan can be confirmed before irreparable harm occurs, then the binding effect of the plan might be a sufficient substitute for the lack of an automatic stay (*see* Section 1327(a)), or alternatively (2) the Court can dismiss the bankruptcy case on its *own motion* and *without* a bar to filing another bankruptcy case. ***See Hernandez pp. 8:4-10:16.***

VII. Definitions. Unless the context suggests otherwise, references to a "Chapter" or "Section" refer to the United States Bankruptcy Code, 11 U.S.C. § 101 et seq. (the "Code"), a "Rule" means the Federal Rules of Bankruptcy Procedure ("FRBP"), Federal Rules of Civil Procedure ("FRCP"), Federal Rules of Evidence ("FRE"), or Local Bankruptcy Rules ("LBR"), and other terms have the meanings provided in the Code and the Rules.

Hon. Catherine E. Bauer

Bankruptcy Judge

Contact Information
U.S. Bankruptcy Court, Central District of California
Courtroom 5D
411 West Fourth Street, Suite 5153
Santa Ana, CA 92701
Courtroom Deputy: (714) 338-5366

Biographical Information

Appointment(s):

- Appointed 02/26/10 by the United States Court of Appeals for the Ninth Circuit. (Current term expires 02/25/24)

Education:

- University of California, Los Angeles, 1982
- University of Southern California, Gould School of Law, J.D., 1985

Career Record:

- 1985-2000: Bank of America N.A., Office of General Counsel
- 2001-2010: United States Attorney's Office, Central District of California
- Admitted to the California Bar, 1985

Professional Memberships:

- American Bankruptcy Institute
- Financial Lawyers Conference
- National Conference of Bankruptcy Judges
- State Bar of California

Awards:

- Most Frequently Chosen Mediator in the Central District
- Most Conferences Settled in Mediation in the Central District
- Hon. William J. Lasarow Award for Outstanding Service
- Public Counsel Advocate of the Year

I. Judge Bauer's Procedures and Practices

A. *Mandatory Use of Local Form 4003-2.4 – Motion for Chapter 13 Debtor Motions to Avoid Junior Lien on Principal Residence*

MANDATORY USE OF LOCAL FORM 4003-2.4-MOTION FOR CHAPTER 13 DEBTOR MOTIONS TO AVOID JUNIOR LIEN ON PRINCIPAL RESIDENCE

Hon. Catherine E. Bauer

Effective January 27, 2011, all motions filed by debtors in Chapter 13 cases to avoid junior liens on the debtor's principal residence (commonly referred to as "lien strip motions," "motions to value," "Lam motions," etc.)[1] must be made on Local Form 4003-2.4-Motion, entitled "Debtor's Motion to Avoid Junior Lien on Principal Residence [11 U.S.C. § 506(d)]." The form may be found on the Court's website, www.cacb.uscourts.gov, by clicking on "Forms/Rules/General Orders," then "Local Bankruptcy Rules & Forms," and scrolling down to F 4003-2.4-MOTION under "Local Bankruptcy Rules Forms."

All debtors filing a motion to avoid a junior lien on the debtor's principal residence must use Local Form 4003-2.4-Motion, including the proof of service. **If a motion to avoid a junior lien on the debtor's principal residence is not filed using Local Form 4003-2.4-Motion, including the proof of service, the motion will not be set for hearing.**

EVIDENCE

As the form indicates, all motions to avoid a junior lien must be supported by evidence regarding the amount and priority of the liens at issue, and the value of the property. Evidence must be admissible and persuasive.

Liens. Without evidence as to the validity and amount of the senior secured loan and the junior secured loan, the requested relief cannot be granted. The debtor's declaration, which contains the debtor's testimony regarding the liens and introduces the documents into evidence, along with a copy of the deed of trust, a loan statement, proof of claim or other statement from the current lender will establish the amount and validity of the lien. No documents will be considered as evidence unless they are accompanied by a declaration. The debtor's testimony alone, with no documentation, will not be sufficient to establish validity and amount (similarly, the debtor's schedules are not sufficient). The court also does not consider a credit report listing amounts owed to be admissible evidence of validity and amount; it is hearsay.

Value. The debtor may testify through a declaration regarding the value of the residence. The declaration should contain the basis for the testimony, which may include, among other factors, the debtor's familiarity with the residence, the neighborhood, and recent sales. It is insufficient for the declaration to state: "I believe that my residence is worth $xxx,xxx." Please note that the debtor may not rely solely on sources from the internet; this is hearsay. Therefore, a declaration stating "I believe my residence is worth $xxx,xxx based on

[1] The form is entitled "Debtor's Motion to Avoid Junior Lien on Principal Residence [11 U.S.C. § 506(d)]." More specifically, the relief sought is the valuation of a secured claim and determination of secured status pursuant to Fed. R. Bankr. P. 3012 and 11 U.S.C. § 506(d). This relief may be obtained through a noticed motion; an adversary proceeding is not necessary.

the attached report from zillow.com [or cyberhomes.com or other similar website]" is not admissible evidence as to value.

While not always necessary, an appraisal can be persuasive evidence of value. To be admissible evidence, the appraisal must be accompanied by a declaration of the debtor or the appraiser.

SERVICE

Use of the proof of service in Local Form 4003-2.4-Motion is mandatory. The proof of service must be completely filled out to indicate what parties were served, how they were served, and when they were served. Be sure to allow sufficient notice of the hearing to comply with LBR 9013-1(d) (notice to be served not later than 21 days before the hearing date). If a hearing date is chosen that is less than 21 days after service, the motion will be continued at least 21 additional days to allow the full notice period to pass.

Proper service of the motion – including compliance with Fed. R. Bankr.P. 7004 and Local Bankr. Rule 4003-2(c) – is critical.

Which parties to serve. The chapter 13 trustee, the affected lienholder, and all other parties asserting a lien on the property must be served. If any party has made an appearance in the case, that party (and counsel, if applicable) must be served at the address used in its notice of appearance.

Compliance with F.R.B.P. 7004(b)(3). This rule applies to domestic and foreign corporations and provides that service may be made by first-class mail upon "an officer, a managing or general agent, or to any other agent authorized by appointment or by law to receive service of process." The address for the corporation and its agent, if any, can usually be found on the corporation's website or the California Secretary of State website.

Compliance with F.R.B.P. 7004(h). Rule 7004(b)(3), discussed above, is generally applicable to corporations, but its lead-in indicates that it applies "[e]xcept as provided in subsection (h)." Rule 7004(h) specifically applies to insured depository institutions (as defined in section 3 of the Federal Deposit Insurance Act). Many lienholders are **FDIC-insured institutions and must be served in accordance with Rule 7004(h)**.

1. Is the lienholder an FDIC-insured institution? The FDIC website has afeature to search for institutions: http://www2.fdic.gov/idasp/main.asp. This feature will provide an address and list of officers for the institution. Please note that many institutions are subsidiaries of FDICinsured institutions (for example, Bank of America Home Loans is a subsidiary of Bank of America, N.A.). In these cases, the FDIC-insured parent must be served in accordance with Rule 7004(h).

2. How to accomplish service in accordance with Rule 7004(h)? Rule 7004(h) requires that service be made by certified mail addressed to an officer of the institution.

   a. Use Certified Mail. Regular first-class mail, overnight mail or courier, or any other delivery method does not comply with Rule 7004(h); certified mail must be used.

   b. Address service to an officer. Remember, an officer of the institution is not the registered agent for service of process, or the FDIC itself. The best sources for finding an officer of an FDIC-insured institution are the FDIC website noted above, and the institution's website. Many courts have held that addressing service to "Officer of the Institution," "Chief Executive Officer," or "President" complies with the rule. If the institution's address is correct, and it is not possible to locate an officer's name, the court will not find that the motion was served incorrectly (although as a practical matter, it would be rare that an officer's name could not be found).

ORDER

When your motion is granted, submit an order within seven days after the hearing date. Use of Local Form 4003-2.4-Order is mandatory (the form replaces the form that was previously on the court's website under Judge Bauer's forms and procedures).

B. Procedures Regarding Telephonic Appearances

PROCEDURES REGARDING TELEPHONIC APPEARANCES

Effective March 1, 2010

Telephonic appearances before Judge Catherine E. Bauer in Courtroom 5D are generally allowed. **No telephone appearances are allowed for the Chapter 13 calendar or any evidentiary hearings.** In order to appear telephonically counsel must adhere to the following procedure:

Standard procedure:

> Telephone appearances may be arranged by calling Court Call, an independent conference call company until the start of the scheduled hearing. Counsel may reach Court Call at (866) 582-6878.

Individuals choosing to appear telephonically do so at their own risk. Hearings generally will not be rescheduled due to missed connections. Furthermore, in deciding to appear telephonically, counsel is agreeing to waive any prejudice attributable to quality deficiencies or irregularities of the record that may result.

Please be advised that poor reception will cause counsel's appearance to be disconnected. Repeated poor connections may cause counsel to be banned from future telephonic appearances.

If an individual schedules a telephonic appearance and then fails to respond to the call of a matter on calendar, the court may pass the matter or may treat the failure to respond as a failure to appear. Scheduling simultaneous telephonic appearances in multiple courts does not excuse a failure to appear when a matter is placed on calendar.

Before appearing, check Judge Bauer's calendar and review any tentative ruling on WebPACER.

C. *Trial and Evidentiary Hearing Procedures*

BRIEFS

LBR Reference: Please comply with LBR 9013-2

Judge's Copy: Please comply with LBR 5005-2(d)
Please comply with Court Manual Sections 2.5, 3.5(b) and Appendix F

EXHIBITS

LBR Reference: Please comply with LBR 9070-1

Identification: Per LBR 9070-1(a)(2):
Numbers: Plaintiff/Movant exhibits must be marked with numbers in increasing order.
Letters: Defendant/Respondent exhibits must be marked with letters in alphabetical order.

Tags: All parties presenting exhibits are responsible for tagging their own exhibits prior to the scheduled trial or evidentiary hearing. The mandatory yellow (Plaintiff) and blue (Defendant) exhibit tabs may be obtained from the Clerk's Office, the Courtroom DECRO, or Judge Bauer's Courtroom Deputy, Susan Kent. Exhibit tags must be placed on the back, bottom left-hand corner, of the last page of each exhibit.

Assembly /Witness List & Exhibit Register: All exhibits must be assembled in a binder or notebook. Each such binder or notebook must include a witness list and an exhibit register. The exhibit register shall be prepared using Form B 3024 "EXHIBIT REGISTER AND NOTICE RE DISPOSITION OF EXHIBITS," which is available on the court's website at www.cacb.uscourts.gov., under "Court Forms."

#of Copies: All parties shall prepare one tagged original set of exhibits to be offered into evidence and (4) sets of conformed copies (1/each counsel, 1/judge, 1/witness). All sets of exhibits shall be delivered to Judge Bauer's Courtroom Deputy, Susan Kent, at least (5) court days prior to the scheduled trial or evidentiary hearing.

Testimony: Each party must present the **direct testimony** of all of its witnesses, including expert witnesses, **by declaration**. Each declaration must set forth the direct testimony that the witness would give as though questions were propounded in the usual fashion. Each statement of fact or opinion must be separately, sequentially numbered and must contain only matters that are admissible under the Federal Rules of Evidence (e.g., avoiding redundancies, hearsay, and other objectionable statements).

All **cross-examination, rebuttal, sur-rebuttal and appropriate**

impeachment evidence must be given by **live testimony**. The oral testimony that may be offered at the proceeding by a party through its own witnesses will be **STRICTLY** limited to rebuttal testimony or such additional testimony on matters relevant to the outcome of the proceeding as may be specifically requested by the court at the time of the proceeding.

The declaration of a witness for a party will be admissible at the proceeding, subject to timely objections, only if the declarant is present at the trial/evidentiary hearing and subject to cross-examination.

Continuance /Settlement: Motions for continuance or stipulation for settlement must be filed and a proposed order lodged with the assigned judge at least five (5) court days prior to the scheduled trial or evidentiary hearing date, with courtesy copies delivered to chambers.

Lodging Orders: Orders that are capable of being lodged electronically shall be lodged via the Court's electronic Lodge Order Upload (LOU) system.

For any further questions regarding Judge Bauer's procedures, please contact Courtroom Deputy Susan Kent at (714) 338-5366.

II. Judge Bauer's Case Management Orders

A. *Standing Order Regarding Time of Chapter 13 Confirmation Hearing*

IN THE UNITED STATES BANKRUPTCY COURT
FOR THE CENTRAL DISTRICT OF CALIFORNIA

In re)
TIME OF CHAPTER 13) **STANDING ORDER**
CONFIRMATION HEARING)
______________________________)

The undersigned Judge of the United States Bankruptcy Court, Central District of California, makes this standing order with respect to the time for the hearing on confirmation of Chapter 13 plans:

I hereby find and accordingly ORDER that it is in the best interests of the creditors and the estate to hold the hearing on the confirmation of the Chapter 13 plan on the same date as the meeting of creditors required under 11 U.S.C. § 341(a). **Any party in interest who objects to that timing of the confirmation hearing shall file a written objection thereto at least 20 calendar days before the scheduled confirmation hearing**; and it is

FURTHER ORDERED that the objecting party shall file the objection with the Court and serve it on the debtor, debtor's counsel, Chapter 13 trustee, and on any creditor who has filed an objection to confirmation, filed a request for special notice, or holds a security interest in the real property of the debtor. If a timely objection is received, the Court will reschedule the confirmation hearing.

DATED: March 22, 2010

____
CATHERINE E. BAUER
United States Bankruptcy Judge

Hon. Sheri Bluebond

Bankruptcy Judge

Contact Information

U.S. Bankruptcy Court, Central District of California
Courtroom 1475
255 E. Temple Street, Suite 1482
Los Angeles, CA 90012
Courtroom Deputy: (213) 894-3688

Biographical Information

Appointment(s):

- Appointed 02/01/01 by the United States Court of Appeals for the Ninth Circuit. (Current term expires 01/31/15.)

Education:

- University of California at Los Angeles, 1982, B.A., (*summa cum laude*) (phi beta kappa);
- University of California at Los Angeles School of Law, 1985, J.D., Law Review.

Career Record:

- 1995-2001, Partner, Irell & Manella LLP, Los Angeles, California;
- 1991-95, Shareholder, Murphy, Weir & Butler, Los Angeles, California;
- 1983-91, Associate, Gendel, Raskoff, Shapiro & Quittner, Los Angeles, California.
- Admitted to the California Bar, 1985.

Publications and Other Media:

- "To File or Not to File," American Bar Association Journal, July 1999;
- "Assessing the Usefulness of Chapter 11 Filing," Business Workouts Manual (Supp. 1999);
- "Insulating Purchasers in Bankruptcy from Successor Liability," The Review of Banking & Financial Services (April 1998).

Professional Memberships:

- Los Angeles County Bar Association;
- Financial Lawyers Conference;
- Los Angeles Bankruptcy Forum;
- American Bankruptcy Institute;
- American Bar Association;
- Jewish Big Brothers Big Sisters of Los Angeles/Camp Max Straus.

I. Judge Bluebond's Procedures and Practices

A. Additional Requirements for Motions for Relief from Stay

ADDITIONAL REQUIREMENTS FOR MOTIONS FOR RELIEF FROM STAY

I. Federal Rule of Bankruptcy Procedure 4001(a) provides that motions for relief from stay shall be served on certain identified parties and "such other entities as the court may direct."

Whenever a lienholder moves for relief from stay the interests of other parties who hold liens against or interests in the property are likely to be affected. Accordingly, Judge Bluebond requires that any motion for relief from stay in which the movant seeks authority to foreclose upon (or to validate a foreclosure sale conducted with regard to) property owned by the debtor or the estate, whether real or personal, tangible or intangible, be served on all parties (other than the movant) identified in the debtor's schedules or the public record as holding a lien against or an interest in the property that is the subject of the motion.

Please note that this rule imposes ***additional*** service requirements for motions for relief from stay and is not intended to replace or supercede the service requirements applicable to motions for relief from stay contained within the Federal Rules of Bankruptcy Procedure and the Local Bankruptcy Rules.

II. Any motion for relief from stay in which the movant seeks authority to foreclose upon (or to validate a foreclosure sale conducted with regard to) property owned by the debtor or the estate, whether real or personal, tangible or intangible, shall include a copy of the Statement of Intent as an Exhibit to the motion. If the Debtor has not filed a Statement of Intent, the movant shall include a statement to this effect in the declaration that it files in support of the motion.

B. Procedures Concerning Motions for Relief from Stay in Dismissed Cases

PROCEDURES CONCERNING MOTIONS FOR RELIEF FROM STAY IN DISMISSED CASES

Bankruptcy cases are generally dismissed as a matter of course by the clerk's office if the debtor fails to file complete case commencement documentation, schedules or other required documents in a timely manner. These dismissals occur even if, prior to the date of the dismissal, a party in interest has filed a motion for relief from the automatic stay in the case. The order and notice of dismissal generated by the clerk's office provides that, "The case is dismissed, the automatic stay is vacated, and all pending motions and adversary proceedings are moot and dismissed."

In most instances, termination of the automatic stay resulting from dismissal will provide sufficient protection to the party that moved for relief from the automatic stay to obviate the need for the Court to proceed to hearing on the motion. However, if the moving party requests extraordinary relief or a 180-day bar on the debtor's refiling, the moving party may wish to proceed to hearing on its motion notwithstanding the dismissal in an effort to obtain these forms of extraordinary relief. Therefore, in order to provide an opportunity for the moving party in such cases to proceed to hearing on its motion notwithstanding the dismissal, while ensuring that the debtor and other parties in interest receive adequate notice of the movant's intention to proceed notwithstanding the dismissal, Judge Bluebond has adopted the following procedures:

Any motion for relief from stay filed prior to the dismissal of a case that has not been resolved before the dismissal of the case will be denied as moot, unless (a) the moving party requested extraordinary relief in its original moving papers and (b) the moving party does both of the following:

1. Serves the following on the debtor, counsel for the debtor (if any), any trustee appointed in the case, the United States Trustee and all other parties entitled to receive notice of the hearing on its motion within 2 business days after the moving party's receipt of notice that the case has been dismissed: (a) a written notice, advising the parties that the moving party intends to proceed to hearing on its motion for relief from stay notwithstanding dismissal of the underlying case, and setting forth the date, time and place of the hearing on the motion; and (b) a copy of this local, local rule.

2. Files with the court, at or before the commencement of the hearing on the motion, a declaration under penalty of perjury evidencing that it has served the documents described in paragraph 1 above in a timely manner upon the appropriate parties.

Provided the moving party satisfies the foregoing conditions, Judge Bluebond will hear the motion for relief notwithstanding dismissal of the underlying case and, if the motion is granted, will vacate the dismissal of the underlying bankruptcy case to the extent necessary to permit the entry of an order granting the motion.

C. Procedures on Orders, Tentative Rulings, and Judge's Copies

JUDGE SHERI BLUEBOND'S PROCEDURES ON ORDERS, TENTATIVE RULINGS, AND JUDGE'S COPIES

1. All orders that are capable of being lodged electronically shall be lodged via the Court's electronic Lodged Order Upload ("LOU") system. Orders should not be lodged more than 2 days prior to the hearing on which they relate unless otherwise instructed by the Court.

2. The Court prepares orders following hearings on Motions for Relief from Stay. Please do not lodge an order relating to a hearing on a Motion for Relief from Stay unless otherwise instructed by the Court.

3. Please note that, even if Judge Bluebond has issued a tentative ruling for a given hearing, unless (1) Judge Bluebond's chambers or calendar clerk has confirmed that no appearance is necessary or (2) the tentative ruling itself states that no appearance is necessary or that appearances have been waived, appearances are required. A moving party's failure to attend the hearing on its motion will result in denial of the motion for failure to prosecute and may result in the issuance of an order to show cause re sanctions. An opposing party who fails to attend the hearing on a motion that it has opposed will be deemed to have withdrawn its opposition to the relief requested in the motion.

4. All Judge's Copies shall be served in accordance with Section 3-F and Appendix F of the Court Manual.

D. Procedures Regarding Telephonic Appearances

PROCEDURES REGARDING TELEPHONIC APPEARANCES

I. A telephonic appearance will be allowed without prior approval from the Court unless the matter on which you would like to appear telephonically is one of the following:

- **A)** Sale Motion
- **B)** Cash Collateral Motion
- **C)** Chapter 11 Plan Confirmation
- **D)** Motion for Approval of Debtor-in-Possession Financing
- **E)** Evidentiary Hearing

If your proceeding falls within one of the five categories listed above, you may appear without prior approval from the Court only if you will be monitoring the proceeding only and do not intend to advance any position or offer any oral argument.

II. A written list of the matter(s) on which you will be making a telephonic appearance must be provided to the Court via email to Marie_Houle@cacb.uscourts.gov AND Nicholas_Koffroth@cacb.uscourts.gov not later than 5 days prior to the hearing and must contain all of the following information within the body of the email:

- **A)** the name of the case and the bankruptcy case number (and adversary number, if applicable);
- **B)** the date and time of the hearing;
- **C)** the calendar number assigned to the matter (or, if a calendar number has not yet been assigned, then a statement so stating);
- **D)** the reason that the requesting party seeks to appear by telephone; and
- **E)** contact information, including email address and telephone number.

After you have received confirmation from the Court that it has noted your telephonic appearance, you must arrange for the conference call yourself through the telephone conferencing contact numbers provided in the "Telephonic Conferencing Procedures" available on the Court's website.

III. In order to obtain approval to appear telephonically on any matter for which prior approval is required, send an email to Marie_Houle@cacb.uscourts.gov AND Nicholas_Koffroth@cacb.uscourts.gov requesting permission to appear telephonically not later than 7 days prior to the hearing and include the information contained in Paragraph II above. The Law Clerk will advise whether your request has been approved. If your request is approved, you will be responsible for making the arrangements for the conferencing call using the telephone conferencing contact numbers provided in the "Telephonic Conferencing Procedures" available on the Court's website.

E. Status Conference Procedures

STATUS CONFERENCE PROCEDURES

A thorough, written status report, filed 14 days in advance, is required before each chapter 11 and adversary status conference, unless one of the following is true:

1. the matter is an adversary proceeding and, prior to the date scheduled for the status conference, the parties have filed and the court has entered an order approving a stipulation that resolves all issues raised by the adversary proceeding and provides either for dismissal of the action in its entirety or the entry of judgment in the action;

2. the matter is an adversary proceeding, defaults have been entered as against all defendants and the plaintiff has filed and served a motion for default judgment prior to the date scheduled for the status conference;

3. the parties have filed and, prior to the date scheduled for the status conference, the court has entered an order approving, a stipulation continuing the status conference to a later date (in which case a written status report must be filed not less than 10 court days in advance of the continued status conference date); or

4. The Court has expressly relieved the parties of the obligation to file a written status report.

In adversary proceedings, use of the court-approved forms is recommended.

Please note also that, pursuant to Local Bankruptcy Rule 7016-1(a)(3), if a defendant has not responded to the complaint or fails to cooperate in the preparation of a joint status report, the plaintiff is required to file a unilateral status report not less than 10 days before the date scheduled for the status conference, which report should include a declaration setting forth the attempts made by the plaintiff to contact or obtain the cooperation of the defendant in the preparation of a joint status report.

Unless one of the four exceptions outlined above applies, Judge Bluebond expects parties to file status reports in a timely manner. Parties that fail to do so will be subject to a minimum sanction of $150, or such other sanctions as may be warranted under the circumstances or allowed under Local Bankruptcy Rule 7016-1(f). Failure to appear for a status conference in an adversary proceeding may result in a minimum sanction of $250, dismissal of the adversary proceeding for failure to prosecute or such other sanctions as may be warranted under the circumstances or allowed under Local Bankruptcy Rule 7016-1(f).

F. *Tentative Ruling Procedures*

TENTATIVE RULING PROCEDURES

In most cases, Judge Bluebond issues tentative rulings 24 to 48 hours prior to the date scheduled for a hearing. These rulings are generally available via the Court's webPACER service and appear on the calendars posted outside the courtroom and placed on counsel tables inside the courtroom.

Please note, however, that, notwithstanding the issuance of a tentative ruling, unless (1) Judge Bluebond's chambers or calendar clerk has confirmed that no appearance is necessary or (2) the tentative ruling itself states that no appearance is necessary, ***appearances are required***. A moving party's failure to attend the hearing on its motion will result in denial of the motion for failure to prosecute and may result in the issuance of an order to show cause re sanctions. An opposing party that fails to attend the hearing on a motion that it has opposed will be deemed to have withdrawn its opposition to the relief requested in the motion.

Hon. Julia W. Brand

Bankruptcy Judge

Contact Information

U.S. Bankruptcy Court, Central District of California
Courtroom 1375
255 E. Temple Street, Suite 1382
Los Angeles, CA 90012
Courtroom Deputy: (213) 894-7341

Biographical Information

Appointment(s):

- Appointed 10/24/11 by the United States Court of Appeals for the Ninth Circuit. (Current term expires 10/23/25.)

Education:

- University of California, Los Angeles, B.A. 1981
- University of Southern California Gould School of Law, J.D. 1985

Career Record:

- Brownstein Hyatt Farber Schreck LLP, 2010-2011
- Danning Gill Diamond & Kollitz LLP, 2009-2010
- Liner Grode Stein Yankelevitz Sunshine Regenstreif & Taylor, LLP, 2007-2009
- Katten Muchin Rosenman, LLP, 1991-2007
- Gendel Raskoff Shapiro & Quittner, 1989-1991
- Bolton Dunn & Moore, 1985-1989
- Admitted to California Bar, 1985

Professional Memberships:

- American Bankruptcy Institute
- American Bar Association
- International Women's Insolvency & Restructuring Confederation

I. Judge Brand's Procedures and Practices

A. Procedures Regarding Telephonic Appearances

PROCEDURES REGARDING TELEPHONIC APPEARANCES

Telephonic appearances before Judge Julia W. Brand in Courtroom 1375 are generally allowed without prior approval. No telephonic appearances are allowed on the following types of matters:

1. Sale Motion
2. Cash Collateral Motion
3. Motion for Post-Petition Financing
4. Chapter 11 Plan Confirmation
5. Evidentiary Hearings.
6. Chapter 13 Plan Confirmation

In order to appear telephonically, counsel must follow the following procedure:

Standard Procedure: Telephone appearances may be arranged by calling Court Call, an independent conference call company no later than 2:00 p.m. on the day prior to the hearing. Court Call may be reached at (888) 882-6878.

Emergency Procedure: If an unexpected emergency arises that prevents counsel from following the Standard Procedure, counsel must telephone chambers and obtain a law clerk's approval to appear telephonically. A law clerk will only approve late requests for legitimate and unanticipated emergencies. Once approved, please notify the courtroom deputy of counsel's approved telephonic appearance. The courtroom deputy may be reached at 213-894-7341.

Once approved, counsel must contact Court Call to arrange a telephonic appearance. If Court Call is not able to accommodate counsel's late request or if the Judge's law clerk denies the request, counsel will not be permitted to appear telephonically and counsel must make an appearance in court.

Individuals choosing to appear telephonically do so at their own risk. Hearings generally will not be rescheduled due to missed connections. Furthermore, in deciding to appear telephonically, counsel is agreeing to waive any prejudice attributable to quality deficiencies or irregularities of the record that may result.

Please be advised that poor reception will cause counsel's appearance to be disconnected. Repeated poor connections may cause counsel to be barred from future telephonic appearances.

If an individual schedules a telephonic appearance and then fails to respond to the call of the matter on calendar, the Court may pass the matter or may treat the failure to respond as a failure to appear.

Before appearing telephonically, please check Judge Brand's calendar and review any tentative rulings which can be found on webPACER.

B. Tentative Ruling Procedures

TENTATIVE RULING PROCEDURES

In most cases, Judge Brand issues tentative rulings 24 to 48 hours prior to the date scheduled for a hearing. These rulings are generally available through the Court's webPACER service and on the Court's website. The tentative rulings also appear on the calendars posted outside the courtroom and placed on counsel tables inside the courtroom.

Please note that, notwithstanding the issuance of a tentative ruling, unless (1) Judge Brand's chambers or calendar clerk has confirmed that no appearance is necessary or (2) the tentative ruling itself states that no appearance is necessary, appearances are required. A moving party's failure to attend the hearing on its motion will result in denial of the motion for failure to prosecute and may result in the issuance of an order to show cause re sanctions. An opposing party that fails to attend the hearing on a motion that it has opposed will be deemed to have withdrawn its opposition to the relief requested in the motion.

Hon. Peter H. Carroll

Chief Bankruptcy Judge

Contact Information
U.S. Bankruptcy Court, Central District of California
Courtroom 1468
255 E. Temple Street, Suite 1460
Los Angeles, CA 90012
Courtroom Deputy: (213) 894-0995

Biographical Information

Appointment(s):

- Appointed 08/01/02 by the United States Court of Appeals for the Ninth Circuit. (Current term expires 07/31/16.)
- Chief Judge, Bankruptcy Court, Central District of California, 2011-2014

Education:

- University of California, Berkeley (California), 1974, B.A.
- St. Mary's University, San Antonio, Texas, 1978, J.D., St. Mary's Law Review

Career Record:

- 1987-1993, Associate then Partner, Brite & Drought, San Antonio, Texas
- 1994-2002, Assistant U. S. Trustee, U. S. Department of Justice, Office of the United States Trustee, Fresno, California
- Admitted to the Texas Bar, 1978; Colorado Bar, 1990; California Bar, 1992; U. S. Court of Appeals for the Ninth Circuit, 1982; U. S. Supreme Court, 1983

Publications and Other Media:

- "Crackdown on Bankruptcy Petition Preparers" in 1997 WILEY BANKRUPTCY LAW UPDATE 383 (Thomas M. Renn, ed., Wiley Law Publications, 1997);
- "No Retention Without Redemption or Reaffirmation Says the Fifth Circuit," ABI Journal, Volume XV, No. 10 (December/January 1997);
- "Statutory Construction by the Ninth Circuit in Recent Bankruptcy Cases," 22 Cal. Bankr. J. 262 (1995); "Literalism: The United States Supreme Court's Methodology for Statutory Construction in Bankruptcy Cases," 25 St. Mary's L.J. 143 (1993);
- "Cramdown of Residential Mortgages in Chapter 13 Cases," The Colorado Lawyer, Volume 20, No. 5 (May 1991); "Discrimination Under Section 525(b) of the Bankruptcy Code," Texas Bar Journal, Volume 54, No. 5 (May 1991).

Awards:

- Director's Award for Management Excellence, U. S. Department of Justice, Office of the United States Trustee, 1999.

Board of Directors:

- California Bankruptcy Forum, 1998-2002.

Professional Memberships:

- National Conference of Bankruptcy Judges;
- American Board of Certification - Board Certified in Business and Consumer Bankruptcy Law;
- Federal Bar Association.

I. Judge Carroll's Procedures and Practices

A. *Notice Regarding Judge Peter H. Carroll's Procedures for Disposition Without Oral Argument and Tentative Rulings*

NOTICE RE JUDGE PETER H. CARROLL'S PROCEDURES FOR DISPOSITIONS WITHOUT ORAL ARGUMENT AND TENTATIVE RULINGS

Unless otherwise ordered by the court, the following procedures govern dispositions without oral argument and tentative rulings in matters pending before Judge Carroll:

1. Dispositions without oral argument and tentative rulings normally are issued not later than 3:00 p.m. on the day preceding the scheduled hearing.

2. Dispositions without oral argument and tentative rulings may be viewed by checking Judge Carroll's calendar on the court's website. To view the calendar, click on "Tentative Rulings" on the court's website, www.cacb.uscourts.gov. Dispositions without oral argument and tentative rulings are also posted outside Judge Carroll's courtroom and placed on counsel tables inside the courtroom.

3. **Dispositions Without Oral Argument.** If the matter has been adequately noticed and no written opposition has been timely filed, the court may decide the matter without oral argument by issuing a "Final Ruling." **NO APPEARANCE IS NECESSARY.** The matter will not be heard by the court. The "Final Ruling" will be incorporated into the minutes. The "Final Ruling," however, may not be a final adjudication of the merits of a matter. If the parties have agreed to a continuance or have resolved the matter by stipulation, they may so advise the Courtroom Deputy at or before the hearing and the "Final Ruling" will be vacated in favor of the continuance or stipulation. Parties who cannot so advise the Courtroom Deputy at or before the hearing must make provision for vacating any order entered by the court based on the "Final Ruling" in the written stipulation or proposed order submitted to the court pursuant to LBR 9021-1(b).

4. **Tentative Rulings.** If written opposition has been timely filed, the court may issue a "Tentative Ruling." Notwithstanding the issuance of a "Tentative Ruling," **APPEARANCES ARE REQUIRED.** The court will call for hearing any matter that has a "Tentative Ruling." The "Tentative Ruling" is subject to change, either as a result of argument presented at the hearing or as a result of further consideration by the court. A moving party's failure to attend the hearing in reliance on a "Tentative Ruling" may result in denial of the motion for failure to prosecute. An opposing party that fails to attend the hearing on a motion that it has opposed will be deemed to have withdrawn its opposition to the relief requested in the motion.

5. Counsel appearing on matters to be called for hearing may arrange to APPEAR TELEPHONICALLY in accordance with Judge Carroll's telephonic appearance procedures. Those appearing telephonically must review and be familiar with the tentative ruling.

6. After the hearing, a proposed order may be submitted electronically via the Lodged Order Upload program ("LOU") in accordance with the LOU Procedures contained in Section 4 of the Court Manual posted on the court's website. **Except as provided**

by LBR 9021-1(b)(1)(B), a proposed order must not be submitted prior to the hearing absent permission of the court.

7. Dispositions without oral argument and tentative rulings WILL NOT be issued on the following matters: (a) confirmation hearings in chapter 11, 12 & 13 cases; (b) status conferences; (c) trials; (d) order to show cause hearings; (e) matters set on shortened notice, and (f) reaffirmation agreements set for hearing.

B. Notice Regarding Judge Peter H. Carroll's Procedures for Telephonic Appearances

NOTICE RE JUDGE PETER H. CARROLL'S PROCEDURES FOR TELEPHONIC APPEARANCES

I. POLICY GOVERNING TELEPHONIC APPEARANCES

Telephonic appearances are allowed in all matters before Judge Carroll, except the following:

1. Trials and Evidentiary Hearings (all counsel and all witnesses *must* appear in person).
2. Chapter 11 Status Conferences (debtor and debtor's counsel *must* appear in person). Other parties in interest may appear telephonically.
3. Chapter 11, 12 & 13 Confirmation Hearings (debtor, debtor's counsel, and all objecting creditors *must* appear in person).
4. Reaffirmation hearings (debtor *must* appear in person). Other parties in interest may appear telephonically.
5. Any matter designated by the court as requiring a personal appearance.

No telephonic appearance will be allowed unless it is made through ***Tele-Court, Inc.***, an independent conference call company, pursuant to the procedures set forth in Section II.

Before requesting a telephonic appearance, you must check Judge Carroll's calendar on the court's website to review any disposition without oral argument or tentative ruling concerning the matter on calendar. Dispositions without oral argument and tentative rulings normally are issued not later than 3:00 p.m. on the day preceding the scheduled hearing. To view the calendar, click on "Tentative Rulings" on the court's website, www.cacb.uscourts.gov.

Dispositions Without Oral Argument. If the matter has been adequately noticed and no written opposition has been timely filed, the court may decide the matter without oral argument by issuing a "Final Ruling." **NO APPEARANCE IS NECESSARY.** The matter will not be heard by the court.

Tentative Rulings. If written opposition has been timely filed, the court may issue a "Tentative Ruling." **APPEARANCES ARE REQUIRED, notwithstanding the issuance of a Tentative Ruling. Each individual who appears telephonically must have reviewed and must be familiar with the Tentative Ruling.**

If an individual schedules a telephonic appearance and then fails to respond to the call of a matter on calendar, the court may pass the matter or may treat the failure to respond as a failure to appear. Scheduling simultaneous telephonic appearances in multiple courts does not excuse a failure to appear when a matter is placed on calendar. Individuals making use of the conference call service are cautioned that they do so at their own risk. Hearings generally will not be rescheduled due to missed connections.

II. PROCEDURES FOR TELEPHONIC APPEARANCE

Telephone appearances may be arranged, not later than 8:30 a.m. the day of the hearing, by calling Tele-Court, Inc. at (800) 924-5680 or going to www.tele-court.com.

Telephonic appearances are connected directly with the courtroom's public address system and electronic recording equipment so that a normal record is produced. **To ensure the quality of the record, the use of car phones, cellular phones, speaker phones, public telephone booths, or phones in other public places is prohibited except in the most extreme emergencies.** Participants should be able to hear all parties without difficulty or echo.

You must be on the line, ready to proceed with your hearing, **before** the judge takes the bench and calls the calendar. You may initially be in the listening mode in which case you will be able to hear the case before yours just as if you were in the courtroom. **You must place your phone on "mute" until your matter is called to ensure the quality of the record and to avoid interfering with other hearings in progress.**

At the time of your hearing, the judge will call the case, request appearances, and direct the manner in which the hearing proceeds. Each time you speak, you should identify yourself for the record. The court's teleconferencing system allows more than one speaker to be heard, so the judge can interrupt a speaker to ask a question or redirect the discussion. When the judge informs the participants that the hearing is completed, you may disconnect and the next case will be called.

Telephonic appearances by multiple participants are only possible when there is compliance with every procedural requirement. Sanctions may be imposed when there is any deviation from the required procedures or the court determines that a person's conduct makes telephonic appearances inappropriate. Sanctions may include dropping a matter from calendar, continuing the hearing, proceeding in the absence of an unavailable participant, a monetary sanction, and/or a permanent prohibition against a person appearing telephonically.

C. *Procedures for Disclosure Statement and Confirmation Hearings*

PROCEDURES FOR DISCLOSURE STATEMENT AND CONFIRMATION HEARINGS

This outline of procedures is intended to assist counsel in preparing for Chapter 11 disclosure statement and confirmation hearings before Judge Peter H. Carroll. These procedures are not inflexible. The court may modify them to accommodate the needs of counsel and any particular Chapter 11 case.

1. Disclosure Statement Hearings

Prior to the disclosure hearing the court reviews each proposed disclosure statement (whether or not objections have been filed). Accordingly, counsel are requested to notify chambers not later the Monday prior to the scheduled hearing if the disclosure statement will be continued.

The court may present a checklist of deficiencies in the proposed disclosure statement at the disclosure hearing. Assuming no other objections have been filed and depending on the extent of the revisions required, the court will either continue the disclosure statement hearing or allow conditional approval of the disclosure statement. When the court has conditionally approved the disclosure statement, the plan proponent will need to present an amended disclosure statement together with a proposed order approving the disclosure statement that conforms to Official Form 13.

If the plan proponent intends to amend its proposed disclosure statement in response to objections that have been filed, a "red-lined" version of the amended disclosure statement should be filed with the court and circulated to opposing counsel not later than the Monday prior to the scheduled disclosure statement hearing. If the plan proponent will require a continuance to prepare the amended disclosure statement, it should notify opposing counsel and the court not later than the Monday prior to the scheduled disclosure statement hearing. If objections cannot be resolved by stipulation and/or amendment of the proposed disclosure statement, the court will consider any unresolved objections at the disclosure statement hearing.

Once a disclosure statement has been approved, the court will schedule the confirmation hearing at the conclusion of the disclosure statement hearing. The plan proponent should prepare a proposed order approving the disclosure statement that conforms to Official Form 13 with the dates supplied by the court at the disclosure statement hearing.

2. Confirmation Hearings

Prior to confirming any proposed plan of reorganization, the court will require evidence of compliance with each requirement of 11 U.S.C. § 1129(a) and, when applicable, § 1129(b). Counsel are cautioned that the failure of a class to vote does not constitute acceptance of the plan. Bell Road Inv. Co. v. M. Long Arabians (In re M. Long Arabians), 103 B.R. 211, 215-16 (9th Cir. BAP 1989). A class must vote affirmatively to accept the plan. See In re Townco Realty, Inc., 81 B.R. 707, 708 (Bankr. S.D. Fla. 1987).

A completed tabulation of ballots should be filed by the plan proponent not later than the Monday prior to the confirmation hearing. If no objections to confirmation have been filed, the plan proponent should also file declarations in support of confirmation that address the elements of § 1129.

If objections to confirmation have been filed, the court will normally treat the confirmation hearing as a scheduling conference. At that hearing, the court will establish a briefing schedule, if appropriate, and set a further evidentiary hearing during which live testimony may be presented.

If the objecting parties and the plan proponent so stipulate, the objections may be resolved based on written evidence and briefs filed with the court prior to the confirmation hearing. The court may also allow live testimony and cross-examination, time permitting, at the initial confirmation hearing upon stipulation of the parties.

Hon. Scott C. Clarkson

Bankruptcy Judge

Contact Information
U.S. Bankruptcy Court, Central District of California
Courtroom 5C
411 West Fourth Street, Suite 5130
Santa Ana, CA 92701
Courtroom Deputy: (951) 774-1097

Biographical Information

Appointment(s):

- Appointed January 20, 2011.

Education:

- Indiana University- Bloomington, BA 1979
- George Mason University School of Law, JD 1982. Articles Editor, Law Review.

Career Record:

- Admitted to the California Bar, 1989; District of Columbia Bar, 1988; Commonwealth of Virginia Bar, 1982.
- Clerk to United States District Judge William L. Hungate (E.D.Mo.)
- Legislative Assistant to United States Representative Harold L. Volkmer, 95th Congress to 97th Congress.

Professional Memberships:

- American Bankruptcy Institute
- National Conference of Bankruptcy Judges
- California Bankruptcy Forum
- Los Angeles County Bar Association

I. Judge Clarkson's Procedures and Practices

A. Appearances in Riverside or Santa Ana Courtrooms

APPEARANCES BOTH IN RIVERSIDE OR SANTA ANA COURTROOMS ALLOWED, WITH EXCEPTIONS

Updated 1/25/2011

Judge Clarkson permanently sits in Santa Ana, but is assigned Riverside division cases. Please note that unless ordered otherwise, counsels and parties may appear at either Judge Clarkson's video courtroom located at the United States Federal Courthouse, Riverside Division, 3420 Twelfth Street, Video Hearing Room 126, Riverside, CA 92501, or live at the United States Bankruptcy Court Ronald Reagan Federal Building and Court House, 411 West Fourth Street, Courtroom 5C, Santa Ana, CA 92701.

NOTE: All Hearings for Judge Clarkson's Riverside Division cases must be noticed with a hearing address of 3420 Twelfth Street, Video Hearing Room 126 Riverside, CA 92501.

B. Failure to Timely File Required Status Reports

FAILURE TO TIMELY FILE REQUIRED STATUS REPORTS – COUNSELS/PARTIES MUST APPEAR IN SANTA ANA

Updated 1/25/2011

All required status reports in adversary proceedings and chapter 11 cases must be filed timely. Please carefully review all Central District Local Bankruptcy Rules and all orders arising in adversary proceedings and Chapter 11 cases for the timing, content and service of such status reports.

Any counsel or party required to file and serve a status report by a date certain pursuant to the Local Bankruptcy Rules or by order of the Court, but fails to do so, must physically appear for hearing in Courtroom 5C at the United States Bankruptcy Court – Ronald Reagan Federal Building and Court House, 411 West Fourth Street, Santa Ana, CA 92701. Video or telephone appearances are not an option.

C. Notice Regarding Telephonic Appearance Procedures

NOTICE RE TELEPHONIC APPEARANCE PROCEDURES FOR JUDGE SCOTT C. CLARKSON'S CASES

EFFECTIVE August 22, 2011

I. POLICY GOVERNING TELEPHONIC APPEARANCES

Telephonic appearances are allowed in **all matters** before Judge Clarkson **with the exception** of Trials and Evidentiary Hearings (all counsel and all witnesses must appear in person in Courtroom 5C located at 411 West Fourth Street, Santa Ana, CA 92701) and such other matters as designated by the Court as requiring a personal appearance.

No telephonic appearance will be allowed unless it is made through **CourtCall**, an independent conference call company, pursuant to the procedures set forth in Section II.

Before the hearing, you should check Judge Clarkson's Calendar on the United States Bankruptcy Court website and review any Tentative Ruling concerning the matter on calendar. If the court has issued a Tentative Ruling prior to the hearing, each individual who appears telephonically should have reviewed the Tentative Ruling prior to the hearing. If an individual schedules a telephonic appearance and then fails to respond to the call of a matter on calendar, the court may treat the failure to respond as a failure to appear. Scheduling simultaneous telephonic appearances in multiple courts does not excuse a failure to appear.

The 3:00 p.m. deadline for scheduling telephonic appearances noted below is independent of the Tentative Rulings process. Late scheduling of a telephonic appearance is not justified by the fact that Tentative Rulings have not been posted on the Court's website by 3:00 p.m. the day before the hearing.

Individuals making use of the conference call service are cautioned that they do so at their own risk. Hearings generally will not be rescheduled due to missed connections.

II. SCHEDULING A TELEPHONIC APPEARANCE.

By Telephone: Absent an emergency, telephone appearances may be arranged by calling **CourtCall at (866) 582-6878** not later than **3:00 p.m.** the court day prior to the hearing date. Any request for a telephonic appearance made after the 3:00 p.m. deadline must be Court approved by contacting Judge Clarkson's Chambers at 714-338-5460.

III. PROCEDURE FOR TELEPHONIC APPEARANCE.

Court Call will provide counsel with written confirmation of a telephonic appearance, and give counsel a number to call to make the telephonic appearance. It is counsel's responsibility to dial into the call not later than 10 minutes prior to the scheduled hearing.

CourtCall does not place a call to counsel.

Telephonic appearances are connected directly with the courtroom's public address system and electronic recording equipment so that a normal record is produced. **To ensure the quality of the record, the use of car phones, cellular phones, speakerphones, public telephone booths, or phones in other public places is prohibited except in the most extreme emergencies.** Participants should be able to hear all parties without difficulty or echo.

After your call is connected to the courtroom, the Judge will call the case, request appearances, and direct the manner in which the hearing proceeds. Each time you speak, you should identify yourself for the record. The court's teleconferencing system allows more than one speaker to be heard, so the Judge can interrupt a speaker to ask a question or redirect the discussion. When the Judge informs the participants that the hearing is completed, you may disconnect.

Telephonic appearances by multiple participants are only possible when there is compliance with every procedural requirement. Sanctions may be imposed when there is any deviation from the required procedures or the Court determines that a person's conduct makes telephonic appearances inappropriate. Sanctions may include dropping a matter from calendar, continuing the hearing, proceeding in the absence of an unavailable participant, a monetary sanction, and/or a permanent prohibition against a person appearing telephonically.

D. Trials and Evidentiary Hearings

JUDGE CLARKSON'S PROCEDURES:
TRIALS and EVIDENTIARY HEARINGS

If these instructions are not followed explicitly, sanctions may be imposed.

A. BRIEFS

LBR Reference	Please comply with LBR 9013-2
Judge's Copy	* Please comply with LBR 5005-2(d)
	* Please comply with Court Manual Sections 2-5(d), 3-5(b) and Appendix F

B. EXHIBITS

LBR Reference	Please comply with LBR 9070-1
Identification	Per LBR 9070-1(a)(2):
	* **Numbers:** plaintiff/movant's exhibits must be marked with numbers in increasing order
	* **Letters:** defendant/respondent's exhibits must be marked with letters in alphabetical order.
	Tags All parties presenting exhibits have the responsibility to tag their own exhibits prior to the start of trial. Exhibit tags may be obtained from the courtroom deputy or the court recorder prior to the trial.
# Copies	* Please bring **one original set** (court recorder)
	* Please bring **at least 4 sets of copies** (1/each counsel, 1/judge, 1/witness)
Exhibit Register	All parties presenting exhibits must prepare an exhibit register on Form B 3024 "EXHIBIT REGISTER AND NOTICE RE DISPOSITION OF EXHIBITS" available on the court's website, www.cacb.uscourts.gov, under "Court Forms."

Hon. Thomas B. Donovan

Bankruptcy Judge

Contact Information

U.S. Bankruptcy Court, Central District of California
Courtroom 1345
255 E. Temple Street, Suite 1352
Los Angeles, CA 90012
Courtroom Deputy: (213) 894-6172

Biographical Information

Appointment(s):

- Appointed 03/21/94 by the United States Court of Appeals for the Ninth Circuit.
- Reappointed 03/21/08 by the United States Court of Appeals for the Ninth Circuit. (Current term expires 03/20/22.)

Personal:

- Married. Two grown children.

Education:

- San Jose State College (California), 1953-55;
- University of California at Berkeley, 1955-57, B.A.;
- Boalt Hall School of Law, Univ. of California at Berkeley, 1959-62, J.D., Law Review.

Military Service:

- Entered active duty as 2LT, U. S. Army in 1957; released as 1LT in 1959 after service with Army Security Agency.

Career Record:

- 1962-63, Associate, Covington and Burling, Washington, DC;
- 1964-69, Associate then Partner, Dinkelspiel and Dinkelspiel, San Francisco, California;
- 1969-93, Partner, Dinkelspiel, Donovan and Reder, San Francisco, California.
- Admitted to the California Bar, 1963; District of Columbia Bar, 1963; U. S. Supreme Court Bar, 1966.

Professional Memberships:

- American Bankruptcy Institute;
- Fellow, American College of Bankruptcy;
- National Conference of Bankruptcy Judges;
- California Bankruptcy Forum;
- Financial Lawyers' Conference;
- Bankruptcy Committee, Los Angeles County Bar Association;
- Los Angeles Association of Business Trial Lawyers.

I. Judge Donovan's Procedures and Practices

A. *Chapter 13 Lien Stripping Motion Suggestions*

CHAPTER 13 LIEN STRIPPING MOTION SUGGESTIONS

We receive many lien stripping motions in chapter 13 cases. The process can be more successful for movants if the following considerations are kept in mind:

Notice: Be sure the affected junior lien creditor is served properly under the rules. Serving a personally-named officer of a bank is best. Mail sent to a street address generally is better than to a post office drop box. Service in accordance with Rule 7004 is the safest. Service addressed as requested in a proof of claim may suffice as well.

Motion: Be sure to attach credible, persuasive evidence of (1) the property value as of the petition date and (2) the current principal balance owed to the senior lien holder. Bank statements reflecting current principal balances are more persuasive than most debtors' conclusory statements.

Prayer: This should be limited and explicit. You may want the following: (1) the second deed of trust (for example) to be deemed unsecured for purposes of chapter 13; (2) to treat any proof of claim filed by the holder of the second to be deemed an unsecured claim within the debtor's chapter 13 plan; (3) upon completion of the chapter 13 plan and entry of a chapter 13 discharge, the second to be treated as void and no longer an encumbrance against the debtor's property; and (4) to add a request that upon completion of the chapter 13 plan and discharge, the holder of the second reconvey the second deed of trust.

In every prayer, you must specify that should the case be dismissed or converted to any other chapter prior to completion of the plan and entry of a chapter 13 discharge, the lien will remain valid.

Points and Authorities generally are not necessary because the court is familiar with current governing lien stripping appellate decisions.

B. Chapter 13 Requirements and Suggestions

CHAPTER 13 REQUIREMENTS AND SUGGESTIONS

The optional form F4003-2.4 MOTION and the accompanying ORDER are mandatory in my court for motions to avoid junior liens on real property pursuant to 11 U.S.C. § 506(d). Parties may supplement the mandatory forms to provide additional information.

Documentary evidence of a tax assessment is strong evidence of real property value.

Broker's price opinions or other evidence is acceptable to Judge Donovan with respect to motions to avoid junior liens, provided the evidence is persuasive and authenticated by a declaration.

Judge Donovan will allow loan modification discussions and agreements. Judge Donovan will not approve terms of loan modification agreements that the parties agree to.

Attorneys should be mindful of the requirements of the LBRs with respect to Notice of Motion, Motion, and proofs of service, as outlined in LBR 9013-1(c)(2), (d)(2), and (e). Judge Donovan is frequently seeing noncompliance with these rules, resulting in delays and disappointment.

C. *Disclosure Statement Review and Approval Procedures*

DISCLOSURE STATEMENT REVIEW AND APPROVAL PROCEDURE

The judge generally employs the following system for reviewing chapter 11 disclosure statements:

When we receive a disclosure statement (and objections), the law clerk looks over the papers and drafts a memorandum of decision outlining all the significant objections, her/his own objections, and her/his recommended response to each objection. The judge reviews the papers and the draft, makes a decision on each objection, adds his own, and inserts an overall comment as to the general quality of the proponent's proposal along with instructions for remediation and further hearing. The direct participants are notified by phone and fax by the law clerk. Usually, no hearing is necessary, though no request for a hearing has been denied. Rarely, Judge Donovan requires a hearing. After the hearing date, the memorandum of decision may be revised and then is signed, entered, and mailed out.

The judge believes this procedure is considerably less time consuming and more helpful to the participants than discussing the objections and proposed changes at a hearing. In our experience, this system typically leads to faster, more effective and economical disclosure statement approval and plan confirmation, especially if debtor's lawyers are doing a conscientious job of representing their client.

Attached is an example of a memorandum of decision documenting (1) strong disapproval and (2) that an order to show cause will be issued based on substantive deficiencies in the proposed disclosure statement. Names of the parties, the case number and dates have been redacted to avoid embarrassing anybody.

Occasionally, unfortunately, a proposed disclosure statement is an unmitigated disaster. In that event, the judge may reject the disclosure statement outright without a detailed memorandum of decision but simply with an order containing instructions for remediation and an order to show cause why the case should not be dismissed or converted.

Sample Disclosure Statement Memorandum of Decision

NOTE: This is a copy of a disclosure statement memorandum of decision. Docket numbers, names of parties and dates have been changed to avoid embarrassing anybody. Altered or deleted names and numbers are shown in brackets.

IN THE UNITED STATES BANKRUPTCY COURT
FOR THE CENTRAL DISTRICT OF CALIFORNIA

In re	)	Case No. LA [__-_____] TD
[ABC DEVELOPERS, INC.]	)	Chapter 11
	)	
Debtor.	)	**MEMORANDUM OF DECISION RE: THE DEBTOR'S ORIGINAL DISCLOSURE STATEMENT; AND ORDER**
______________________________	)	

DATE: [_______]
TIME: 11:00 a.m.
PLACE: Courtroom 1345

CONTINUED HEARING DATE:
DATE: [________]
TIME: 11:00 a.m.
PLACE: Courtroom 1345

The Debtor filed a voluntary chapter 11 petition on [_______]. This is a single asset real estate case and the Debtor has proposed a Plan of Reorganization (plan). The court has received objections to approval of the Debtor's Original Disclosure Statement (disclosure statement) from the Office of the United States Trustee (OUST), and from two secured creditors: the [County] and the [Bank]. These objections convincingly reflect that the disclosure statement is seriously deficient.

Section 1125 governs approval of a disclosure statement. Section 1125(b) states that

> [a]n acceptance or rejection of a plan may not be solicited . . . from a holder of a claim or interest with respect to such claim or interest, unless, at the time of or before such solicitation, there is transmitted to such holder the plan or summary of the plan, and a written disclosure statement approved after notice and a hearing, by the court as containing adequate information.

Section 1125 governs approval of a disclosure statement. Section 1125(a)(1) provides:

> "adequate information" means information of a kind, and in sufficient detail, as far as is reasonably practicable in light of the nature and history of the debtor and the condition of the debtor's books and records, that would enable a hypothetical reasonable investor typical of holders of claims or interests of the relevant class to make an informed judgment about the plan . . . .

The court finds the disclosure statement to lack adequate information and hereby continues the matter to afford the Debtor an opportunity to amend and improve upon the content of the disclosure statement, as well as the plan. Aside from the detailed corrections that need to be made pursuant to the objections sustained as outlined below, the disclosure statement needs to present to creditors a more comprehensive, objective view of the factors that will have an effect on any prospective reorganization.

Objections of the OUST

The OUST does not believe that the disclosure statement contains "adequate information." All of the OUST's objections are sustained and the disclosure statement must be amended in light of these objections.

1. The technical errors and inconsistencies in the disclosure statement need to be amended.

2. The disclosure statement should be amended to explain why the Debtor filed its bankruptcy petition in the Central District of California, despite the fact that it operates property located in [a distant state].

3. The status of [John Doe's] ownership interest in the Debtor and his involvement in management of the Debtor under the plan, if any, needs to be fully disclosed in a comprehensive manner, as opposed to the present piecemeal fashion. The Debtor also needs to explain [John Doe's] past and present relationship to the Debtor and any related entities in order to assist creditors to better understand why [John Doe] has refused to provide certain financial statements to the Bank and to sign certain documents for extension of the Bank loan.

4. The disclosure statement should be amended to include the definition of "Effective Date."

5. The disclosure statement must be amended to explain, specifically, why Classes Three and Four are "not impaired."

6. Disclosure is required regarding whether the security deposits, which are listed as priority unsecured claims pursuant to §507(a)(6), have been segregated, the exact amount of such security deposits collected, as well as the exact amount of such claims.

The court adds to the OUST's objection that the disclosure statement should provide the language of [distant] state law that will determine the payment of such claims.

7. The description of the treatment of Class Six needs to be amended to indicate whether payments are to be monthly, quarterly, annually or some other time interval.

8. The Debtor is proposing to cram down on non-consenting classes. If more than 50% of Class Six agrees to receive payment of 60% of their claim, then that whole class would be paid 60% of their claim. At the same time, interest holders (Class Seven) retain 100% of their interest. This appears to violate the absolute priority rule. The disclosure statement and the plan must account for this possible violation and the disclosure statement must explain to creditors, in a clear, comprehensible fashion, what the violation is and whether and how the Debtor's plan is feasible and confirmable despite the violation.

9. The partnership administration fee is disclosed to be $12,500 each quarter.

The disclosure statement should describe what services are provided entitling [X Properties, Inc. (XP)], the Debtor's general partner, to this fee. Also, the disclosure statement should clarify that [XP] will suspend its "administrative fee" until all creditors are paid in full.

10. Classes Two and Three are undersecured. The plan appears to treat them differently than other unsecured creditors, absent the 1111(b) election. This is a violation of §1122(b) and must be addressed and/or amended in both the plan and the disclosure statement.

11. The disclosure statement needs to discuss the circumstances of all of the notes and amounts due and how they will be treated under the plan. Specifically, the balance sheet dated 9/30/97 lists as a liability a note due to "GP" in the amount of $70,000 which is not included in the plan and is not disclosed anywhere in the disclosure statement. The same is true for the $100,000 listed as a liability owed to "Affiliates." The identity and nature of the relationship(s) of the "Affiliates" to the Debtor also should be disclosed. To the extent that any amounts have been paid to these apparently related persons in the year prior to filing, those amounts also should be disclosed.

12. Both the disclosure statement and the plan need to address the calculation and payment of post-confirmation quarterly fees and clearly state who the responsible parties for payment will be.

13. The Debtor indicates that any shortfall of necessary funds will be made up from a loan by [XP]. There needs to be a discussion of [XP's] financial condition and the wherewithal of [XP] to make those loans. In addition, under §723, the chapter 7 trustee has certain rights against the general partner. Therefore, the assets and liabilities of [XP] must be disclosed and considered in any liquidation analysis.

Objections of the County

The County's objection to the interest rate of 6% on payment of its claim pursuant to the plan is sustained. However, the County's suggestion of an interest rate of 10% will not be imposed on the Debtor by the court absent evidence that 10% is a reasonable rate.

Objections of the Bank

The Bank has taken the position that the court should deny approval of the disclosure statement because it fails to provide "adequate information" and is premised on an unconfirmable plan. The Bank's objections with respect to the disclosure statement's failure to provide adequate information are sustained and must be addressed by the Debtor in amending the disclosure statement.

1. The Debtor must completely describe the low-income housing tax credit program, as well as the Form 8609 Low Income Housing Credit Allocation Certification (Form 8609), and disclose the impact of both on the plan. Accordingly, there must be full disclosure of the Debtor's past and present status with respect to such tax credits and issuance of the Form 8609, as well as the probability that the Debtor will become eligible for use of such credits and/or the Form 8609. A complete and coherent explanation of any disputes or problems involving the Debtor, which have or will affect the tax credits and/or issuance of the Form 8609 is also required. More specifically, the Debtor must address the allegations made by the Bank with respect to these issues and why the Bank believes the Debtor has been precluded from obtaining permanent financing to date.

2. Considering that the heart of the plan is the Debtor's ability to obtain a permanent "take out" loan, the Debtor has failed to disclose sufficient information to permit creditors to make a reasoned decision concerning plan feasibility or whether the plan provides for an adequate means of implementation or to evaluate whether confirmation is likely to be followed by liquidation of the need for future financial reorganization. The court concurs strongly with this objection and will not approve the disclosure statement absent coherent and full disclosure of such critical information.

The Debtor must amend the disclosure statement to provide all information regarding the procedure to obtain such a loan, as well as what the Debtor has done and/or will do to obtain such a loan and why the Debtor believes that it will succeed in doing so.

Moreover, the disclosure statement must set forth, in detail, a time line for the steps the Debtor will take to obtain the loan and what will happen if the Debtor fails to do so by a definite date. The disclosure statement must clarify who the "back-up take-out lenders" are. The Debtor alleges to have "arranged to pursue" with such lenders if the loan with [ABC Mortgage Co.] falls through. The disclosure statement also must set forth whether and why the Debtor will be able to perform under such loan (or any loan, for that matter), in light of the Debtor's history of defaults under present loans.

3. The disclosure statement must explain in detail how the Debtor will raise between $400,000 and $700,000 in additional equity to secure "take-out" financing from a new source. In order for creditors to estimate the feasibility and possibility of success of this plan, complete and specific disclosure of the following is required: who are the securities brokers and investors who gave the Debtor a "positive response about refinancing options and further syndication of the tax credits to raise this additional equity" and exactly what were their comments; who will further syndicate the tax credits; whether existing equity holders or other investors will purchase the tax credits; and any current commitments to infuse additional capital.

4. References in the disclosure statement to different fair market valuations of the subject property must be supported by admissible evidence.

5. The disclosure statement must be further supplemented with historical and projected financial information concerning the Debtor and, specifically, the operating income and expenses of the subject property.

Additional Comments of the Court

1. The supporting affidavit of [Sam Smith] is fragmentary, piecemeal, evasive and inadequate. All factual statements in the disclosure statement must be supported by a complete, unqualified declaration executed by the principal(s) of the Debtor under penalty of perjury .

2. The Debtor should fully disclose the nature of the County's secured claim.

3. The disclosure statement must be amended to clearly state the full amount of each claim.

4. Exhibits B, C and D are incomplete and confusing. The exhibits must be amended to provide accurate information that is consistent with the information provided in the body of the disclosure statement.

5. All pages of the disclosure statement, including attached exhibits, must be numbered consecutively at the bottom of each page pursuant to Local Rule 1002-1(4)(c).

6. The Debtor failed to satisfy the notice requirements for approval of a disclosure statement pursuant to Fed. R. Bankr. P. 2002(b)(1). The Debtor must comply with all notice requirements for future hearings.

Conclusion

The Debtor is required to amend the disclosure statement pursuant to the aforementioned rulings. Furthermore, in light of the serious substantive deficiencies outlined above, an order to show cause will be entered by the court. The hearing on approval of the Debtor's disclosure statement and the status conference hearing are continued to [______] at 11:00 a.m. The Debtor is directed to file and serve both red-lined and clean copies of its First Amended Disclosure Statement on the OUST, the Bank and the County, and to provide conformed courtesy copies delivered to chambers no later than [________]. Objections to the First Amended Disclosure Statement shall be filed, with conformed courtesy copies to chambers, no later than [______].

DATED: [_______]

____
THOMAS B. DONOVAN
United States Bankruptcy Judge

ORDER

IT IS SO ORDERED.

DATED: [_______]

____
THOMAS B. DONOVAN
United States Bankruptcy Judge

D. *Helpful Hints for Legal Assistants, Paralegals, and Lawyers from Judge Donovan's Chambers*

HELPFUL HINTS FOR LEGAL ASSISTANTS, PARALEGALS AND LAWYERS FROM JUDGE DONOVAN'S CHAMBERS

Forms:

We encourage the use of current, court-approved forms, for plans, motions, status conference reports, and orders. They are great time savers and help eliminate many ambiguities, evidentiary oversights, and delays. The forms can be found on the court's website: www.cacb.uscourts.gov.

Motions:

Notices of motions, motions and proofs of service should be filed at the same time. Judge's Copies must be mailed or delivered directly to chambers when motion papers are filed. **Motions will not be placed on the calendar until the Judge's Copies are received in chambers.**

Tabs on the Judge's Copy for exhibits and declarations or other attachments are very important, particularly if the papers are lengthy or complicated. Tabs should be visible at a glance and should be durable.

Motions not supported by declarations or persuasive evidence will be denied.

If the judge issues a tentative ruling on an uncontested matter and excuses the movant's appearance, but a party appears in court to contest the motion, the judge may either allow the tentative ruling to stand or continue the matter so that absent parties can be afforded an opportunity to be heard. If the matter is continued, the courtroom deputy will call the moving party with the date and time of the continued hearing. The moving party should give notice of the continued hearing.

The judge changes tentative rulings, occasionally.

Declarants normally are not required to be present at hearings on motions.

Oral testimony seldom is required or allowed unless the judge has agreed in advance to hear oral testimony. If live cross examination is essential, be sure to make arrangements for cross examination in advance, with opposing counsel first, and then through the judge's law clerk Brook Gotberg at (213) 894-1577.

If a matter is settled or will be withdrawn, continued or taken off calendar, please inform the judge's law clerk Brook Gotberg at (213) 894-1577 or the judge's courtroom deputy Pat Pennington Jones at (213) 894-6172 as soon as possible and file and serve an appropriate notice.

Relief From Stay - Unlawful Detainer and Questionable Real Estate Transfers:

The judge hears relief from stay motions on 14 days' notice when they involve (1) residential unlawful detainer; (2) post-petition transfers of real property; or (3) prepetition transfers of real property to the debtor either (a) within 90 days of the petition date or (b) involving fractionalized transfers of real property. An order shortening time is not required in any such instance. Pleadings should be filed and served at least 14 days prior to the hearing.

Proof of service should be filed when the pleadings are filed, if possible.

Rule 9019 Motions Affecting Adversary Proceedings:

While a motion for approval of a proposed compromise sometimes must be filed in the main bankruptcy case, please be sure to follow up promptly with a separate motion or application in the adversary to dismiss the adversary once the compromise has been approved by the court.

Emergency and Ex Parte Applications:

Emergency hearings should be requested only when a true emergency exists that was not self-inflicted. A moving party should file an ex parte application only if there is a very good reason to warrant a hearing on shortened time.

When filing an emergency motion, the moving party should telephone the judge's law clerk Brook Gotberg ahead of time to alert him to expect the papers.

The judge usually requires moving papers before he sets an emergency hearing, except in Chapter 11 case "first day" or other urgent matters.

If an ex parte application to hear a matter on shortened time is granted, notice by electronic means, overnight delivery, telephone and/or fax usually is required.

Status Conferences:

A thorough, written status report, filed 14 days in advance, is required before each chapter 11 status conference hearing and 14 days in advance before each adversary status conference hearing. In adversary proceedings, use of court-approved status conference report forms is strongly recommended.

Objections to Proof of Claims:

On objections to proof of claim, the judge requires admissible evidence and legal grounds to be set forth as required by the Bankruptcy Code, Bankruptcy Rules, and especially Local Bankruptcy Rule 3007-1.

Orders:

The judge normally signs orders promptly. If more than a week has passed since you submitted the order, you should check CM/ECF, or you may, if necessary, telephone the judge's administrative law clerk Candace Crociani at (213) 894-3728 to check on the status of the proposed order.

Please lodge an order promptly through L.O.U. or at the filing window in the clerk's office. The moving party or the prevailing party may drop off the proposed order in the courtroom on the day of the hearing.

Appearances:

The judge generally allows telephone appearances, as a courtesy, not as a right. It is the requester's duty to make arrangements and to place the call. Requests should be made by calling CourtCall at (866) 582-6878.[1] When appearing by phone, speak directly into the phone,

[1] After October 1, 2010, the telephonic appearance provider will be Tele-Court.

do not use cell phones (except in an real emergency) or speaker phones (ever).

Attorneys may request second call by calling the judges law clerk Candace Crociani at (213) 894-3728 or by making the request personally to the court recorder before the calendar call. The judge normally will honor reasonable requests for a limited amount of time, subject to balancing the reason for the request against the inconvenience to other parties.

Attorneys may request priority when they check in with the judge's court recorder Wanda Toliver just before the calendar call. Within reason, such requests usually are granted, especially if the matter can be dealt with very briefly.

Requests for Transcripts:

You may order a transcript of a hearing by contacting the judge's court recorder Wanda Toliver at (213) 894-5011.

Common Problems and Suggestions:

Lawyers who wish to introduce business records in evidence should pay close attention to Rule 803(6) of the Federal Rules of Evidence.

Please submit a proposed order granting an ex parte application for an order shortening time when the ex parte application is filed, preferably, filled out with your proposed hearing date and notice and service requirements normally required by the court, to the best of your knowledge.

Be sure to move to reopen the case under § 350 when bringing a motion to avoid a lien discovered after the debtor has been discharged and the case has been closed.

Be sure to use F 9021-1.1 for the required Notice of Entered Order.

Please staple pleadings only once, in the upper left hand corner.

Please throw away staplers that don't work. Open staples are a constant nuisance.

Note the Judge's Copy rules and Court Manual instructions. Judge's copies are required and must be delivered timely to be of any use or to be actually read by the court. In the Judge's Copy, you **must use tabs for exhibits and declarations, always**!

E. *Telephonic Appearance Procedures*

TELEPHONIC PROCEDURE FOR
HONORABLE THOMAS B. DONOVAN
Updated 09/28/2010

The judge generally allows telephone appearances, as a courtesy, not as a right.

It is the requester's duty to make arrangements using the judge's designated conference call provider, Tele-Court.

To appear telephonically, you must go to www.tele-court.com or call (800) 924-5680.

When appearing by phone, mind your mute button to avoid interfering with other hearings in progress.

No speaker phones allowed ever!

No cell phones allowed without a very good reason.

F. Tentative Ruling Procedure

TENTATIVE RULING PROCEDURE

The judge issues tentative rulings whenever possible and appropriate prior to the scheduled hearing date. Tentatives are available via the court's website (www.cacb.uscourts.gov). Please do not call chambers to inquire if no tentative has been posted.

In most situations where tentative rulings are issued, an appearance is not required, but any party not in agreement with the tentative ruling may request a hearing at the scheduled time by telephoning Judge Donovan's law clerk Brook Gotberg at (213) 894-1577 the day before the hearing. If a hearing is requested, that party must notify all other interested parties of its intent to appear at the hearing not later than the business day before the hearing.

If the judge issues a tentative ruling in an uncontested matter and excuses the movant's appearance, but a party appears in court to contest the motion, the judge may either allow the tentative ruling to stand or continue the hearing to allow the absent parties to be heard. If the hearing is continued, the courtroom deputy, Pat Pennington Jones, will call the moving party with the date and time of the continued hearing.

The moving party must either (a) upload an order on L.O.U or (b) lodge a proposed order that conforms to the judge's tentative ruling, accompanied by a notice of entered order, the appropriate number of copies of the proposed order, and addressed, stamped envelopes bearing the names and addresses of those who are to receive a copy of the signed, entered order.

Attorneys are strongly encouraged to upload all orders through L.O.U. Otherwise, you may deposit the proposed lodged order and notice of entered order, along with all the copies and envelopes, in the courtroom or in the Judge's Copy box located outside of chambers on the day of the hearing. All proposed orders submitted after the hearing date must be lodged through L.O.U. or at the filing window.

G. Trial Procedures

TRIAL PROCEDURES

When the judge sets a case for trial, plaintiff's counsel normally must prepare and lodge a proposed scheduling order. If the case is to be tried based on written declarations, the judge will prepare the scheduling order outlining trial procedures. Trial dates will be adhered to strictly. Requests for continuances are discouraged unless the request is accompanied by a very good explanation.

The judge normally schedules several cases for trial one week per month, starting at 10 a.m. on Monday of the trial week (or Tuesday if Monday is a holiday).

The court will contact counsel the week before the scheduled trial date to determine whether the case has settled (or is going to settle) or the prospects that the case will be tried and, if the latter, counsels' current trial time estimates. If you reach a settlement, please let us know promptly at (213) 894-1577. Written stipulations and proposed orders must be filed at least two days before the trial date (excluding weekends or holidays) or personal appearance will be required at the time set for trial.

If possible, the judge will furnish counsel with a more definite starting date and time for the trial. The first trial of the week will begin promptly on Monday morning. As to cases that will be tried on Monday morning, counsel will be advised by the preceding Friday, and counsel and witnesses for such cases should be present on Monday morning at 10 a.m. Counsel should show up before that time to prepare exhibit tags for all expected trial exhibits. The court expects counsel and witnesses in later scheduled trials to be available on 2-3 hours telephone notice for the remainder of the week.

Trial exhibits and deposition transcripts should be marked in advance. Please follow the local rules carefully and prepare at least five exhibits sets (for counsel, opposing counsel, court files, Judge's Copies, and the witness). If the exhibits are longer than 10 pages, they should be assembled in loose leaf 3-ring binders and tabbed on the right (with exhibit numbers for the plaintiff and letters for the defendant). An exhibit register also should be filed, following the local rules. Deliver a complete set of Judge's Copies to chambers, in tabbed binders as required by these instructions.

All trial briefs and proposed findings and conclusions should be filed and served not less than one calendar week in advance of the trial date, with Judge's Copies delivered to chambers.

Opening statements are welcome (but usually are not necessary). Counsel should be prepared to complete closing argument as soon as the parties have rested. Post-trial briefs seldom are requested by the court, or allowed.

Hon. Mark D. Houle

Bankruptcy Judge

Contact Information

U.S. Bankruptcy Court, Central District of California
Courtroom 303
3420 Twelfth Street, Suite 365
Riverside, CA 92501
Courtroom Deputy: (951) 774-1085

Biographical Information

Appointment(s):

- Appointed 02/17/12 by the United States Court of Appeals for the Ninth Circuit. (Current term expires 02/16/2026.)

Education:

- Salem State College, 1993, B.S. (summa cum laude)
- Boston College Law School, 1996, J.D.

Military Service:

- United States Air Force, 1985 -1989
- Massachusetts Air National Guard, 1989 - 1993

Career Record:

- 1996 - 1998, Rotating Law Clerk, U. S. Bankruptcy Court, Santa Ana Division for the Honorable Lynne Riddle, James N. Barr, John J. Wilson, and Robert W. Alberts
- 1998 - 2000, Associate, Winthrop Couchot, PC
- 2000 - 2011, Counsel, Pillsbury Winthrop Shaw Pittman, LLP
- Admitted to the California Bar, 1998

Private Practice Specialization:

- Practiced exclusively in the areas of bankruptcy and insolvency. Primarily represented secured and unsecured creditors, asset purchasers, and other parties in bankruptcy cases, adversary proceedings, pre-bankruptcy workouts, and related state and federal litigation.

I. Judge Houle's Procedures and Practices

A. *Early Meeting of Counsel and Status Conference Instructions*

EARLY MEETING OF COUNSEL AND STATUS CONFERENCE INSTRUCTIONS

Effective February 17, 2012

1. **Service of Order.** A copy of this Order Re: Rule 26(f) Meeting, Initial Disclosures, and Scheduling Conference must be served with the summons and complaint. The proof of service of the summons and complaint must indicate that a copy of this order was served therewith.

2. **Local Bankruptcy Rule 7026-1.** Compliance with Local Bankruptcy Rule 7026-1 ("LBR 7026-1") is required in ALL adversary proceedings.

3. **Rule 26(f) Meeting.** Unless all defendants default, the parties must meet and confer pursuant to Rule 26(f) of the Federal Rules of Civil Procedure ("Rule 26(f) Meeting") at least 21 days before the status conference date set forth in the summons. **The status conference set forth in the summons shall also serve as the initial Rule 16(b) Scheduling Conference in this adversary proceeding.**

   The parties are jointly responsible for arranging and attending the Rule 26(f) Meeting, which may be conducted in person or by telephone. During the Rule 26(f) Meeting, the parties must, at a minimum: (a) discuss the nature and basis of their claims and defenses and the possibilities for a prompt settlement or resolution of the case; (b) make or arrange for the initial disclosures required by Rule 26(a)(1); and (c) develop a proposed discovery plan. The discussion of claims and defenses must be substantive and meaningful. The parties are directed to approach the Rule 26(f) Meeting cooperatively and in good faith.

4. **Initial Disclosures.** Rule 26(a)(1) states that a party must, without awaiting a discovery request, provide to other parties:

   a. The name and, if known, the address and telephone number of each individual likely to have discoverable information – along with the subjects of that information – that the disclosing party may use to support its claims or defenses, unless the use would be solely for impeachment;

   b. A copy of – or a description by category and location – of all documents, electronically stored information, and tangible things that the disclosing party has in its possession, custody, or control and may use to support its claims or defenses, unless the use would be solely for impeachment;

   c. A computation of each category of damages claimed by the disclosing party – who must also make available for inspection and copying as under Rule 34 the documents or other evidentiary material, unless privileged or protected from disclosure, on which each computation is based, including materials bearing on the nature and extent of injuries suffered; and

   d. For inspection and copying as under Rule 34, any insurance agreement under which an insurance business may be liable to satisfy all or part of a possible judgment in the action or to indemnify or reimburse for payments made to satisfy the judgment.

F.R.Civ.P. 26(a)(1)(A). Rule 26(a)(1) requires a party to make its initial disclosures based on the information then reasonably available to it. A party is not excused from making its disclosures because it has not fully completed its investigation of the case or because it challenges the sufficiency of another party's disclosures or because another party has not made its disclosures. F.R.Civ.P. 26(a)(1)(E).

5. **Alternative Dispute Resolution ("ADR").** The parties must explore the feasibility of ADR to reach a settlement or early resolution of the adversary proceeding. The specific reasons for any decision not to participate in a form of early ADR must be explained in the Joint Status Report. If the parties elect not to participate in an early ADR effort, the court may nonetheless direct the parties to ADR before trial.

6. **Discovery Plan.** At the Rule 26(f) Meeting, the parties must also discuss any issues about preserving discoverable information and develop a proposed discovery plan. The discussion regarding discovery following the initial disclosures must address the relevance of the discovery sought and the sequence and timing of such discovery, including whether the discovery will be conducted informally or formally. The deadlines in the discovery plan must be mutually agreeable, with a view to achieving resolution of the case with a minimum of expense and delay.

7. **Joint Status Report.** Not later than 7 days before the status conference/Rule 16(b) Scheduling Conference date set forth in the summons, the parties must file a Joint Status Report in a form substantively identical to LBR **Form F 7016-1.1**. The Joint Status Report must contain the information set forth in LBR 7016-1(a)(2), and a statement that the parties have completed the Rule 26(f) Meeting and made the initial disclosures required by Rule 26(a)(1). The Joint Status Report shall also serve as the written report of the Rule 26(f) Meeting.

8. **Status Conference/Rule 16(b) Scheduling Conference.** At the Rule 16(b) Scheduling Conference, the court will review the discovery plan set forth in the Joint Status Report and set appropriate deadlines. The court seeks to try all adversary proceedings not later than 18 months of the filing of the complaint. Consequently, all deadlines in the schedule, including the dispositive motion deadline, must be met within 12 to 14 months of the filing of the complaint to afford adequate time for briefing and ruling prior to the final pretrial conference and trial date.

   Counsel representing any party in conjunction with the Rule 26(f) Meeting, Joint Status Report, and Rule 16(b) Scheduling Conference must be authorized to bind the party on all matters to be covered.

9. **Default.** If no response to the complaint is timely filed, plaintiff should request entry of default by the clerk <u>prior</u> to the status conference date set forth in the summons. F.R.Civ.P. 55(a). Plaintiff may also request entry of a default judgment by filing and serving an appropriate motion. F.R.Civ.P. 55(b)(2).

10. **Sanctions.** Failure to comply with these instructions may subject the responsible party and/or counsel to sanctions. The failure of either party to cooperate in the preparation and filing of a Joint Status Report or appear at the status conference may result in the imposition of sanctions under LBR 7016-1(f) or (g).

B. Mandatory Use of Local Form 4003-2.4–Motion, Regarding Chapter 13 Debtor Motions to Avoid Junior Lien on Principal Residence

MANDATORY USE OF LOCAL FORM 4003-2.4 – MOTION, RE CHAPTER 13 DEBTOR MOTIONS TO AVOID JUNIOR LIEN ON PRINCIPAL RESIDENCE

Effective February 17, 2012

All motions filed by debtors in Chapter 13 cases to avoid junior liens on the debtor's principal residence (commonly referred to as "lien strip motions," "motions to value," "Lam motions," etc.)[1] must be made on Local Form 4003-2.4-Motion, entitled "Debtor's Motion to Avoid Junior Lien on Principal Residence [11 U.S.C. § 506(d)]." The form may be found on the Court's website, www.cacb.uscourts.gov, by clicking on "Forms/Rules/General Orders," then "Local Bankruptcy Rules & Forms," and scrolling down to F 4003-2.4-MOTION under "Local Bankruptcy Rules Forms."

All debtors filing a motion to avoid a junior lien on the debtor's principal residence must use Local Form 4003-2.4-Motion, including the proof of service. **If a motion to avoid a junior lien on the debtor's principal residence is not filed using Local Form 4003-2.4-Motion, including the proof of service, the motion will not be set for hearing.**

EVIDENCE

As the form indicates, all motions to avoid a junior lien must be supported by evidence regarding the amount and priority of the liens at issue, and the value of the property. Evidence must be admissible and persuasive.

Liens. Without evidence as to the validity and amount of the senior secured loan and the junior secured loan, the requested relief cannot be granted. The debtor's declaration, which contains the debtor's testimony regarding the liens and introduces the documents into evidence, along with a copy of the deed of trust, a loan statement, proof of claim or other statement from the current lender will establish the amount and validity of the lien. No documents will be considered as evidence unless they are accompanied by a declaration. The debtor's testimony alone, with no documentation, will not be sufficient to establish validity and amount (similarly, the debtor's schedules are not sufficient). The court also does not consider a credit report listing amounts owed to be admissible evidence of validity and amount; it is hearsay.

Value. The debtor may testify through a declaration regarding the value of the residence. The declaration should contain the basis for the testimony, which may include, among other factors, the debtor's familiarity with the residence, the neighborhood, and recent sales. It is insufficient for the declaration to state: "I believe that my residence is worth $xxx,xxx." Please note that the debtor may not rely solely on sources from the internet; this is hearsay. Therefore, a declaration stating "I believe my residence is worth $xxx,xxx based on the attached report from zillow.com [or cyberhomes.com or other similar website]" is not admissible evidence as to value.

---

1 The form is entitled "Debtor's Motion to Avoid Junior Lien on Principal Residence [11 U.S.C. § 506(d)]." More specifically, the relief sought is the valuation of a secured claim and determination of secured status pursuant to Fed. R. Bankr. P. 3012 and 11 U.S.C. § 506(d). This relief may be obtained through a noticed motion; an adversary proceeding is not necessary.

While not always necessary, an appraisal can be persuasive evidence of value. To be admissible evidence, the appraisal must be accompanied by a declaration of the debtor or the appraiser.

SERVICE

Use of the proof of service in Local Form 4003-2.4-Motion is mandatory. The proof of service must be completely filled out to indicate what parties were served, how they were served, and when they were served. Be sure to allow sufficient notice of the hearing to comply with LBR 9013-1(d) (notice to be served not later than 21 days before the hearing date). If a hearing date is chosen that is less than 21 days after service, the motion will be continued at least 21 additional days to allow the full notice period to pass.

Proper service of the motion – including compliance with Fed. R. Bankr. P. 7004 and Local Bankr. Rule 4003-2(c) – is critical.

Which parties to serve. The chapter 13 trustee, the affected lienholder, and all other parties asserting a lien on the property must be served. If any party has made an appearance in the case, that party (and counsel, if applicable) must be served at the address used in its notice of appearance.

Compliance with F.R.B.P. 7004(b)(3). This rule applies to domestic and foreign corporations and provides that service may be made by first-class mail upon "an officer, a managing or general agent, or to any other agent authorized by appointment or by law to receive service of process." The address for the corporation and its agent, if any, can usually be found on the corporation's website or the California Secretary of State website.

Compliance with F.R.B.P. 7004(h). Rule 7004(b)(3), discussed above, is generally applicable to corporations, but its lead-in indicates that it applies "[e]xcept as provided in subsection (h)." Rule 7004(h) specifically applies to insured depository institutions (as defined in section 3 of the Federal Deposit Insurance Act). Many lienholders are **FDIC-insured institutions and must be served in accordance with Rule 7004(h)**.

1. Is the lienholder an FDIC-insured institution? The FDIC website has a feature to search for institutions: http://www2.fdic.gov/idasp/main.asp. This feature will provide an address and list of officers for the institution. Please note that many institutions are subsidiaries of FDIC-insured institutions (for example, Bank of America Home Loans is a subsidiary of Bank of America, N.A.). In these cases, the FDIC-insured parent must be served in accordance with Rule 7004(h).
2. How to accomplish service in accordance with Rule 7004(h)? Rule 7004(h) requires that service be made by certified mail addressed to an officer of the institution.
   a. Use Certified Mail. Regular first-class mail, overnight mail or courier, or any other delivery method does not comply with Rule 7004(h); certified mail must be used.
   b. Address service to an officer. Remember, an officer of the institution is not the registered agent for service of process, or the FDIC itself. The best sources for finding an officer of an FDIC-insured institution are the FDIC website noted above, and the institution's website. Many courts have held that addressing service to "Officer of the Institution," "Chief Executive Officer,"

or "President" complies with the rule. If the institution's address is correct, and it is not possible to locate an officer's name, the court will not find that the motion was served incorrectly (although as a practical matter, it would be rare that an officer's name could not be found).

ORDER

When your motion is granted, submit an order within seven days after the hearing date. Use of Local Form 4003-2.4-Order is mandatory.

C. *Procedures Regarding Telephonic Appearances*

PROCEDURES REGARDING TELEPHONIC APPEARANCES

Effective February 17, 2012

Telephonic appearances are allowed in matters before Judge Mark D. Houle in Courtroom 303, except the following:

1. Trials and evidentiary hearings (all counsel and all witnesses must appear in person).
2. Chapter 11 status conferences (debtor's counsel must appear in person; other parties in interest may appear telephonically).
3. Adversary proceeding initial status conferences and pretrial conferences (all trial counsel must appear in person).
4. Chapter 11 and 13 confirmation hearings (debtor, debtor's counsel, and all objecting parties must appear in person).
5. Reaffirmation hearings (debtor and debtor's counsel must appear in person; other parties in interest may appear telephonically).
6. Any matter designated by the court as requiring a personal appearance.

In order to appear telephonically counsel must adhere to the following procedure:

Standard procedure:
Telephone appearances may be arranged by calling Court Call, an independent conference call company no later than 2:00 p.m. the day prior to the hearing. Counsel may reach Court Call at (888) 882-6878.

Emergency Procedure:
If an unexpected emergency arises that prevents counsel from following the standard procedure detailed above, counsel must telephone chambers and obtain a law clerk's approval to appear telephonically. A law clerk will only approve late requests for legitimate and unanticipated emergencies. Once approved, counsel must notify the courtroom deputy of counsel's approved telephonic appearance. The courtroom deputy may be reached at (951) 774-1085.

Once approved, counsel must also contact Court Call to arrange a telephonic appearance. If Court Call is not able to accommodate counsel's late request or if the Judge's law clerk denies the request, counsel will not be permitted to appear telephonically and counsel must make an appearance in court, as usual.

Individuals choosing to appear telephonically do so at their own risk. Hearings generally will not be rescheduled due to missed connections. Furthermore, in deciding to appear telephonically, counsel is agreeing to waive any prejudice attributable to quality deficiencies or irregularities of the record that may result.

To ensure the quality of the record, the use of cellular phones is prohibited except in the most extreme emergencies. If an individual's cellular phone is causing any interference, the court may ask that individual to disconnect from the hearing, and that individual will be deemed to have waived his or her appearance in the matter. Similarly, if a cellular phone disconnects during a hearing, the party appearing on cellular phone will be deemed to have waived his or her appearance.

D. *Trial and Evidentiary Hearing Procedures*

Trial and Evidentiary Hearing Procedures

Effective February 17, 2012

Briefs

LBR Reference: Please comply with LBR 9013-2

Judge's Copy: Please comply with LBR 5005-2(d)
Please comply with Court Manual Sections 2.5, 3.5(b) and Appendix F

Exhibits

LBR Reference: Please comply with LBR 9070-1

Identification: Per LBR 9070-1(a)(2):
Numbers: Plaintiff/Movant exhibits must be marked with numbers in increasing order.
Letters: Defendant/Respondent exhibits must be marked with letters in alphabetical order.

Tags: All parties presenting exhibits are responsible for tagging their own exhibits prior to the scheduled trial or evidentiary hearing. The mandatory yellow (Plaintiff) and blue (Defendant) exhibit tabs may be obtained from the Clerk's Office, the Courtroom DECRO, or Judge Houle's Courtroom Deputy, Rita Cargill. Exhibit tags must be placed on the back, bottom left-hand corner, of the last page of each exhibit.

Assembly /Witness List & Exhibit Register: All exhibits must be assembled in a binder or notebook. Each such binder or notebook must include a witness list and an exhibit register. The exhibit register shall be prepared using Form B 3024 "EXHIBIT REGISTER AND NOTICE RE DISPOSITION OF EXHIBITS," which is available on the court's website at www.cacb.uscourts.gov., under "Court Forms."

#of Copies: All parties shall prepare one tagged original set of exhibits to be offered into evidence and four sets of conformed copies (one for each counsel, one for the judge, one for the witness). All sets of exhibits shall be delivered to Judge Houle's Courtroom Deputy, Rita Cargill, at least five court days prior to the scheduled trial or evidentiary hearing.

Continuance /Settlement: Motions for continuance or stipulations for settlement must be filed and a proposed order lodged with the court at least five (5) court days prior to the scheduled trial or evidentiary hearing date, with courtesy copies delivered to chambers.

Lodging Orders: Orders that are capable of being lodged electronically shall be lodged via the Court's electronic Lodge Order Upload (LOU) system.

For any further questions regarding Judge Houle's procedures, please contact Courtroom Deputy, Rita Cargill at (951) 774-1085.

II. Judge Houle's Case Management Orders

A. *Standing Order Regarding Time of Chapter 13 Confirmation Hearing*

IN THE UNITED STATES BANKRUPTCY COURT
FOR THE CENTRAL DISTRICT OF CALIFORNIA

RE TIME OF CHAPTER 13 CONFIRMATION HEARING	)	**STANDING ORDER**

The undersigned Judge of the United States Bankruptcy Court, Central District of California, makes this standing order with respect to the time for the hearing on confirmation of Chapter 13 plans:

I hereby find and accordingly ORDER that it is in the best interests of the creditors and the estate to hold the hearing on the confirmation of the Chapter 13 plan on the same date as the meeting of creditors required under 11 U.S.C. § 341(a). **Any party in interest who objects to that timing of the confirmation hearing shall file a written objection thereto at least 20 calendar days before the scheduled confirmation hearing**; and it is

FURTHER ORDERED that the objecting party shall file the objection with the Court and serve it on the debtor, debtor's counsel, Chapter 13 trustee, and on any creditor who has filed an objection to confirmation, filed a request for special notice, or holds a security interest in the real property of the debtor. If a timely objection is received, the Court will reschedule the confirmation hearing.

DATED: February 17, 2012

____
MARK HOULE
United States Bankruptcy Judge

Hon. Wayne E. Johnson

Bankruptcy Judge

Contact Information
U.S. Bankruptcy Court, Central District of California
Courtroom 302
3420 Twelfth Street, Suite 345
Riverside, CA 92501
Courtroom Deputy: (951) 774-1098

Biographical Information

Appointment(s):

- Appointed 02/28/11 by the United States Court of Appeals for the Ninth Circuit. (Current term expires 02/27/25.)

Education:

- University of Pennsylvania Law School (J.D., 1992)
- Cornell University (B.A., magna cum laude 1989)

Career Record:

- 2003-2011, Law Office of Wayne Johnson, A Professional Corporation
- 1999-2001, Adjunct Professor of Law, Trinity Law School, Santa Ana, California
- 1996-2003, Brobeck, Phleger & Harrison LLP
- 1994-1996, Lewis, D'Amato, Brisbois & Bisgaard
- 1992-1994, Law Clerk to the Honorable David N. Naugle, U.S. Bankruptcy Court Central District of California
- 1992, Admitted to the Calilfornia State Bar

Publications:

- *Bad Laws for Bad Times*, Riverside Lawyer, Volume 59, Number 1 (2009)
- *Bankruptcy Basics*, California Lawyer (1997)
- *The Negotiated Rates Act of 1993: Congress Curtails Undercharge Litigation in Bankruptcy by Amending the Filed Rate Doctrine*, 68 American Bankruptcy Law Journal 319 (1994)
- *Discharging Unscheduled Debts: Creating Equal Justice for Creditors by Restoring Integrity to Section 523(a)(3)*, 10 Bankruptcy Developments Journal 571 (1994)
- *The embattled California Homestead Exemption*, 21 California Bankruptcy Journal 305 (1993)
- *In Re Bonner Mall Partnership: The Ninth Circuit Embraces the New Value Exception*, 21 California Bankruptcy Journal 259 (1993)
- *Effect of Decision Lingers Despite Code Changes*, Los Angeles Daily Journal (1996)
- *Slight Tremor: Quake Case Should Have Minor Impact on Lenders*, Los Angeles Daily Journal (1995)

- *No Preference: Avoiding a Bankruptcy-Reimbursement Suite*, Los Angeles Daily Journal (1995)
- *California Homestead Exemption Lives On in Bankruptcy*, Los Angeles Daily Journal (1994)
- *Courts Split Over Lender's Right to Sue for Fraud*, Los Angeles Daily Journal (1994)
- *The Power and the Glory of the Automatic Stay in Bankruptcy*, Los Angeles Daily Journal (1994)
- *Acting to Protect Security Interests in Bankruptcy Proceedings*, Los Angeles Daily Journal (1994)
- *Dueling Courts: Discharging Divorce Debts and Bankruptcy*, Los Angeles Daily Journal (1993)

I. Judge Johnson's Procedures and Practices

A. *Chapter 13 – General Guidelines*

CHAPTER 13 GUIDELINES

(June 14, 2011)

The following procedures apply to chapter 13 cases.

1. Follow the local rules and timely provide all required documents to the trustee and timely file all required documents with the court (including proofs of service). The failure to timely deliver or timely file documents (including proofs of service) will usually result in the dismissal of a case.

2. Timely make all plan payments and all secured debt payments. Failure to timely make required payments will usually result in the dismissal of a case.

3. Judge Johnson has posted on the Court's website separate guidelines regarding motions to value junior liens secured by real property (also known as "lien strip motions," "motions to extinguish junior liens," "motions to value," "*Lam* motions," etc.). All valuation motions must be filed and served in such a manner so that they are timely heard on or before the date of the initial confirmation hearing. This procedure applies to both real property and personal property. If, for example, a debtor intends to "cramdown" a creditor holding a lien against a vehicle (or other personal property) or otherwise attempt a "lien strip" of any kind in chapter 13, the debtor must file and serve a valuation motion with respect to that creditor and its collateral in such a manner so that the motion is timely heard on or before the date of the initial confirmation hearing.

4. Payment History Declaration.

(a) Judge Johnson has posted a form document entitled "Declaration Of Debtors Regarding Secured Debt Payment History" ("Payment History Declaration"). This declaration should be completed, filed and served between seven to fourteen days prior to the confirmation hearing. It should be served upon the chapter 13 trustee and all creditors holding consensual liens against the property identified in the declaration.

(b) As set forth in the form, the Payment History Declaration should provide information regarding monthly payments covering the period from (i) January 1st of the calendar year preceding the year in which the bankruptcy case is filed to (ii) the petition date.

(c) The Payment History Declaration applies to encumbered real property only. It is never required for personal property.

(d) The Payment History Declaration is required when the debtor intends to modify in any manner a debt secured by real property (i.e. to cure an arrearage, lien strip or otherwise). It is not required if the chapter 13 case does not involve any real property. The declaration does not apply to unencumbered real property. The declaration is not required if the chapter 13 case involves encumbered real property but the debtor does not intend to modify any debt secured by the real property.

(e) For example, if the debtor intends to surrender or abandon real property, the Payment History Declaration is not required with respect to that property. Likewise, if the debtor intends to keep real property but the debtor is current on all debts secured by the real property (and does not intend to cure any arrearage, lien strip or otherwise modify such debts), the Payment History Declaration is not required with respect to that property.

5. Local Bankruptcy Rule 3015-1(m) requires debtors to file and serve a declaration of post-petition payments using mandatory court form 3015-1.4 prior to every confirmation hearing. However, this rule has not always been enforced in the Riverside Division. Judge Johnson requires compliance with this rule to the following extent.

   (a) The form is not required in cases that do not involve any encumbered real property or only involve encumbered real property that the debtor intends to surrender or abandon.

   (b) Likewise, if the debtor intends to keep real property but the debtor is current on all debts secured by the real property (and does not intend to cure any arrearage, lien strip or otherwise modify such debts), the form is not required with respect to that property.

   (c) In chapter 13 cases involving real property secured by debts that debtors intend to modify, debtors have two options. They may (a) submit a Payment History Declaration that covers the period from January 1st of the prior year to a date between seven to fourteen days prior to the initial confirmation hearing (i.e., a declaration that covers the pre-petition and post-petition period) and not file Form 3015-1.14 or (b) file a Payment History Declaration that covers the period from January 1st of the prior year to the petition date and a Form 3015-1.14 that covers the entire post-petition period. If an initial confirmation hearing is continued, the Court will usually require the filing of another Payment History Declaration between seven to fourteen days prior to the continued hearing date.

B. Chapter 13 – Guidelines Regarding Valuation Motions

CHAPTER 13 GUIDELINES REGARDING MOTIONS TO VALUE (AKA "LAM" MOTIONS)

(April 15, 2011)

I. INTRODUCTION.

Applicable law provides that a chapter 13 debtor may avoid a junior lien on the debtor's residence under certain circumstances. *Zimmer v. PSB Lending Corp. (In re Zimmer)*, 313 F.3d 1220, 1227 (9th Cir. 2002); *Lam v. Investors Thrift (In re Lam)*, 211 B.R. 36, 41 (9th Cir. BAP 1997), *appeal dismissed*, 192 F.3d 1309 (9th Cir. 1999). The procedure for obtaining this relief has multiple steps in chapter 13 cases. First, if a debtor wishes to confirm a chapter 13 plan that treats a junior lienholder as unsecured, the debtor must file a motion pursuant to Rule 3012 of the Federal Rules of Bankruptcy Procedure to obtain a court order finding that the claim of the junior lienholder is not a secured claim. This motion must be filed and heard prior to confirmation of the chapter 13 plan.

Second, if the Court grants the motion and confirms the chapter 13 plan, the debtor must fully perform under the terms of the plan. If the debtor does so, then an adversary proceeding can be filed to avoid the lien. Rule 7001(2) of the Federal Rules of Bankruptcy Procedure requires an adversary proceeding to avoid a lien. Given that only approximately 8% of chapter 13 cases are successful (i.e. result in a confirmed chapter 13 plan that is fully performed), the number of valuation motions filed pursuant to Rule 3012 vastly exceeds the number of instances in which a lien is actually avoided.

The problem of the large volume of valuation motions is compounded by a lack of uniformity among the motions. The titles of motions by debtors in chapter 13 cases to avoid junior liens secured by their principal residence (i.e. "lien strip motions," "motions to extinguish junior liens," "motions to value," "Lam motions," etc.) are as varied as their content. Throughout these guidelines, however, all such motions shall be described as "Valuation Motions."

Given the considerable volume of Valuation Motions, use of a standardized form is necessary to more quickly and efficiently process such motions. The issues arising in a Valuation Motion are typically quite discrete (i.e. the value of collateral and the amount of existing liens) and can be easily presented in a uniform fashion. Just as motions for relief from stay (another type of motion filed in very large quantities) have been standardized, Valuation Motions in chapter 13 cases should also be uniform.

This is especially true given that 92% of chapter 13 cases fail (i.e. fail to achieve confirmation or default occurs thereafter). When a chapter 13 case fails, the time and energy expended by the Court in considering the Valuation Motion becomes pointless. Unlike motions for relief from stay (which provide some benefit for the moving party even in a failed bankruptcy case), Valuation Motions serve little purpose in a chapter 13 case that fails and, as stated above, the vast majority of them fail.

As a result, the Court has developed Form 4003-2.4-Motion, entitled "Debtor's Motion to Avoid Junior Lien on Principal Residence [11 U.S.C. § 506(d)]." The form may be found on the Court's website, www.cacb.uscourts.gov, by clicking on "Forms/Rules/General

Orders," then "Local Bankruptcy Rules & Forms," and scrolling down to F 4003-2.4 MOTION under "Local Bankruptcy Rules Forms." While no form is perfect in character or form, it is being widely used. Indeed, other judges have established guidelines requiring its use.

Accordingly, effective April 15, 2011, all Valuation Motions filed by debtors in chapter 13 cases pending before Judge Johnson must be made using Form 4003-2.4-Motion including the proof of service. If a Valuation Motion is not filed using Form 4003-2.4-Motion, including the proof of service, the motion will be denied.

In addition, all motions must be accompanied with a notice of the motion. Most local forms have been created with a notice included within the motion but, for unknown reasons, Form 4003-2.4-Motion does not include one. Therefore, counsel must complete and attach to the front of Form 4003-2.4-Motion the court's standard notice of a motion: Form 9013-1.1. The combined document (Form 9013-1.1 and Form 4003-2.4-Motion) should be filed and served as one document.

Use of Form 4003-2.4-Motion for purposes of the pre-confirmation Rule 3012 motion to value collateral is mandatory notwithstanding the fact that, as discussed above, an adversary proceeding is ultimately required to avoid the lien. Some courts use Form 4003-2.4-Motion in lieu of an adversary proceeding to permit avoidance of a junior lien on a conditional basis. As stated above, Judge Johnson does not follow that procedure based on the provisions of F.R.B.P. Rule 7001(2). However, because Form 4003-2.4-Motion has been developed by the Court and the form is widely used already (particularly in the Riverside Division), it makes sense to use the form in the interests of promoting consistency and judicial economy.

Nevertheless, consistent with F.R.B.P. Rule 3007(b), to the extent that the title of the Valuation Motion or the content of the motion seek relief avoiding, extinguishing, attacking or otherwise modifying any lien, that language and relief will not be approved by the court. The relief that will be granted will be limited solely to valuing the collateral of a junior lienholder and determining the treatment of its claims in the bankruptcy case. Nothing in the order granting the Valuation Motion shall be construed to avoid a lien or determine the extent, validity, or priority of a lien or security interest. The lien of the junior lienholder will remain of record and the junior lienholder shall retain all rights under the lien unless and until the Court enters a further order or judgment avoiding the lien. If the Court confirms a plan of reorganization and the debtor timely performs all obligations under the confirmed plan, the debtor may thereafter initiate an adversary proceeding pursuant to F.R.B.P. Rule 7001(2) to obtain a further order or judgment extinguishing or avoiding the junior lien.

II. EVIDENCE.

A large number of Valuation Motions are not granted due to a failure to provide proper evidence or to properly serve the motions. Debtors and their counsel should fill out the form completely and accurately, including the proof of service, file and serve their papers in a timely manner in accordance with all applicable Federal Rules of Bankruptcy Procedure and Local Bankruptcy Rules, deliver a judge's copy (with tabs) to chambers, and follow the additional guidelines below.

As the form indicates, all Valuation Motions must be supported by evidence regarding the amount and priority of the liens at issue, and the value of the property. Evidence must be admissible and persuasive.

Liens. Without evidence as to the validity and amount of the senior secured loan and the junior secured loan, the requested relief cannot be granted. The debtor's declaration, which contains the debtor's testimony regarding the liens and introduces the documents into evidence, along with a copy of the deed of trust, a loan statement, proof of claim or other statement from the current lender may establish the amount and validity of the lien. No documents will be considered as evidence unless they are accompanied by a declaration of the debtor. The debtor's testimony alone, with no documentation, will not be sufficient to establish validity and amount (similarly, the debtor's schedules are not sufficient). The court also does not consider a credit report listing amounts owed to be admissible evidence of validity and amount; it is hearsay.

Historical Information. Any declaration submitted by a debtor should include (among other information) the date of the original purchase of the residence, the original purchase price of the residence and the original amount of the secured debt against the residence. If the debtor obtained new financing secured by the residence either by entirely refinancing the original debt or obtaining new junior liens (i.e. obtaining a second or third mortgage), the declaration should also include the date of each new financing and the total amount of the debt secured by the residence upon completion of the new financing.

Current Value. A current appraisal of the property provides evidence of its present value. However, an appraisal must be authenticated by the appraiser in a declaration. (Neither the debtor nor counsel for the debtor can authenticate an appraisal). The declaration of the appraiser should also establish the credentials of the appraiser and contain an opinion of value.

The motion must be complete and must be supported by admissible and persuasive evidence. The failure to provide adequate evidence in support of the motion will result in denial of the motion.

III. SERVICE.

Use of the proof of service form in Form 4003-2.4-Motion is mandatory. The proof of service must be completely filled out to indicate which parties were served, how they were served, and when they were served. Be sure to allow sufficient notice of the hearing to comply with Rule 9013-1(d) of the Local Bankruptcy Rules (notice to be served not later than twenty one days before the hearing date). If a hearing date is chosen that is less than twenty-one days after service, the motion will be denied.

Proper service of the motion (especially complying with Rule 7004 of the Federal Rules of Bankruptcy Procedure) is critical. A large portion of Valuation Motions are denied due to improper service.

A. Who To Serve.

The following parties must be served with Valuation Motions: the chapter 13 trustee, the senior lienholder, the affected junior lienholder, any servicing agent for the affected junior lienholder, and all other parties asserting a lien against the property.

In order to evaluate whether service is proper (and to provide evidence of the current amount of secured debt), the debtor must submit the most recent billing statement received from the senior mortgage holder and the most recent billing statement received from the holder of the mortgage that is the subject of the Valuation Motion. Both of these documents must be attached as exhibits to the motion. However, if either the senior mortgage holder or the junior mortgage holder has filed a proof of claim in the existing bankruptcy case, the proof of claim may be submitted in lieu of the monthly billing statement. A recent proof of claim is often the best form of evidence regarding the identity of a lienholder, the amount of its debt and the proper address for service of the motion.

If billing statements or a proof of claim are not attached (or the billing statements are not recent), the motion will likely be denied.

B. Method of Service.

When serving a creditor with the motion, if any attorney has appeared for the creditor in the case, serve the creditor by serving its attorney of record. See, e.g., F.R.B.P. Rule 7005; Rule 5(b)(1) of the Federal Rules of Civil Procedure; F.R.B.P. Rule 7004(h)(1).

If no attorney has appeared in the case for the creditor but the creditor has filed a proof of claim in the bankruptcy case, serve the creditor at the address indicated on the proof of claim to the attention of the person who signed the proof of claim.

If the creditor has not filed a proof of claim and no attorney has appeared then service must be made in accordance with F.R.B.P. Rule 7004 (discussed below).

Compliance with F.R.B.P. 7004(b)(3). Rule 7004(b)(3) applies to domestic and foreign corporations, partnerships and other unincorporated associations and provides that service may be made by first-class mail upon "an officer, a managing or general agent, or to any other agent authorized by appointment or by law to receive service of process." The address for the corporation and its agent, if any, can usually be found on the California Secretary of State website or the corporation's website.

When serving the junior lienholder who is the target of the motion, the debtor should serve the agent for service of process for the junior lienholder as designated in the records of the California Secretary of State. If no agent for service of process has been designated in the records of the California Secretary of State, then service may be made upon "an officer, a managing or general agent, or to any other agent authorized by appointment or by law to receive service of process."

Compliance with F.R.B.P. 7004(h). As discussed above, Rule 7004(b)(3), is generally applicable to most businesses, but introductory language states that it applies "[e]xcept as provided in subsection (h)." Rule 7004(h) specifically applies to insured depository institutions (as defined in section 3 of the Federal Deposit Insurance Act). Many lienholders are FDIC insured institutions and must be served in accordance with Rule 7004(h).

Parties researching whether a lienholder is an FDIC-insured institution should consult the FDIC website (http://www.fdic.gov) which has a feature to search for institutions. The website will provide an address for the institution. Information regarding the identity of officers can often be found on the institution's website. Please note that many institutions are subsidiaries of FDIC-insured institutions (for example, Bank of America Home Loans is a subsidiary of Bank of America, N.A.). In these cases, the FDIC-insured parent must also be served in accordance with Rule 7004(h).

Rule 7004(h) requires that service be made by certified mail addressed to an officer of the institution. Regular first-class mail does not comply with Rule 7004(h); certified mail must be used.

If an FDIC-insured entity has also designated an agent for service of process with the California Secretary of State then, in addition to serving the FDIC-insured entity in the manner indicated above, you should also serve the agent for service of process (by certified mail).

As a general rule, if there is any doubt as to whether service needs to comply with Rule 7004(h), serve your motion by certified mail to (1) the agent for service of process listed on the California Secretary of State website, (2) any other address used for communication with the lienholder (i.e. from a billing statement) and (3) to an officer of the institution using the address listed on the FDIC website.

Ultimately, it is to the debtor's benefit to ensure that service is correct. Federal law (including, but not limited to, Rule 60(b)(4) of the Federal Rules of Civil Procedure and Rule 9024 of the Federal Rules of Bankruptcy Procedure) allows a party to challenge any court order as void if the order was obtained as a result of insufficient service of process of the Valuation Motion. If the Court grants a Valuation Motion that is not properly served, the party who is purportedly bound by the order may later seek to set aside the order as void.

C. Evidence of Method of Service.

Evidence should be attached to the motion that demonstrates that the address and name information on the proof of service is accurate. For example, whenever service is accomplished using information from the California Secretary of State, a copy of the document used (i.e. a website printout or other record) should be attached as an exhibit to the motion. Whenever service is accomplished using information from the FDIC, a copy of the document used (i.e. a website printout or other record) should be attached as an exhibit to the motion. Whenever service is accomplished using information obtained from the junior lienholder's website or some other source, a copy of the document used should be attached to the motion. In particular, when service must be made upon an officer, evidence should be provided that demonstrates that the person served is an officer of the served party. Whenever service is accomplished by using a proof of claim, the proof of claim should be attached.

IV. IDENTITY OF JUNIOR LIENHOLDER.

Finally, if a Valuation Motion is properly served and contains sufficient evidence, it will be granted but only with respect to the creditor specifically identified in the motion. The order granting the motion shall be binding upon the specifically identified creditor (and any successors-in-interest to or assignees of the creditor) but not upon any other creditor, any affiliate of the creditor or any other party. Therefore, if necessary, the debtor should take appropriate steps (prior to filing the bankruptcy case) to research the identity of the junior lienholder, such as obtaining a title report, making a RESPA demand seeking information set forth in 12 U.S.C. § 2605(k)(1)(D), etc.

V. FORM OF ORDER.

When Valuations Motions are granted by the Court, local form F 4003-2.4.ORDER should not be used. Instead, a form of order has been posted with these guidelines and counsel for the debtor should submit an order using that form of order.

C. *Notice Regarding Appearing by Telephone*

NOTICE REGARDING APPEARING BY TELEPHONE

(April 15, 2011)

I. POLICY GOVERNING APPEARANCES BY TELEPHONE.

Appearances by telephone are allowed in all matters before Judge Johnson, except the following:

1. Trials and evidentiary hearings (all counsel and all witnesses must appear in person).

2. Chapter 11 status conferences (debtor and debtor's counsel must appear in person). Other parties in interest may appear by telephone.

3. Chapter 11, 12 & 13 confirmation hearings (debtor, debtor's counsel, and all objecting creditors must appear in person).

4. Reaffirmation hearings (debtor must appear in person). Other parties in interest may appear by telephone.

No appearance by telephone will be allowed unless it is made through ***Tele-Court, Inc.***, an independent conference call company, pursuant to the procedures set forth in Section II. Before requesting an appearance by telephone, you should check Judge Johnson's calendar on the court's website to review any disposition without oral argument or tentative ruling concerning the matter on calendar. Dispositions without oral argument and tentative rulings normally are issued by 3:00 p.m. on the day preceding the scheduled hearing.

Dispositions Without Oral Argument. If the matter has been adequately noticed and no written opposition has been timely filed, the court may decide the matter without oral argument by issuing a "Final Ruling" that states no appearance is necessary. In such instances, the matter will not be heard by the court.

Tentative Rulings. If written opposition has been timely filed, the court may issue a "Tentative Ruling" that states appearances are required. Each individual who appears by telephone must have reviewed and must be familiar with the tentative ruling.

If an individual schedules an appearance by telephone and then fails to respond to the call of a matter on calendar, the court may pass the matter or may treat the failure to respond as a failure to appear. Scheduling simultaneous appearances by telephone in multiple courts does not excuse a failure to appear when a matter is placed on calendar. Individuals making use of the conference call service are cautioned that they do so at their own risk. Hearings are usually not rescheduled due to missed connections.

II. PROCEDURES FOR APPEARING BY TELEPHONE.

Telephone appearances may be arranged, not later than 8:30 a.m. the day of the hearing, by calling Tele-Court, Inc. at (800) 924-5680 or going to www.tele-court.com. Appearances by telephone are connected directly with the courtroom's public address system and electronic recording equipment so that a normal record is produced. To ensure the quality of the record, the use of car phones, cellular phones, speaker phones, public telephone booths, or phones in other public places is prohibited except in the most extreme emergencies.

Participants should be able to hear all parties without difficulty or echo.

You must be on the line, ready to proceed with your hearing, before the judge takes the bench and calls the calendar. You may initially be in the listening mode in which case you will be able to hear the case before yours just as if you were in the courtroom. You must place your phone on "mute" until your matter is called to ensure the quality of the record and to avoid interfering with other hearings in progress.

At the time of your hearing, the judge will call the case, request appearances, and direct the manner in which the hearing proceeds. Each time you speak, you should identify yourself for the record. The court's teleconferencing system allows more than one speaker to be heard, so the judge can interrupt a speaker to ask a question or redirect the discussion. When the judge informs the participants that the hearing is completed, you may disconnect and the next case will be called.

Appearances by telephone by multiple participants are only possible when there is compliance with every procedural requirement. Sanctions may be imposed when there is any deviation from the required procedures or the court determines that a person's conduct makes appearances by telephone inappropriate. Sanctions may include dropping a matter from calendar, continuing the hearing, proceeding in the absence of an unavailable participant, a monetary sanction, and/or a permanent prohibition against a person appearing by telephone.

II. Judge Johnson's Case Management Orders

A. *Chapter 13 – Standing Order Regarding the Timing of Confirmation Hearings*

IN THE UNITED STATES BANKRUPTCY COURT
FOR THE CENTRAL DISTRICT OF CALIFORNIA

RE TIME OF CHAPTER 13 CONFIRMATION HEARING	)	**STANDING ORDER**

The undersigned Judge of the United States Bankruptcy Court, Central District of California, makes this standing order with respect to the time for the hearing on confirmation of Chapter 13 plans:

I hereby find and accordingly ORDER that it is in the best interests of the creditors and the estate to hold the hearing on the confirmation of the Chapter 13 plan on the same date as the meeting of creditors required under 11 U.S.C. § 341(a). **Any party in interest who objects to that timing of the confirmation hearing shall file a written objection thereto at least 20 calendar days before the scheduled confirmation hearing**; and it is

FURTHER ORDERED that the objecting party shall file the objection with the Court and serve it on the debtor, debtor's counsel, Chapter 13 trustee, and on any creditor who has filed an objection to confirmation, filed a request for special notice, or holds a security interest in the real property of the debtor. If a timely objection is received, the Court will reschedule the confirmation hearing.

DATED: February 28, 2011

WAYNE E. JOHNSON
United States Bankruptcy Court

Hon. Meredith A. Jury

Bankruptcy Judge

Contact Information
U.S. Bankruptcy Court, Central District of California
Courtroom 301
3420 Twelfth Street, Suite 325
Riverside, CA 92501
Courtroom Deputy: (951) 774-1091

Biographical Information

Appointment(s):

- Appointed 11/24/97 by the United States Court of Appeals for the Ninth Circuit. (Current term expires 11/23/11.)

Education:

- University of Colorado, Boulder, 1969, B.A. (*cum laude*) in English, Phi Beta Kappa;
- University of Wisconsin, Madison, 1971, M.A. in Economics, 1972, M.S. in English Education;
- University of California Law School, Los Angeles, 1976, J.D.

Career Record:

- 1976-97, Associate-Partner, Best Best and Krieger, LLP, Riverside, California
- Admitted to the California State Bar and U. S. District Court for the Central District of California, 1976; U. S. Court of Appeals for the Ninth Circuit, 1980

Professional Memberships:

- Federal, California, and Riverside County Bar Associations

I. Judge Jury's Procedures and Practices

A. Instructions Regarding Telephonic Appearances for Judge Jury

INSTRUCTIONS REGARDING TELEPHONIC APPEARANCES FOR JUDGE JURY

1. A written request must be mailed or called into the Courtroom Deputy (951) 774-1091 or the Judicial Assistant (951) 774-1043 at least three (3) days prior to the hearing:

Hon. Meredith A. Jury
United States Bankruptcy Court
3420 Twelfth Street, Suite 345
Riverside, CA 92501-3819
Attention: Judicial Assistant

2. The written or verbal information must contain the following information:

a) the name of the case and the bankruptcy case number;

b) the date and the time of the hearing and the type of matter to be heard;

c) the reason for the telephonic appearance and name of the person who will make the appearance; and

d) contact information including address, telephone and fax numbers.

3. Once the Judge has granted the request, the Judicial Assistant will call and advise that personal appearance is required or fax you information that telephonic appearance has been authorized. The "Telephonic Conferencing Procedures" will be faxed to you. You must arrange for the conference call yourself through the telephone conferencing contact numbers provided by the Judicial Assistant. **YOU ARE RESPONSIBLE FOR FOLLOWING UP AND MAKING THE ARRANGEMENTS FOR THIS CALL.**

4. The Judicial Assistant will advise the Courtroom Recorder and Courtroom Deputy of the approval of the request, so that they are aware of the telephonic appearance.

II. Judge Jury's Case Management Orders

A. *Standing Order Regarding Time of Chapter 13 Confirmation Hearing*

IN THE UNITED STATES BANKRUPTCY COURT
FOR THE CENTRAL DISTRICT OF CALIFORNIA

RE TIME OF CHAPTER 13 CONFIRMATION HEARING	**STANDING ORDER**

The undersigned Judge of the United States Bankruptcy Court, Central District of California, makes this standing order with respect to the time for the hearing on confirmation of Chapter 13 plans:

I hereby find **and accordingly ORDER** that it is in the best interests of the creditors and the estate to hold the hearing on the confirmation of the Chapter 13 plan on the same date as the meeting of creditors required under **11 U.S.C. § 341(a). Any party in interest who objects to that timing of the confirmation hearing shall file a written objection thereto at least 20 calendar days before the scheduled confirmation hearing; and it is**

FURTHER ORDERED that the objecting party shall file the objection with the Court and serve it on the debtor, debtor's counsel, Chapter 13 trustee, **and on any creditor who has filed an objection to confirmation, filed a request for special notice, or holds a security interest in the real property of the debtor.** If a **timely** objection is received, **the Court will reschedule** the confirmation hearing.

DATED: April 5, 2006

MEREDITH JURY
United States Bankruptcy Court

Hon. Victoria S. Kaufman

Bankruptcy Judge

Contact Information
U.S. Bankruptcy Court, Central District of California
Courtroom 301
21041 Burbank Boulevard, Suite 354
Woodland Hills, CA 91367
Courtroom Deputy: (818) 587-2850

Attention: All San Fernando Valley hearings will be held in Courtroom 301 of the San Fernando Valley Division.

Biographical Information

Appointment(s):

- Appointed 05/02/06 by the United States Court of Appeals for the Ninth Circuit. (Current term expires 05/01/20.)

Education:

- Bryn Mawr College, B.A., 1986, *magna cum laude*
- Harvard Law School, J.D., 1989

Career Record:

- 2004-2006: Of Counsel, Paul, Hastings, Janofsky & Walker LLP
- 1996-1997; 1999-2004: Of Counsel, Jeffer, Mangels, Butler & Marmaro LLP
- 1994-1996: Counsel, McCutchen, Doyle, Brown & Enersen LLP
- 1991-1994: Associate, Levene & Eisenberg P.C.
- 1989-1991: Associate, Latham & Watkins LLP
- Admitted to the California Bar, 1989

Professional Memberships:

- State Bar of California
- National Conference of Bankruptcy Judges

I. Judge Kaufman's Procedures and Practices

A. Consequences of Failure to Comply with Local Bankruptcy Rule 5005-2(d) Regarding Chapter 13 Plan Objections

CONSEQUENCES OF FAILURE TO COMPLY WITH LOCAL BANKRUPTCY RULE 5005-2(d) REGARDING CHAPTER 13 PLAN OBJECTIONS

Local Bankruptcy Rule 5005-2(d) requires that a **paper copy** of any document filed at the Court's San Fernando Valley division, either electronically or in paper format, must be marked "Judge's Copy" and be served on the judge in chambers in the manner and not later than the deadline set forth in the Court Manual. However, after they file a confirmation objection electronically, counsel for creditors in chapter 13 cases often do not provide a paper copy of the objection. This conduct overburdens the Court's staff and impedes the Court's timely review of objections filed in chapter 13 cases.

A COMPLETE JUDGE'S COPY OF ANY OBJECTION TO CONFIRMATION OF A CHAPTER 13 PLAN MUST BE SERVED NO LATER THAN 24 HOURS AFTER THE OBJECTION WAS FILED.

FOR CONFIRMATION HEARINGS HELD ON AND AFTER OCTOBER 8, 2008, IF YOU DO NOT TIMELY SERVE A PAPER "JUDGE'S COPY" OF YOUR OBJECTION TO CONFIRMATION OF A CHAPTER 13 PLAN, UNLESS THE COURT FINDS GOOD CAUSE, THE COURT WILL ISSUE SANCTIONS AGAINST THE RESPONSIBLE ATTORNEY IN THE AMOUNT OF $100.00 PER OBJECTION.

These sanctions may be increased for those persons who repeatedly fail to serve a paper "Judge's Copy" of an objection to chapter 13 plan confirmation.

B. Notice Regarding Telephonic Appearance Procedures

NOTICE RE TELEPHONIC APPEARANCE PROCEDURES FOR JUDGE VICTORIA S. KAUFMAN'S CASES

I. POLICIES GOVERNING TELEPHONIC APPEARANCES.

Telephonic appearances are allowed in all matters before Judge Kaufman in Courtroom # 301 of the San Fernando Valley Division, **EXCEPT** the following:

1. Trials and evidentiary hearings (Counsel for all parties must appear in person. Witnesses must also appear in person where requested or if they are to be crossexamined).
2. Chapter 11 Status Conferences (Debtor, debtor's counsel, and counsel for creditors' committee, if any, must appear in person). Other parties in interest may appear telephonically.
3. Adversary Proceeding Initial Status Conferences and Pretrial Conferences (all trial counsel must appear in person unless JUDGE KAUFMAN has authorized appearance by telephone for the adversary proceeding at issue).
4. Chapter 11 and 12 confirmation hearings (Debtor, debtor's counsel, and all objecting creditors must appear in person).
5. Chapter 13 contested matters, other than motions for relief from stay and motions to dismiss filed by the chapter 13 trustee.
6. Any matter designated by the Court as requiring a personal appearance.

No telephonic appearance will be allowed unless it is made through *Court Call*, an independent conference call company, pursuant to the procedures set forth in **Section II**.

If an individual schedules a telephonic appearance and fails to respond when the matter is called on calendar, the Court may pass the matter or may treat the failure to respond as a failure to appear. Scheduling simultaneous telephonic appearances in multiple courts does not excuse a failure to appear when a matter placed on the calendar is called.

Individuals making use of the conference call service are cautioned that they do so at their own risk. Hearings generally will not be rescheduled due to missed connections.

II. SCHEDULING A TELEPHONIC APPEARANCE.

A. Contact *Court Call*

By Telephone: Telephone appearances may be arranged by calling *Court Call* at (866) 582-6878 no later than **3:00 p.m. the court day prior to the hearing date**. Any request for a telephonic appearance made to *Court Call* after this deadline must be Court approved by contacting Judge Kaufman's chambers at (818) 587-2823.

By Written Request: Written requests may only be done if the request is made at least **two (2) court days** in advance of the hearing date. The facsimile telephone number at *Court Call* is (866) 533-2946.

III. PROCEDURE FOR TELEPHONIC APPEARANCE.

Court Call will provide counsel with written confirmation of a telephonic appearance and give counsel a number to call to make the telephonic appearance. It is counsel's responsibility to dial into the call not later than 10 minutes prior to the scheduled hearing. ***Court Call* does not place a call to counsel.** The billing schedule for a *Court Call* appearance is as follows: (a) 0-45 minutes - $30.00; (b) 46-60 minutes - $37; (c) 60 minutes and above is an additional $7 for each 15 minute increment. If you do not call and connect with the *Court Call* operator timely, you will be billed for the call and the hearing may proceed in your absence.

Telephonic appearances are connected directly with the courtroom's public address system and electronic recording equipment so that a normal record is produced. To ensure the quality of the record, the use of car phones, cellular phones, speaker phones, public telephone booths, or phones in other public places is prohibited except in the most extreme emergencies. Participants should be able to hear all parties without difficulty or echo.

At the time of your hearing, you may be placed in a listening mode initially and will be able to hear the case before yours just as if you were in the courtroom. After your call is connected to the courtroom, the Judge will call the case, request appearances, and direct the manner in which the hearing proceeds. **Each time you speak, you should identify yourself for the record.** The court's teleconferencing system allows more than one speaker to be heard so the Judge can interrupt a speaker to ask a question or redirect the discussion. When the Judge informs the participants that the hearing is completed, you may disconnect and the next case will be called.

Telephonic appearances by multiple participants are only possible when there is compliance with every procedural requirement. Sanctions may be imposed upon any deviation from the required procedures or the Court determines that a person's conduct makes telephonic appearances inappropriate. Sanctions may include dropping a matter from calendar, continuing the hearing, proceeding in the absence of an unavailable participant, a monetary sanction, and/or a permanent prohibition against a person appearing telephonically.

C. *Status Conference Instructions*

STATUS CONFERENCE INSTRUCTIONS

1. A copy of these instructions must be attached to the copy of the complaint served upon each party, and the proof of service must state that these instructions, as well as a copy of the summons and complaint, was served.

2. Plaintiff must serve, with the summons and complaint, a notice in compliance with Local Bankruptcy Rule 7026-1(a)(1). Plaintiff must also file proof of service of the notice with proof of service of the summons and complaint as required by Local Bankruptcy Rule 7026-1(a)(2).

3. Counsel for the parties **MUST TIMELY MEET TO DISCUSS SETTLEMENT AND TO EXCHANGE DOCUMENTS, OTHER EVIDENCE AND LISTS OF WITNESSES AND PRELIMINARY DISCOVERY SCHEDULES AS PROVIDED IN FED. R. BANKR. P. 7026.**

4. Pursuant to Local Bankruptcy Rule 7016-1(a)(2), all parties must file a Joint Status Report at least fourteen (14) days before the date set for each status conference. The Joint Status Report should be in a form substantially similar to Exhibit A attached hereto, *i.e.*, Local Form 7016-1.1.[*] Failure to file such a Joint Status Report may result in the imposition of monetary sanctions and/or the status conference being continued and parties being ordered to redo the status report to conform to Exhibit A. If cooperation in the filing of a Joint Status Report cannot reasonably be obtained, each appearing party must file a Unilateral Status Report and Declaration which comply with Local Bankruptcy Rule 7016-1(a)(3).

5. If a response to the complaint is not timely filed:

A. The plaintiff should file a request for entry of default by the clerk. The plaintiff also may request entry of a default judgment by filing and serving (if necessary) an appropriate motion; see Fed. R. Bankr. P. 7055 and Local Bankruptcy Rule 7055-1(b);

AND

B. No later than seven (7) days prior to the status conference, each appearing party must file a Unilateral Status Report (completing Sections A-E of Exhibit A attached hereto) as required by Local Bankruptcy Rule 7016-1(a)(3).

6. If the parties dispute whether the adversary proceeding is "core" within the meaning of 28 U.S.C. § 157(b), they must file points and authorities in support of their positions. Any party who contends that the proceeding is "non-core" must file and serve a memorandum of points and authorities and evidence in support of his/her/its position no less than fourteen (14) days before the status conference. Any response must be filed at least

* [Editor's Note: Exhibit A (Local Form 7016-1.1) can be downloaded at the court's website at http://www.cacb.uscourts.gov.]

seven (7) days before the status conference. **If a party does not timely file and serve his/her/its papers, that failure may be deemed a consent to whatever determination the Court makes.**

7. Any party claiming a right to trial by jury must make a timely demand as set forth in Local Bankruptcy Rule 9015-2. If the parties dispute whether a party has a right to a jury trial, they must file points and authorities in support of their positions. Any party who contends that he/she/it has a right to a jury trial must file and serve a memorandum of points and authorities and evidence in support of his/her/its position no less than fourteen (14) days before the status conference. Any response must be filed at least seven (7) days before the status conference. **If a party does not timely file and serve his/her/its papers, that failure may be deemed a consent to whatever determination the Court makes.**

8. **Counsel for each party and any party who does not have counsel must appear in person at the first status conference, unless JUDGE KAUFMAN has authorized appearance by telephone for the adversary proceeding at issue.** With respect to subsequent status conferences, counsel for each party and any party who does not have counsel may appear by telephone if they make timely arrangements to do so in accordance with Judge Kaufman's telephonic appearance procedures, which can be accessed by clicking "Information" on the upper left-hand corner of the Court's website at www.cacb.uscourts.gov. If a party has questions about these procedures or cannot locate them on the Court's website, the party may contact Judge Kaufman's Courtroom Deputy, Patty Garcia, at (818) 587-2850.

9. Unless otherwise ordered by the Court, within seven (7) court days after the status conference, the plaintiff must submit a Scheduling Order which complies with Local Bankruptcy Rule 7016-1(a)(4).

10. Extensions of time to respond to a pleading are ineffective by stipulation of the parties unless approved by the Court. The Court is likely to deny requests to extend the response deadline to a date within five (5) days of the hearing date unless the hearing date is continued to a date which permits the Court adequate time to consider the pleadings. The Court will not grant a request to continue a hearing unless the request states adequate cause for the continuance.

11. Failure to comply with these instructions may subject the responsible party to a sanction of $150, or such other sanctions as may be warranted under the circumstances or allowed under Local Bankruptcy Rule 7016-1(f).

12. Failure of counsel for any party to appear at a status conference may be considered an abandonment or failure to prosecute or defend diligently and may result in dismissal of the proceeding or judgment entered against the defaulting party without further hearing, or such other sanctions as may be warranted under the circumstances or allowed under Local Bankruptcy Rule 7016-1(g).

Hon. Victoria S. Kaufman
United States Bankruptcy Judge

D. Tentative Ruling Procedures

TENTATIVE RULING PROCEDURES FOR JUDGE VICTORIA S. KAUFMAN

Judge Kaufman may issue tentative rulings 24 to 48 hours prior to the scheduled hearing date. These rulings are available via the court's webPACER service and on the court's webpage, www.cacb.uscourts.gov, by clicking "Tentative Rulings" on the lower, left hand corner of the court's home page, selecting judge VK and clicking on the relevant hearing date. Please do not call chambers to inquire if no tentative has been posted.

Please note, however, that, notwithstanding the issuance of a tentative ruling, unless (1) Judge Kaufman's chambers or Courtroom Deputy has confirmed that no appearance is necessary or (2) the tentative ruling itself states that no appearance is necessary, **appearances are required**. A moving party's failure to attend the hearing on its motion may result in denial of the motion for failure to prosecute and in the issuance of an order to show cause re sanctions. An opposing party that fails to attend the hearing on a motion that it has opposed will be deemed to have withdrawn its opposition to the relief requested in the motion.

If the Judge issues a tentative ruling in an uncontested matter and excuses the movant's appearance, but a party appears in court to contest the motion, the Judge will listen briefly and either allow the tentative ruling to stand or continue the hearing to allow the absent parties to be heard. If the hearing is continued, a member of Judge Kaufman's chambers or the Courtroom Deputy will inform the moving party of the date and time of the continued hearing.

Unless otherwise provided in the tentative ruling, the moving party must lodge a proposed order that conforms to the Judge's tentative ruling, accompanied by a proof of service that the proposed form of order was served on all required parties and, unless the proposed order is lodged using the court's Electronic Lodged Order Upload ("LOU") procedures and those procedures provide otherwise, a notice of entry, the appropriate number of copies of the proposed order and stamped, pre-addressed envelopes bearing the names and addresses of those who are to receive a copy of the signed, entered order.

On the date of the hearing, you may deposit the proposed order and notice of entry, along with all the copies and envelopes, in the courtroom. All proposed orders submitted after the hearing date must be lodged at the court's filing window, located at the San Fernando Valley Division, 21041 Burbank Boulevard, Woodland Hills, CA 91367, or submitted through the court's LOU procedures.

E. *Trial Procedures Supplemental to Local Rules*

TRIAL PROCEDURES SUPPLEMENTAL TO LOCAL RULES

1. Trial Briefs: **Unless otherwise ordered by the Court, plaintiff's trial brief shall be filed and served at least thirty (30) days before the trial date, defendant's trial brief shall be filed and served at least twenty-one (21) days before the trial date and any reply brief by plaintiff (which is not required) shall be filed and served at least fourteen (14) days before the trial date.** Courtesy copies of the trial briefs must be delivered to chambers, Suite 354, on the same date as the relevant trial brief is filed. The parties are encouraged to include a brief statement of the pertinent facts in their briefs, with citation to exhibits.

2. Direct Testimony By Declaration: Unless otherwise permitted by the Court, parties are required to submit all direct testimony by declaration, under penalty of perjury, unless:

   A. the witness is adverse or refuses to give testimony by declaration;

   B. the testimony is offered to impeach or rebut; or

   C. the Court, either on its own or upon the request of a party at or prior to the last scheduled pre-trial conference or trial-setting conference, waives this requirement.

   If a party is unable to obtain a declaration of a witness, counsel for the party shall file a declaration stating the name of the witness and a detailed summary of the expected testimony and why counsel was unable to obtain the witness' declaration.

   Plaintiff shall file and serve its declarations at least thirty (30) days before the trial date. Defendant shall file and serve its declarations at least twenty-one (21) days before the trial date. Plaintiff shall file and serve any reply declarations at least fourteen (14) days before the trial date.

   If a portion of a witness' declaration concerns an exhibit to be admitted into evidence at trial, the exhibit must be attached to the declaration.

   The parties may request permission to offer oral testimony supplementing matters covered in the declarations or present portions of the testimony in the declaration orally, and the Court may grant such a request in the interest of justice.

   The declaration of a witness for a party will be admissible at trial, subject to timely objections. Witnesses whose declarations are offered must be present at the trial and subject to cross-examination when the declarations are offered into evidence (unless the parties agree otherwise).

   Unless the parties stipulate in the pre-trial order to the admittance of an exhibit, foundation for admittance of exhibits (other than for impeachment or rebuttal purposes) shall be established in the declarations, although the Court may allow oral testimony for this purpose. Exhibits referenced in any declaration shall be offered into evidence when the declaration is offered into evidence.

   Any evidentiary objections to plaintiff's initial declarations shall be filed and served at least twenty-one (21) days before the trial date. Any evidentiary

objections to defendant's declarations must be filed and served at least fourteen (14) days before the trial date. Any evidentiary objections to plaintiff's reply declarations shall be served at least seven (7) days before the trial date.

Courtesy copies of the declarations and evidentiary objections must be delivered to chambers, Suite 354, on the same date as the relevant declarations and evidentiary objections are filed.

Important: The failure to file declarations timely may result in the dismissal of the case, the entry of a default judgment, or the imposition of monetary sanctions.

3. Exhibits: All trial exhibits shall be numbered and marked as required by Local Rule 9013-2(b). **At least seven (7) days before trial, each counsel shall deliver to chambers the original and one copy of a notebook containing all trial exhibits.** The original exhibits shall be tagged as required by Local Rule 9013-2(b). Counsel shall deliver to chambers an "exhibit register," on the form available from the Clerk's Office, at the same time. Counsel shall exchange all exhibits on or before the date of the delivery to chambers. The Exhibit Books shall include all exhibits anticipated to be used at the trial, including all rebuttal exhibits. Exhibits to be used for impeachment only need not be included. At trial, counsel shall have sufficient conformed sets of exhibits for opposing counsel's witnesses and for each party in the proceeding. Counsel shall also have copies of exhibits used for impeachment purposes or rebuttal for opposing counsel, witnesses and, with respect to impeachment exhibits not included in the two Exhibit Books delivered to chambers, the Court.

4. Continuance/Postponement of Trial: As a general rule, scheduled trials will not be continued prior to or at trial. Motions/Stipulations for continuance of trial must be submitted in writing at least two (2) court days prior to the scheduled trial date. The parties will be contacted by the judge's law clerk or judicial assistant as to whether the continuance has been granted or denied.

5. Settlement: In the event of a settlement prior to trial, the parties shall immediately contact and advise the judge's law clerk.

6. Service: Service of briefs, declarations and evidentiary objections discussed herein shall be on counsel for the opposing party, or if the opposing party is appearing *pro se*, on the opposing party.

Hon. Sandra R. Klein

Bankruptcy Judge

Contact Information

U.S. Bankruptcy Court, Central District of California
Courtroom 1575
255 E. Temple Street, Suite 1582
Los Angeles, CA 90012
Courtroom Deputy: (213) 894-5856

Biographical Information

Appointment(s):

- Appointed April 22, 2011, the United States Court of Appeals for the Ninth Circuit.

Education:

- University of California Los Angeles, Anderson School of Management, M.B.A., 2009, UCLA Anderson School of a Management Honor Society.
- Loyola Law School, Los Angeles, CA, J.D., 1992, Magna Cum Laude, Order of the Coif, Senior Note & Comment Editor, Loyola Int'l & Comp. L.J., 1991 – 92.
- University of Massachusetts, Lowell, MA (formerly University of Lowell, Lowell, MA), B.M., Music Education, 1982, Magna Cum Laude.

Career Record:

- 1997 – 2011, United States Department of Justice.
- 2009 – 2011, Acting Assistant Director of Office of Criminal Enforcement, United States Trustee Program.
- 2003 – 2009, Bankruptcy Fraud Criminal Coordinator, United States Trustee Program
- 1997 – 2003, Special Assistant United States Attorney, United States Attorney's Office, Central District of California (on permanent detail from the United States Trustee Program).
- 1995 – 1997, Associate, O'Melveny & Myers, LLP, Los Angeles, CA.
- 1994 – 1995, Judicial Law Clerk, Honorable Arthur L. Alarcon, United States Court of Appeals for the Ninth Circuit.
- 1992 – 1994, Judicial Law Clerk, Honorable Lourdes G. Baird, United States District Court for the Central District of California.

Professional Memberships:

- American Bankruptcy Institute
- American Bar Association
- Federal Bar Association
- Los Angeles County Bar Association
- National Conference of Bankruptcy Judges
- Women Lawyers Association of Los Angeles

I. Judge Klein's Procedures and Practices

A. *Chapter 13 Procedures*

CHAPTER 13 PROCEDURES

Effective April 22, 2011, the following procedures will be followed for all chapter 13 cases assigned or reassigned to Judge Sandra R. Klein:

1. All confirmation hearings will start promptly at the time listed on the court calendar.

2. Pursuant to Local Bankruptcy Rule (LBR) 1001-1(d), the court **waives** application of LBR 3015-1(m)(6) & (7). Therefore, debtors are not required to file with the court and serve on the chapter 13 trustee and all secured creditors a declaration on court-mandated Form F 3015-1.4, entitled, "Declaration Setting Forth Postpetition, Preconfirmation Deed of Trust Payments [Local Bankruptcy Rule 3015-1(m)]" commonly referred to as a "mortgage declaration."

3. All **new** requests to value and avoid liens in chapter 13 cases **must** be brought via motion pursuant to Federal Rule of Bankruptcy Procedure 9014. Such motions (commonly referred to as "lien strip motions," "motions to value," "Lam motions,"[1] etc.) **must** be made on Local Form 4003-2.4-MOTION, entitled "Debtor's Motion to Avoid Junior Lien on Principal Residence [11 U.S.C. § 506(d)]" (Motion to Avoid Junior Lien). The form may be found on the Court's website, www.cacb.uscourts.gov, by clicking on "Forms/Rules/General Orders," then "Local Bankruptcy Rules & Forms," and scrolling down to F 4003-2.4-MOTION. For additional information, please see "Judge Sandra R. Klein's Guidelines for Valuing and Avoiding Liens in Chapter 13 Cases," which is posted on Judge Klein's website.

   a. **After April 22, 2011, if a Lam motion is not filed using Local Form 4003-2.4-MOTION, including the proof of service, the motion will not be set for hearing.**

4. Any **pending** adversary proceedings to value and avoid liens in chapter 13 cases that are reassigned to Judge Klein may, in the discretion of the plaintiff, continue to be adjudicated in an adversary proceeding or may be dismissed and refiled using Local Form 4003-2.4-MOTION. If a pending adversary is dismissed and refiled using Local Form 4003-2.4-MOTION, the motion must be supported by admissible evidence and there must be sufficient notice and service to comply with the Federal Rules of Bankruptcy Procedure and Local Bankruptcy Rules. For additional information regarding motions to value and avoid liens in chapter 13 cases, please see "Judge Sandra R. Klein's Guidelines for Valuing and Avoiding Liens in Chapter 13 Cases," which is posted on Judge Klein's website.

   a. If the plaintiff chooses to continue litigating a pending adversary proceeding to value and avoid liens in a chapter 13 case, the plaintiff **must** utilize Local Form 4003-2.5.DEFAULT.MOTION, entitled

---

[1] Lam v. Thrift Investors (In re Lam), 211 B.R. 36 (9th Cir. B.A.P. 1997).

"Debtor's Motion for Default Judgment Re Complaint to Avoid Junior Lien on Principal Residence [11 U.S.C. § 506(a),(d), FRBP 3012]" as well as Local Form 4003-2.5.DEFAULT JUDGMENT, entitled "Default Judgment Re Complaint to Avoid Junior Lien on Principal Residence [11 U.S.C. § 506(a)(d), FRBP 3012]." These forms may also be found on the Court's website, www.cacb.uscourts.gov. For additional information, please see "Judge Sandra R. Klein's Guidelines for Valuing and Avoiding Liens in Chapter 13 Cases," which is posted on Judge Klein's website.

5. All motions to value and avoid liens before Judge Klein must be scheduled for hearing **before** the date scheduled for confirmation of the chapter 13 plan. If a lien strip motion cannot be scheduled for a hearing **before** the date scheduled for confirmation, Debtor or where applicable, Debtor's counsel, **must** contact the chapter 13 trustee at least 3 days before the date scheduled for the confirmation hearing and Debtor or where applicable, Debtor's counsel, **must** obtain an oral stipulation to continue the confirmation hearing until after the date scheduled for the hearing to value and avoid the lien.

B. Guidelines for Valuing and Avoiding Liens in Chapter 13 Cases

GUIDELINES FOR VALUING AND AVOIDING LIENS IN CHAPTER 13 CASES

Effective April 22, 2011, all **new** requests to value and avoid liens in chapter 13 cases **must** be brought via motion pursuant to Federal Rule of Bankruptcy Procedure 9014. Such motions (commonly referred to as "lien strip motions," "motions to value," "Lam motions,"[1] etc.) **must** be made on Local Form 4003-2.4-MOTION, entitled "Debtor's Motion to Avoid Junior Lien on Principal Residence [11 U.S.C. § 506(d)]" (Motion to Avoid Junior Lien). This form may be found on the Court's website, www.cacb.uscourts.gov, by clicking on "Forms/Rules/General Orders," then "Local Bankruptcy Rules & Forms," and scrolling down to F 4003-2.4-MOTION.

Effective April 22, 2011, any **pending** adversary proceedings to value and avoid liens in chapter 13 cases that are reassigned to Judge Klein may, in the discretion of the plaintiff, continue to be adjudicated in an adversary proceeding or may be dismissed and refiled using Local Form 4003-2.4-MOTION. If a pending adversary is dismissed and refiled using Local Form 4003-2.4-MOTION, the motion must be supported by admissible evidence and there must be sufficient notice and service to comply with the Federal Rules of Bankruptcy Procedure and Local Bankruptcy Rules as outlined below.

If the plaintiff chooses to continue litigating a pending adversary proceeding to value and avoid liens in a chapter 13 case, the plaintiff **must** utilize Local Form 4003-2.5.DEFAULT.MOTION, entitled "Debtor's Motion for Default Judgment Re Complaint to Avoid Junior Lien on Principal Residence [11 U.S.C. § 506(a),(d), FRBP 3012]" for the Default Judgment Motion. This form may be found on the Court's website, www.cacb.uscourts.gov, by clicking on "Forms/Rules/General Orders," then "Local Bankruptcy Rules & Forms," and scrolling down to F 4003-2.5.DEFAULT.MOTION. If the court grants Plaintiff's Default Judgment Motion, Plaintiff **must** submit a proposed Default Judgment Order within seven calendar days electronically, using Local Form 4003-2.5.DEFAULT JUDGMENT, entitled "Default Judgment re Complaint to Avoid Junior Lien on Principal Residence [11 U.S.C. § 506(a)(d), FRBP 3012]." The Default Judgment Order must be submitted via the Lodged Order Upload program ("LOU") in accordance with the LOU Procedures contained in Section 4 of the Court Manual posted on the court's website. Use of Local Form 4003-2.4.DEFAULT.JUDGMENT is **mandatory**.

After April 22, 2011, if a Lam motion is not filed using Local Form 4003-2.4-MOTION, including the proof of service, the motion will not be set for hearing.

EVIDENCE

As Local Form 4003-2.4-MOTION indicates, a Motion to Avoid a Junior Lien must be supported by admissible evidence regarding the amount and priority of the liens at issue and the value of the property. Evidence must be admissible under the Federal Rules of Evidence and persuasive.

---

1 Lam v. Thrift Investors (In re Lam), 211 B.R. 36 (9th Cir. B.A.P. 1997).

1. **Liens.** Without evidence as to the validity and amount of the senior secured loan and the junior secured loan, the requested relief cannot be granted. The debtor's declaration, which contains the debtor's testimony regarding the liens and introduces the documents into evidence, along with a copy of the deed of trust, a loan statement, proof of claim or other statement from the current lender will establish the amount and validity of the lien. No documents will be considered as evidence unless they are accompanied by a declaration. The debtor's testimony alone, without supporting documentation, will not be sufficient to establish the validity and the amount of liens (similarly, the debtor's schedules are not sufficient). The court also does not consider a credit report listing amounts owed to be admissible evidence of validity and amount; it is hearsay.

2. **Value.** The debtor may testify through a declaration regarding the value of the residence. The declaration should contain the basis for the testimony, which may include, among other factors, the debtor's familiarity with the residence, the neighborhood, and recent sales. It is insufficient for the declaration to state: "I believe that my residence is worth $xxx,xxx." Please note that the debtor may not rely solely on Internet sources, which are inadmissible hearsay. Therefore, a declaration stating "I believe my residence is worth $xxx,xxx based on the attached report from zillow.com [or cyberhomes.com or any other website]" is not admissible evidence regarding value.

While not required, an appraisal can be persuasive evidence of value. To be admissible, the appraisal must be accompanied by a declaration of the debtor or the appraiser.

SERVICE

Use of the proof of service in Local Form 4003-2.4-MOTION is **mandatory**. The proof of service must be completely filled out to indicate what parties were served, how they were served, and when they were served. Be sure to allow sufficient notice of the hearing date to comply with LBR 9013-1(d) (notice to be served not later than 21 days before the hearing date). If a hearing date is chosen that is less than 21 days after service, the motion will be continued at least 21 additional days to allow for the full notice period.

Proper service of the Motion to Avoid Junior Lien – including compliance with Federal Rule of Bankruptcy Procedure 7004 and Local Bankruptcy Rule 4003-2(c) – is critical.

1. **Parties to serve.** The chapter 13 trustee, the affected lienholder, and all other parties asserting a lien on the property must be served. If any party has made an appearance in the case, that party (and counsel, if applicable) must be served at the address used in its notice of appearance.

2. **Compliance with F.R.B.P. 7004(b)(3).** This rule applies to domestic and foreign corporations and provides that service may be made by first-class mail upon "an officer, a managing or general agent, or to any other agent authorized by appointment or by law to receive service of process." The address for the corporation and its agent, if any, can usually be found on the corporation's website or the California Secretary of State website.

3. **Compliance with F.R.B.P. 7004(h).** Rule 7004(b)(3) generally applies to corporations, although it does not apply if a party is an insured depository institution. In such a case, Rule 7004(h) applies. Many lienholders are **FDIC-insured institutions and must be served in accordance with Rule 7004(h).**

a. **Is the lienholder an FDIC-insured institution?** The FDIC website has a feature to search for institutions: http://www2.fdic.gov/idasp/main.asp. This feature will provide an address and list of officers for the institution. Please note that many institutions are subsidiaries of FDIC-insured institutions (for example, Bank of America Home Loans is a subsidiary of Bank of America, N.A.). In these cases, the FDIC-insured parent must be served in accordance with Rule 7004(h).

b. **How to accomplish service in accordance with Rule 7004(h)?** Rule 7004(h) requires that service be made by **certified mail** addressed to an officer of the institution.

   i. **Use Certified Mail.** Regular first-class mail, overnight mail or courier, or any other delivery method does not comply with Rule 7004(h); certified mail must be used.

   ii. **Address service to an officer.** An officer of the institution is not the registered agent for service of process, or the FDIC itself. The best sources for finding an officer of an FDIC-insured institution are the FDIC website noted above and the institution's website. Many courts have held that addressing service to "Officer of the Institution,""Chief Executive Officer," or "President" complies with the rule. If the institution's address is correct, and it is not possible to locate an officer's name, the court will not find that the motion was served incorrectly (although as a practical matter, it would be rare that an officer's name could not be found).

ORDER

If the court grants a Motion to Avoid Junior Lien, the debtor **must** submit a proposed order, using Local Form 4003-2.4.ORDER, within seven calendar days electronically via the Lodged Order Upload program ("LOU") in accordance with the LOU Procedures contained in Section 4 of the Court Manual posted on the court's website. Use of Local Form 4003-2.4.ORDER is **mandatory**.

C. *Instructions for Telephoning Chambers*

INSTRUCTIONS FOR TELEPHONING CHAMBERS

The court is experiencing an unprecedented number of bankruptcy filings. Consequently it is not possible to answer every phone call because that takes time away from preparing for hearings and processing orders in a timely manner. It is inappropriate for the court to answer legal or procedural questions or assist a party in obtaining relief against another party. Please read these instructions carefully before you place a call to chambers.

A. PHONE CALLS THAT WILL NOT BE RETURNED

1. **Status of Cases, Result of Hearings:** Judge Klein's staff will not return calls asking about the status of a case or the result of a hearing. It is inappropriate for the court to provide explanations over the phone about what is happening in a case or what happened at a hearing. Such information can be obtained from the CM/ECF docket, a party who participated in the case or hearing, or by obtaining an audio or written transcript of a proceeding. Instructions for obtaining an audio or written transcript are posted on the court's website on the "Court Forms" page under the links "Audio Recording of Court Proceedings Order Form" or "Transcripts Order Form and Instructions."

2. **Status of Orders:** Judge Klein's staff will not return calls regarding the status of an order if less than14 days have passed since the order was lodged.

3. **Seeking Advice:** Judge Klein's staff will not to return calls asking how to file or respond to pleadings, which procedures to follow, which rules apply, etc.

4. **Inquiring if a Hearing was Continued or if an Appearance is Necessary:** Judge Klein's staff will not return calls asking whether a hearing was "taken off calendar." All hearings remain on the calendar, although appearances may not be required in certain cases so all parties should review Judge Klein's tentative rulings that will generally be posted by 2:00 p.m. the day before the hearing.

   a. **Motion or Stipulation to Continue Hearing:** Judge Klein follows LBR 9013-1(m) which requires a stipulation or motion to continue a hearing to be filed (and a proposed ordered lodged) at least 3 days before a hearing. Attorneys who file electronically will receive email notification (NEF) of entry of the order.

   b. **Stipulation Resolving a Motion or Adversary Proceeding:** Judge Klein requires compliance with LBR 9071-1, LBR 9013-1(k) and FRBP 7041, if applicable. On any stipulation and proposed order, please include the date of the next hearing or status conference. Proposed orders lacking a hearing date will be marked unused.

   c. **Serving a Judge's Copy of a Stipulation/Motion and Order Resolving a Hearing:** To ensure your stipulation/motion is promptly ruled upon, a judge's copy must be delivered to chambers. Please comply with LBR 5005-2(d) by using tabs for all exhibits and declarations, and stapling/binding the copy. Court Manual Appendix F indicates how to list the judge on the Proof of Service, and identifies delivery addresses for all judges in the Central District of California.

5. **Special Procedures and Required Forms for Judge Klein:** Special procedures and required forms for Judge Klein are posted on her section of the website at www.cacb.uscourts.gov. If a special procedure is not posted, Judge Klein requires compliance with the applicable Local Bankruptcy Rules.

6. **Problems Filing or Lodging Documents:** If you have an issue with electronically filing or lodging a document, please call the CM/ECF Help Desk at (213) 894-2365. If you received an email about making an error on a docket, please contact Judge Klein's courtroom deputy, Thais May, at (213) 894-5856.

B. PHONE CALLS THAT WILL BE RETURNED

1. **Requesting Emergency Hearings:** Judge Klein requires compliance with LBR 9075-1. If you seek a hearing on less than 48 hours notice under LBR 9075-1(a), please leave a message and a law clerk will call you back to discuss the situation and determine whether the court will set a hearing without the emergency motion being filed first. If you are seeking an application for an order setting a hearing on shortened time your phone call will not be returned and you must file the papers before a hearing date can be set under LBR 9075-1(b).

2. **Placing a Hearing on Second Call:** If you are calling to place a matter on second call, please identify the calendar number of your matter by checking the tentative ruling calendar on the main page of the court's website, www.cacb.uscourts.gov. Please indicate how late the attorney or litigant will be, the reason for the delay and whether you have notified the other parties who are appearing on the same matter.

D. No Longer Allows Telephonic Appearances

EFFECTIVE JUNE 27, 2011, JUDGE SANDRA R. KLEIN NO LONGER ALLOWS TELEPHONIC APPEARANCES

Although Judge Sandra R. Klein previously allowed telephonic appearances, counsel repeatedly ignored the criteria for appearing telephonically, which was posted on Judge Klein's and Tele-Court's websites. This caused hearings to be delayed and increased the burden on Judge Klein's already overworked staff. Therefore, effective June 27, 2011, Judge Klein will no longer allow telephonic appearances in any matter.

In most cases, Judge Klein issues tentative rulings by 2:00 p.m. the day before the hearing date. These rulings are generally available via the Court's webPACER service. Unless the tentative ruling states explicitly that no appearance is required, appearances are required by all parties to the matter.

A moving party's failure to attend a hearing on its motion will result in denial of the motion for failure to prosecute and may result in the issuance of an order to show cause re: sanctions. An opposing party's failure to attend a hearing on a motion that it has opposed will be deemed to have withdrawn its opposition to the relief requested in the motion.

E. Notice Regarding Failure to Timely Appear for Scheduled Hearing

NOTICE REGARDING FAILURE TO TIMELY APPEAR
FOR SCHEDULED HEARING

PLEASE NOTE

ALL HEARINGS BEFORE THE
HONORABLE SANDRA R. KLEIN START ON TIME.

IF A PARTY OR A PARTY'S ATTORNEY HAS NOT CHECKED IN WITH JUDGE KLEIN'S COURT RECORDER BEFORE THE HEARING IS SCHEDULED TO BEGIN, THE COURT MAY DISMISS THE MATTER FOR FAILURE TO PROSECUTE, IMPOSE MONETARY SANCTIONS, OR BOTH.

F. *Notice Regarding Posting on Courtroom Bulletin Board*

NOTICE REGARDING POSTING ON COURTROOM BULLETIN BOARD

PLEASE NOTE

NO NOTICES, FLYERS, PAMPHLETS OR ANY OTHER DOCUMENTS MAY BE POSTED ON THE BULLETIN BOARD OUTSIDE OF COURTROOM 1575 WITHOUT PRIOR APPROVAL OF JUDGE SANDRA R. KLEIN'S STAFF.

G. Procedure for Approval of Disclosure Statement and Confirmation of Chapter 11 Plan When the Debtor Is not an Individual

PROCEDURE FOR APPROVAL OF DISCLOSURE STATEMENT AND CONFIRMATION OF CHAPTER 11 PLAN WHEN THE DEBTOR IS NOT AN INDIVIDUAL

A. Requests for orders approving disclosure statements pursuant to 11 U.S.C. § 1125 and for orders confirming plans of reorganization pursuant to 11 U.S.C. § 1129 are motions within the meaning of Federal Rules of Bankruptcy Procedure 9013 and 9014. All motions must be supported by evidence admissible under the Federal Rules of Evidence and in compliance with Local Bankruptcy Rule 9013-1(i).

B. **Unless the court orders otherwise, the proponent of any reorganization plan must use the Combined Disclosure Statement and Plan of Reorganization, which is located in the "Forms" section of Judge Klein's website and called "Combined Disclosure Statement and Plan of Reorganization."**

Please note that the "Combined Disclosure Statement and Plan of Reorganization" utilized by Judge Klein is different from the separate Chapter 11 Disclosure Statement and Chapter 11 Plan adopted by the Central District of California as forms F 3017-1 and F 3018-1, respectively.

C. Hearings on approval of disclosure statements must be set on at least 36 days notice, unless the court prescribes a shorter period. The plan proponent must serve with the disclosure statement a notice of:

1. The disclosure statement hearing date; and
2. The requirement that objections to disclosure statements must be filed and served on the proponent at least 14 days before the hearing.

Please note that the court reviews each proposed disclosure statement before the disclosure hearing, regardless of whether any objections have been filed. Accordingly, counsel are required to notify chambers no later than the Monday before the scheduled hearing if the disclosure statement hearing will be continued.

D. An amended disclosure statement shall not be filed before the initial hearing on the adequacy of the original disclosure statement. **The court strongly encourages all plan proponents to submit a copy of the disclosure statement to creditors, the United States trustee, and any committee prior to filing the disclosure statement with the court, to permit changes pursuant to comments made by these parties in interest.**

If a hearing on approval of the disclosure statement is continued to permit revision of the disclosure statement, the plan proponent shall make all necessary changes and prepare, in anticipation of the next hearing, "redlined" copies of the amended disclosure statement. A "redlined" copy and a "clean" copy must be filed with the court and served on all other parties who appeared at the previous hearing.

E. After granting a disclosure statement motion, the court will set the following:

1. A hearing date for the Motion to Confirm the Plan (Confirmation Motion);
2. A deadline for serving the approved disclosure statement and the notice of hearing for the Confirmation Motion;
3. A deadline for filing of claims and for objecting to claims, if not already set; and
4. A deadline for creditors and equity security holders to transmit ballots.

F. A Confirmation Motion must be prepared, filed and served in accordance with Local Bankruptcy Rule 9013-1 and therefore must meet at least the following criteria:

1. Be supported by evidence demonstrating that the plan is confirmable under 11 U.S.C. § 1129;
2. Be served at least 21 days before the confirmation hearing on the United States trustee, any official committee, and all impaired creditors and equity security holders who rejected the plan; and
3. The plan proponent must serve with the Confirmation Motion a notice of the confirmation hearing date and of the requirement that any party opposing the Motion must file and serve, at least 14 days before the confirmation hearing date, its written opposition supported by admissible evidence.

NOTE: Because the Confirmation Motion ordinarily must be served at least 21 days before the confirmation hearing, the proponent should select a confirmation hearing date so that sufficient time is given for ballots to be returned and for the preparation of the Motion.

G. Unless otherwise ordered, every order confirming a chapter 11 plan must contain the language required by Local Bankruptcy Rule 3020-1(b). The proposed order shall be accompanied by proof of payment of any special charges due the Clerk's Office as described in Local Bankruptcy Rule 3020-1(a).

H. *Requirement of Individual Chapter 11 Debtors To Use Local Bankruptcy Rules Forms*

REQUIREMENT OF INDIVIDUAL CHAPTER 11 DEBTORS TO USE LOCAL BANKRUPTCY RULES FORMS

Effective December 1, 2011, use of the following Local Bankruptcy Rules Forms in individual chapter 11 cases is mandatory:

- F 2081-1.4.MOTION.UTILITIES – Notice of Motion and Motion in Individual Chapter 11 Case for Order Authorizing Debtor to Provide Adequate Assurance of Payment to Utility Service Providers [11 U.S.C. § 366];
- F 2081-1.4.ORDER.UTILITIES – Order Re Notice of Motion and Motion in Individual Chapter 11 Case for Order Authorizing Debtor to Provide Adequate Assurance of Payment to Utility Service Providers [11 U.S.C. § 366].

These forms may be found on the Court's website, www.cacb.uscourts.gov, by clicking on "Forms/Rules/General Orders," then "Local Bankruptcy Rules & Forms" and scrolling down to the appropriate form.

After December 1, 2011, if an individual chapter 11 debtor does not use these forms, the matter will not be set for hearing and/or the order will not be signed.

Effective July 1, 2011, use of the following Local Bankruptcy Rules Forms in individual chapter 11 cases is **mandatory**:

- Form 2081-1.DISCLSR.STMT - Individual Debtor's Disclosure Statement in Support of Plan of Reorganization;
- Form 2081-1.PLAN - Individual Debtor's Chapter 11 Plan of Reorganization;
- F 2081-1.1.MOTION.CASH.COLLATERAL - Notice of Motion and Motion in Individual Chapter 11 Case for Order Authorizing Interim Use of Cash Collateral [11 U.S.C. § 363];
- F 2081-1.1.ORDER.CASH.COLLATERAL - Order Re: Notice of Motion and Motion in Individual Chapter 11 Case for Order Authorizing Interim Use of Cash Collateral [11 U.S.C. § 363];
- F 2081-1.2.MOTION.BUDGET - Notice of Motion and Motion in Individual Chapter 11 Case for Order Setting Budget for Interim Use of Estate Property as Defined in 11 U.S.C. § 1115;
- F 2081-1.2.ORDER.BUDGET - Order Re: Notice of Motion and Motion in Individual Chapter 11 Case for Order Pursuant to 11 U.S.C. § 363(b) Setting Budget for Interim Use of Estate Property as Defined in 11 U.S.C. § 1115;
- F 2081-1.3.MOTION.PAYROLL - Notice of Motion and Motion in Individual Chapter 11 Case for Order Authorizing Payment of Prepetition Payroll and to Honor Prepetition Employment Procedures: LBR 2081-1(a)(6); and
- F 2081-1.3.ORDER.PAYROLL - Order Authorizing Payment of Prepetition

Payroll and to Honor Prepetition Employment Procedures: LBR 2081-1(a)(6).

These forms may be found on the Court's website, www.cacb.uscourts.gov, by clicking on "Forms/Rules/General Orders," then "Local Bankruptcy Rules & Forms" and scrolling down to the appropriate form.

After July 1, 2011, if an individual chapter 11 debtor does not use these forms, the matter will not be set for hearing and/or the order will not be signed.

I. Tentative Ruling Procedures

TENTATIVE RULING PROCEDURES

In most cases, Judge Klein issues tentative rulings by 2:00 p.m. the day before the hearing date. These rulings are generally available via the Court's webPACER service and will appear on the calendars posted outside the courtroom and placed on counsel tables inside the courtroom on the date scheduled for the hearing.

Please note that even if the court has issued a tentative ruling **appearances are still required** unless:

1. The tentative ruling states explicitly that no appearance is required; or
2. Judge Klein's chambers or calendar clerk has confirmed that no appearance is necessary.

A moving party's failure to attend a hearing on its motion will result in denial of the motion for failure to prosecute and may result in the issuance of an order to show cause re: sanctions. An opposing party's failure to attend a hearing on a motion that it has opposed will be deemed to have withdrawn its opposition to the relief requested in the motion.

J. Trial Procedures Supplement to Local Rules

TRIAL PROCEDURES SUPPLEMENT TO LOCAL RULES

I. TRIAL BRIEFS

Unless otherwise ordered by the court, trial briefs are required. Trial briefs must be filed at least seven (7) calendar days before trial. Judge's copies of the trial briefs **must** be delivered to Judge Klein's chambers on the same day the briefs are filed.

The trial briefs **must** contain:

(1) a concise statement of the facts of the case;

(2) a short statement of any relevant procedural history, including the resolution of all motions;

(3) a summary of the relevant law involved with supporting authorities;

(4) a summary of the disputed issues of fact and the testimony that such party plans to introduce in an effort to prove its version of the disputed facts; and

(5) a brief discussion of any anticipated evidentiary or other issues that the party believes are likely to arise at trial.

Unless specifically requested by the court, no additional trial briefs will be considered.

II. PRETRIAL ORDER

Unless otherwise ordered by the court, the parties must prepare and file a written joint pretrial order pursuant to Local Bankruptcy Rule (LBR) 7016-1(b) through (f) not later than seven (7) calendar days before trial. A judge's copy **must** be delivered to chambers the same day. The pretrial order must contain the statements and information required by LBR 7016-1(b)(2).

In conjunction with the pretrial order, the parties must meet and confer to attempt to stipulate to the authenticity and possible admissibility (without the necessity for live testimony) of the documents that have been exchanged. The court expects the parties to make good faith efforts to resolve all evidentiary issues.

III. PRESENTATION OF DIRECT TESTIMONY BY DECLARATION

The purpose of this procedure is to facilitate pretrial preparation and to streamline the trial process without sacrificing due process and a fair trial.

A. Except as provided herein, each party **must present the direct testimony of all of its witnesses, including expert witnesses, through the declarations of said witnesses**. The declarations must be signed under penalty of perjury and be otherwise admissible under the Federal Rules of Evidence. See, e.g., Lee-Benner v. Gergely (In re Gergely), 110 F.3d 1448, 1452 (9th Cir. 1997); Adair v. Sunwest Bank (In re Adair), 965 F.2d 777, 779-80 (9th Cir. 1992). Each declaration must set forth the direct testimony that the witness would give as though questions were propounded in the usual fashion. Each statement of fact or opinion must be separately, sequentially numbered and must contain only matters that are admissible under the Federal Rules of Evidence (e.g., avoiding redundancies, hearsay, and other objectionable statements).

B. All cross-examination, rebuttal, surrebuttal and appropriate impeachment evidence must be given by live testimony. The only oral testimony that may be offered at trial by a party through its own witnesses will be **STRICTLY** limited to rebuttal testimony or such additional testimony on matters relevant to the outcome of the proceeding as may be specifically requested by the court at the time of trial.

C. If a witness refers in their declaration to an exhibit to be admitted into evidence, the exhibit must be identified in the declaration by exhibit number or letter. The exhibit itself need not be attached to the witnesses' declaration, but must be included in the exhibit binder or notebook and properly marked for identification. (See section IV). Unless the parties stipulate to the admittance of an exhibit, the foundation for admittance of exhibits (other than for impeachment or rebuttal purposes) must be established in the declaration. Exhibits referenced in a declaration should be offered into evidence when the declaration is offered into evidence.

D. If a party is unable to obtain a declaration of a witness (such as, for example, in the case of a hostile witness), counsel for that party must file (by the applicable deadline for the filing of the witness' declaration) a declaration stating the name of the witness, a detailed summary of the expected testimony and why counsel was unable to obtain the witness' declaration. Failure to make every reasonable effort to obtain the declaration of a witness will result in the exclusion of such witness' oral testimony.

E. A party may present the direct testimony of a witness in the form of a transcript of a deposition of the witness, in which event the party must submit a declaration authenticating the excerpts from the transcript that contain the testimony the party wishes to introduce. (Only the portions of the transcript that the party wishes to introduce should be attached to the declaration).

F. The declaration of a witness for a party will be admissible at trial, subject to timely objections, only if the declarant is present at trial and subject to cross-examination.

IV. EXHIBITS

A. All exhibits must be marked for identification before the trial begins. Each exhibit must be marked for identification at the bottom (right) of the first page of the exhibit. Unless the parties agree upon a unified, joint set of exhibits, the Plaintiff's exhibits must be marked in numerical order, and the Defendant's exhibits must be marked in alphabetical order (e.g., Plaintiff's Exhibit 1, etc., Defendant's Exhibit A, etc.). If the parties agree on a unified, joint set of exhibits, the exhibits must be marked in numerical order.

B. All exhibits must be assembled in a binder or notebook. Each such binder or notebook must include as its first page an exhibit register. The exhibit register must include the following information for each exhibit:

Exhibit #	Brief Description	Date Admitted?	How Admitted? (Stipulation; Name of Witness, etc.)	How was Exhibit Used During Trial?

C. At the beginning of trial, the parties must be prepared to stipulate into evidence all exhibits that are admissible for at least one purpose. Bona fide objections may be reserved, with the issue of admissibility deferred, until the exhibit is offered into evidence.

D. Immediately after the trial's conclusion, the parties must complete the exhibit register to indicate the date each exhibit was admitted, how it was admitted, and how the exhibit was actually used during trial. The completed exhibit register **must** be submitted to the court within one business day after the conclusion of trial. Please note that the court will only consider exhibits that were admitted AND that were used during trial. For example, if the parties stipulated to the admissibility of an exhibit, but the exhibit was not referred to by a witness or otherwise used during trial, the exhibit will not be considered by the court.

V. DEADLINES FOR SUBMISSION OF DECLARATIONS, EXHIBITS AND OBJECTIONS

A. Plaintiff must submit to opposing counsel all declarations and exhibits comprising the Plaintiff's case in chief not later than thirty (30) days before the trial date.

B. Defendant must submit to opposing counsel all declarations and exhibits comprising the Defendant's case, together with any written objections to the admission of any of Plaintiff's exhibits or to the testimony contained in any of Plaintiff's witness declarations, not later than twenty-one (21) days before the trial date.

C. Plaintiff must submit to opposing counsel any written objections to the admission of any of Defendant's exhibits or to the testimony contained in any of Defendant's witness declarations not later than fourteen (14) days before the trial date.

D. All witness declarations and exhibits, together with any written objections to the admission of any of the exhibits or to any of the declarations or any portion thereof, must be lodged with Judge Klein's Courtroom Deputy at least seven (7) days before the trial date. Each party must lodge sufficient copies of its exhibit binder (containing the exhibit register and all exhibits), for all parties, the witness stand, the court recorder, and the judge.

E. At trial, each party must also have sufficient copies of exhibits, which the party expects to be used for impeachment or rebuttal, so that copies of such exhibits can be provided to the opposing party, the witness and the judge.

F. Evidentiary objections will be adjudicated at the time a witness declaration or exhibit is offered into evidence. Any evidentiary objections to declaration testimony, which are not raised in a written objection filed within the applicable time limit set forth above, shall be deemed waived.

G. **NO OTHER DECLARATIONS WILL BE ALLOWED.** The only additional evidence that a party may offer at trial is rebuttal evidence. If the court concludes that testimony a party seeks to offer should more accurately be characterized as direct testimony than as rebuttal evidence, that testimony will be excluded.

VI. EXCERPTS FROM DISCOVERY DOCUMENTS

A. **Deposition Transcripts.** Each party intending to offer any evidence by way of deposition testimony pursuant to Fed. R. Civ. P. 32, other than for impeachment or rebuttal, must lodge with Judge Klein's Courtroom Deputy the original deposition transcript, together with a copy of the transcript or pages from the transcript to be offered, marked to reflect the portions to be offered, pursuant to LBR 7030-1(b) not later than the applicable deadline for submission of declarations, exhibits and objections set forth in Section V. Transcripts may be bound on the left side and do not have to be hole-punched or blue-backed.

B. **Other Discovery Documents.** Excerpts from interrogatories, requests for admissions, or other discovery documents to be offered at trial, other than those to be used for impeachment or rebuttal, must be filed pursuant to LBR 7026-2(c) not later than the applicable deadline for submission of declarations, exhibits and objections set forth in Section V.

VII. CONTINUANCE/POSTPONEMENT OF TRIAL DATE

Trials will begin promptly at the scheduled date and time. Trial dates **will not be** continued or vacated absent good cause, on noticed motion, supported by competent evidence. If a motion is filed requesting that a trial be continued, the parties will be contacted by Judge Klein's law clerk regarding whether the continuance has been granted or denied.

Parties are further advised that during the week before trial, the court may move the starting time or day. Judge Klein's Courtroom Deputy will advise the parties of any such change by telephone. All parties will be required to adjust their schedules accordingly.

VIII. SETTLEMENT

Not later than five (5) calendar days before the trial date, counsel for Plaintiff must telephone Judge Klein's Courtroom Deputy at (213) 894-5856 to report:

(a) whether the parties intend to go forward with trial as scheduled;

(b) if settlement is likely;

(c) whether the time reserved for trial is realistic; and

(d) any other relevant information.

Stipulations for settlement must be in writing, executed by each party or their counsel, and delivered to chambers before the trial date. If time constraints prevent reducing a settlement to writing before trial, all the parties, or their counsel, must (a) advise chambers of the settlement, and (b) appear at the time set for trial to recite the stipulation on the record.

IX. COMPLIANCE

Failure to comply with these trial procedure instructions may result in the imposition of sanctions, including but not limited to, removal of the trial from the court's calendar or the exclusion of evidence (e.g., witnesses who were not timely identified or exhibits that were not timely submitted).

Hon. Robert Kwan

Bankruptcy Judge

Contact Information

U.S. Bankruptcy Court, Central District of California
Courtroom 1675
255 E. Temple Street, Suite 1682
Los Angeles, CA 90012
Courtroom Deputy: (213) 894-3385

Biographical Information

Appointment(s):

- Appointed 02/05/07 by the United States Court of Appeals for the Ninth Circuit (Current term expires 02/04/21).

Education:

- Yale College, B.A., 1975
- Hastings College of the Law, University of California, J.D., 1979
- Georgetown University Law Center, LL.M (Taxation), 1985

Career Record:

- 1989-2007: Assistant United States Attorney, Deputy Chief, Tax Division, U.S. Attorney's Office, Central District of California
- 1987-1989: Associate, Law Offices of Wellington Y. Kwan
- 1983-1987: Trial Attorney, Tax Division, U.S. Department of Justice
- 1979-1983, Trial Attorney, Civil Rights Division, U.S. Department of Justice
- Admitted to the California Bar, 1979, and District of Columbia Bar, 1981

Professional Memberships:

- Los Angeles County Bar Association
- American Bankruptcy Institute
- Financial Lawyers Conference
- Los Angeles Bankruptcy Forum
- Orange County Bankruptcy Forum
- National Conference of Bankruptcy Judges

I. Judge Kwan's Procedures and Practices

A. *Mandatory Use of L.O.U. for Section 362 Orders*

MANDATORY USE OF L.O.U. FOR SECTION 362 ORDERS

Effective January 1, 2009

These guidelines apply to orders on motions: (1) for relief from the automatic stay; (2) to impose the stay; or (3) to continue the stay (collectively "Section 362 Orders").

The guidelines will add certainty to the process and minimize costs/delay by:

1) Utilizing electronic processes of filing documents ("CM/ECF"), Lodged Order Upload ("LOU"), and service by Notice of Electronic Filing ("NEF");

2) Clarifying the "Service List for Entered Order"; and

3) Eliminating the need to provide envelopes and copies of orders.

A. Check Tentative Rulings

Judge Kwan posts tentative rulings one court day prior to hearings. Check to see if relief will be granted without a hearing, and if so, what relief. Go to www.cacb.uscourts.gov. The Tentative Rulings link is on the bottom left-hand corner of page one.

B. Lodge Proposed Orders via LOU

All CM/ECF users must lodge Section 362 Orders via LOU. **NO** exceptions.

C. When Should a Proposed Order be Lodged?

Lodged via LOU – Proposed orders may be lodged via LOU after tentative rulings are posted; if a tentative ruling is not posted, lodge the proposed order after the hearing.

Lodged at Intake Window – Non CM/ECF users may only lodge proposed orders after the hearing.

D. Are F 4001-1 Form Orders Mandatory?

MANDATORY FORMS – All Section 362 Orders must be prepared using a mandatory F 4001-1 order available at www.cacb.uscourts.gov under Local Bankruptcy Rules ("LBR") and Forms.

E. Preparing Proof of Service of Proposed Order

1. **Proposed Orders on Unopposed Motions** – There is no obligation to serve a proposed form of order on any person, entity, or attorney ***who did not file an opposition to the motion. This includes a case trustee or the United States trustee.***

2. **Proposed Orders on Opposed Motions** – Pursuant to LBR 9021-1(b)(4) and 9021-1(b)(3)(A), a proposed order must be served only upon any person, entity, or attorney who filed an opposition to the motion. ***There is no obligation to serve the proposed order on any other person or entity.***

F. Prepare Service List for Entered Order

Parties who will be served by the Court:

- Debtor

- Debtor's Counsel (if any)
- Case Trustee
- U.S. Trustee
- Movant
- Any person, entity, or attorney who filed an opposition to the motion

METHOD OF SERVICE

1. **Served Electronically by the Court** – List the names and email addresses *only* of attorneys who are listed in CM/ECF on the Electronic Mail Notice List to receive an email notice. ***The U.S. trustee and case trustee will always be in this category.*** (*See* the Court Manual for help in determining who receives electronic service.)

2. **Served via U.S. Mail by the Court** – list the names and mailing addresses of persons, entities, and/or attorneys listed in CM/ECF under Manual Notice List. ***The debtor will always be in this category.*** **DO NOT** list any of the same people being served electronically. **DO NOT** list anyone who is not one of the **Parties who will be served by the Court**. (*See* the Court Manual for help in determining who receives manual – U.S. Mail – service.)

3. **Service by Movant** – If Movant desires to serve a copy of the entered order on persons or entities not listed in **Parties who will be served by the Court**, movant may do so. Movant must then file a Declaration re proof of service listing the parties' names addresses and method of service. Under this category, Movant can list other lien holders, co-borrowers, or persons/entities they want to serve.

G. Copies of Proposed Order; Envelopes

All Section 362 Orders are served electronically by the Court via NEF to case trustees, the United States trustee, and to attorneys who are on the Electronic Mail Notice List for the particular bankruptcy case.

All Section 362 Orders are served by the Bankruptcy Noticing Center ("BNC") in Herndon, Virginia via U.S. Mail to debtor and to persons or entities that are on the Manual Notice List for the particular bankruptcy case.

1. Copies of All Proposed Orders, Regardless of How Lodged

DO NOT provide any copies of the proposed order for mailing, because copies will be printed either by the BNC (for all relevant addresses on the Manual Notice List) or by the court (in the rare, unique case).

ONLY SEND ONE COPY to the court along with the LOU receipt per the LOU procedures, and do so the same day that the proposed order is lodged.

2. Stamped, Addressed Envelopes, Regardless of How Proposed Order Is Lodged

DO NOT provide envelopes for the debtor or other Manual Notice parties, as the BNC will prepare envelopes for them.

DO NOT provide envelopes for the case trustee or U.S. trustee or other Electronic Mail Notice parties, as they will be served electronically via NEF.

DO NOT provide envelopes for any other person or entity as it is the responsibility of the Movant to serve the entered order and provide the Court with a Declaration re proof of service.

B. Notice to Practitioners Regarding LBR 7016-2(a)(2)

NOTICE TO PRACTITIONERS – SANTA ANA DIVISION REGARDING REQUIREMENT FOR TIMELY FILING OF STATUS CONFERENCE REPORTS IN ADVERSARY PROCEEDINGS AND IMPOSITION OF SANCTIONS

The Judges of the Santa Ana Division have noticed a steady increase in the number of parties failing to file either timely or at all the status conference reports required under Local Bankruptcy Rule 7016-1(a)(2). The Rule requires a filing of the status conference report *at least 14 days* before the status conference and provides for imposition of sanctions under Local Rule 7016-1(f) for noncompliance. Until now the Judges have merely exhorted practitioners to remember the Rule and have threatened imposition of sanctions for noncompliance, but have rarely actually imposed sanctions. However, these measures appear to have been ineffective. Failure to abide by the Rule severely interferes with the processes of the Court and last-minute filing of status conference reports imposes an undue burden on the Court and its staff. **Therefore, please take notice that commencing January 2009 sanctions will be imposed** as the rule rather than the exception for failure to comply with Local Rule 7016-1.

C. *Telephonic Appearance Procedures*

TELEPHONIC APPEARANCE PROCEDURES

SECTION ONE: POLICY GOVERNING TELEPHONE APPEARANCES

Telephone appearances are permitted in all matters before Judge Kwan in Courtroom 1675 with the exception of trials and evidentiary hearings (for which all attorneys and all witnesses must appear in person), Chapter 11 confirmation hearings (for which all attorneys and parties for the plan proponent(s) and any objecting parties must appear in person), and such other matters as designated by the Court as requiring a personal appearance.

No telephone appearance will be allowed unless it is made through CourtCall, an independent conference call company, pursuant to the procedures set forth below in Section Two, or otherwise permitted by the Court.

Before the hearing, you should check Judge Kwan's hearing calendar posted on the court's website, www.cacb.uscourts.gov, and review any tentative ruling for the matter on calendar.

If an attorney or a party who schedules a telephonic appearance fails to respond to the call of a matter on calendar, the court may pass the matter or may treat the failure to respond as a failure to appear. Scheduling simultaneous telephone appearances in multiple courts does not excuse a failure to appear.

Attorneys and parties making use of the conference call service are cautioned that they do so at their own risk. Hearings generally will not be rescheduled due to missed connections.

SECTION TWO: SCHEDULING A TELEPHONE APPEARANCE

Telephone appearances may be arranged by calling **CourtCall at (866) 582-6878**. You may arrange for a telephone appearance up until the starting time of the scheduled hearing.

SECTION THREE: PROCEDURE FOR TELEPHONE APPEARANCE

Any attorney or party making a telephone appearance must make arrangements with CourtCall for the appearance, including for payment of any charges for CourtCall's services. CourtCall will provide the attorney or the party with written confirmation of a telephone appearance, and give the attorney or party a telephone number to call to make the telephone appearance. It is the responsibility of the attorney or party making a telephone appearance to call CourtCall not later than 10 minutes before the scheduled hearing. CourtCall does NOT place a call to the attorney or party. If you do not timely call and connect with the CourtCall operator, you may be billed for the call and the hearing may proceed in your absence.

Telephone appearances are connected directly with the Court's public address system and electronic recording equipment so that a normal audio record is produced. To ensure the quality of the audio record:

- NO speaker phones;
- NO cellular phones;
- NO car phones;
- NO public telephone booths, or phones in other public places;

Exceptions only in the most extreme emergencies.

At the time of your hearing, you may initially be in the listening mode in which case you will be able to hear the case before yours just as if you were in the courtroom. After your call is connected to the courtroom, the judge will call the case, request appearances, and direct the manner in which the hearing is to proceed. Each time you speak, you should identify yourself for the record. The court's teleconferencing system allows more than one speaker to be heard, so the judge can interrupt a speaker to ask a question or redirect the discussion. When the judge informs the hearing participants that the hearing is completed, you may disconnect from the call, and the next case will be called.

Telephone appearances by multiple participants are only possible when there is compliance with every procedural requirement. Sanctions may be imposed when there is any deviation from the required procedures of the Court determines that a person's conduct makes telephone appearances inappropriate. Sanctions may include dropping a matter from calendar, continuing the hearing, proceeding in the absence of an unavailable participant, a monetary sanction, and/or a permanent prohibition against an attorney or party appearing by telephone.

D. *Tentative Ruling Procedures*

TENTATIVE RULING PROCEDURES

1. The court intends to issue tentative rulings by 4:00 p.m. on the day before the scheduled hearings.

2. The public may access Judge Kwan's tentative rulings on the court's website at www.cacb.uscourts.gov by selecting the Tentative Rulings icon on the main page of the website. Alternatively, tentative rulings may be accessed through the court's electronic filing system – CM/ECF – also located at www.cacb.uscourts.gov under Electronic Systems and Status.

3. If the particular matter is unopposed, a party or counsel may submit on the tentative ruling without an appearance. The party or counsel wishing to submit on the tentative ruling should call Judge Kwan's law clerk at (213) 894-2775 and leave a message stating:

   a) the case name;

   b) the calendar number and hearing time;

   c) the name of the party submitting on the tentative; and

   d) the phone number of a responsible party in case there are any questions from chambers.

4. If a tentative ruling is issued and no appearances are made at the hearing, the court will assume that the parties are submitting on the court's tentative ruling and the court will adopt its tentative ruling as its order. If a party submits on the tentative ruling and the court subsequently decides to consider a late-filed document or an opposing party appears, the court may continue the matter for further hearing. The party making the appearance will be responsible for providing notice of the continuance of the hearing.

5. If the particular matter is opposed or if no tentative ruling issued, appearances are required. However, parties or counsel may arrange to appear telephonically in accordance with Judge Kwan's telephonic appearance procedures.

6. If a party or counsel submits on the tentative ruling and prevails either on the merits or by default, that party or counsel is required to submit a proposed order for review and approval by the court in accordance with Local Bankruptcy Rule 9021-1.

7. The court generally will not issue tentative rulings on disclosure statements, plan confirmation, status conferences, trials, hearings on orders to show cause, or any proceeding set for hearing on shortened time.

8. Any questions regarding Judge Kwan's tentative ruling procedures should be directed to his law clerk at (213) 894-2775.

E. Trial and Evidentiary Hearing Procedures

TRIAL AND EVIDENTIARY HEARING PROCEDURES

All parties, whether represented by counsel or self-represented ("you"), must follow these procedures for all trials and evidentiary hearings before Judge Kwan. However, these procedures are not meant to supersede the Federal Rules of Bankruptcy Procedure ("FRBP") or the Local Bankruptcy Rules ("LBR").

TRIAL BRIEFS

Optional, but encouraged because they may help the court prepare for your trial. You must comply with LBR 9013-2 if you file a trial brief.

EXHIBITS

Exhibit Tags

LBR 9070-1 requires you to number and mark all trial exhibits for identification with official court exhibit tags before trial starts. Exhibit tags may be stapled to, or stuck on, a cover page for an exhibit or on the back of the first page of the exhibit. Official court exhibit tags are available upon request from the courtroom deputy or the Clerk's Office on the second floor. If you have more than 10 exhibits, you must put them in a three-ring binder with a printed index of exhibits. You must comply with LBR 7026-2(c) if you are offering discovery documents as trial exhibits.

Required Sets of Exhibits

On the first day of trial, you must deliver the original set of your tagged exhibits and a duplicate set of copies of the exhibits to the court recorder as required by LBR 9070-1. The original set of exhibits is the official copy of the exhibits, and the duplicate set of exhibits is for the judge's use during the trial. Per LBR 9070-1, you must deliver duplicate sets for each other party, and you should have a set of exhibits for your use.

Exhibit Register

LBR 9070-1 requires you to prepare and submit an exhibit register on Form B 3024 "EXHIBIT REGISTER AND NOTICE RE DEPOSITION OF EXHIBITS." The exhibit register is used by the clerk to keep track of the dates of identification and admission of your exhibits during trial. The exhibit register form is available on the court's website at www.cacb.uscourts.gov, under "Court Forms."

WITNESS TESTIMONY

You must submit declarations under penalty of perjury for the direct testimony of all witnesses called by you unless the witnesses are: (1) adverse to you, (2) unwilling to cooperate in preparing a written declaration, or (3) providing impeachment or rebuttal testimony.

Plaintiffs/movants must serve the direct testimony declarations of their witnesses no later than 21 days before the first day of trial. Defendants/respondents must serve the direct testimony declarations of their witnesses no later than 14 days before the first day of trial. You must file and serve written evidentiary objections to any declaration no later than 7 days before the first day of trial, or otherwise, your objections may be deemed waived.

Your witnesses must appear at trial for cross-examination by other parties. If your witnesses fail to appear at trial, their written testimony may be excluded from being considered by the court. When in doubt that witnesses may not appear, you should serve them with a subpoena to compel their attendance, if necessary.

If you are offering deposition transcripts as evidence, you must follow the procedures of LBR 7030-1(b), including marking of the deposition transcripts. Otherwise, the deposition transcripts may be excluded.

TRIAL CONTINUANCES

Trial dates are considered firm and will be continued only upon a compelling showing of good cause and furtherance of the interest of justice. A stipulation or properly noticed motion must be submitted and supported by declaration(s) under penalty of perjury stating the justification for a continuance of a trial. Even after a stipulation or noticed motion has been filed, the parties are required to appear at the trial as scheduled and to comply with these procedures unless explicitly instructed otherwise by chambers, posted tentative ruling, or order of the court.

SETTLEMENT

If you settle a matter before trial, you must immediately notify the judge's law clerk by calling 714-338-5450. Even after the law clerk is notified of the settlement, you are required to appear at the trial as scheduled and to comply with these procedures unless explicitly instructed otherwise by the court or by posted tentative ruling.

ORDERS

You must submit orders that are capable of being lodged electronically through the court's electronic Lodged Order Upload (LOU) system.

TRIAL RULINGS

At the conclusion of the trial, the court may do any of the following: issue oral findings of fact and conclusions of law; set a further hearing at which time it will announce its decision; or take the matter under submission for written decision. If the court directs you to submit proposed findings of fact and conclusions of law, you must comply with LBR 7052-1.

Hon. Geraldine Mund
Bankruptcy Judge

Contact Information
U.S. Bankruptcy Court, Central District of California
Courtroom 303
21041 Burbank Boulevard, Suite 342
Woodland Hills, CA 91367
Courtroom Deputy: (818) 587-2832

Biographical Information
Appointment(s):

- Appointed to the Court 02/09/84 by the United States District Court Judges;
- Reappointed 08/27/86 and 08/27/00 by the United States Court of Appeals for the Ninth Circuit. (Current term expires 08/26/14.)
- Chief Judge, Bankruptcy Court, Central District of California, 1997-2002

Career Record:

- 1977-84, practicing attorney, Beverly Hills, California
- Admitted to the California Bar, 1977

I. Judge Mund's Procedures and Practices

A. Emergency Motions

EMERGENCY MOTIONS PROCEDURES

To obtain a hearing date for a motion on an emergency basis, the movant must file the following documents with the Clerk's Office:

1. Application for an order setting the hearing date for a motion on an emergency basis and a proposed order thereon;

2. Supporting declaration(s) justifying the setting of a hearing on an emergency basis; and

3. Motion, including all supporting papers, for which the movant seeks an emergency hearing.

To expedite the process of obtaining an emergency motion hearing date, when the movant files the documents with the Bankruptcy Court Clerk's Office, they should also place courtesy copies of all the pleadings in the courtesy copy box adjacent to the elevators on the third floor of the SAN FERNANDO DIVISIONAL OFFICE, 21041 Burbank Boulevard, Woodland Hills, CA 91367.

Judge Mund's Law clerk will call the movant within 48 hours of the documents being filed. If the movant is not contacted by Judge Mund's law clerk within 48 hours of filing the emergency motion, the movant shall call Judge Mund's law clerk at (818) 587-2843.

B. Reaffirmation Agreement Information and Notice

INFORMATION REGARDING REAFFIRMATION AGREEMENTS

You have signed a reaffirmation agreement with one of your creditors. It is not valid unless you come to Court and I approve it. You can still decide not to reaffirm this debt, so it is important for you to understand what the effect of the reaffirmation agreement is.

Your discharge in bankruptcy relieves you of a legal liability to pay debts that are discharged. You may decide that you voluntarily want to pay a debt that has been discharged and there is no prohibition against you doing this. You are not required to reaffirm any debt or sign any agreement regarding a debt that has been or will be discharged in your bankruptcy.

Even though the discharge means you do not have to pay the debts that are discharged, sometimes a creditor will have a security interest in some property the creditor will be able to take in you do not pay the debt. A creditor can have a security interest in real property or in personal property (such as your furniture, or car). Often, for example, a merchant who sells you something on its credit card has a security interest in the item or items purchased.

If a creditor has a security interest, it can enforce that security interest if the loan is in default. Usually that means it can foreclose or "take" whatever it is that is the subject of the security interest. Just going into bankruptcy in not a default that a creditor can enforce. Defaults usually arise out of missed payments or lack of insurance or something of that nature.

If I approve this reaffirmation agreement, the debt that you are reaffirming will not be discharged in the bankruptcy. You will be stuck with the payments. If you can't make the payments, the creditor can repossess the property in which it has a security interest (the collateral), can sell it, and may sue you for a judgment for the difference between the amount that is receives on the sale and the amount that you owe on the loan. If there is no collateral for the loan, the creditor can sue you and obtain a judgment for the balance owed and this is not effected by your bankruptcy discharge. For this reason, the bankruptcy law requires me to conduct an inquiry with you as to whether you understand what you are agreeing to, whether you are likely to be able to keep up with the agreement, whether the payments will be a hardship to you and your reason for reaffirming this debt.

Therefore, I need to know the answer to those and some other questions to help me decide whether to approve your agreement or not. At the hearing I will ask you several questions. I will want to know if the creditor with whom you have made this reaffirmation agreement holds some kind of security for the debt. If so, I will want to know what is the security interest in. Do you still have the property that is collateral for this debt? If so, do you want to keep it? Why? How much is it worth?

If the creditor does not have collateral for the debt, I will want to know why you want to be legally obligated to pay it. What do you think you will get out of it? Has the creditor made any promises to you? If so, are they in writing?

Whether there is collateral for the debt or not, I will want to know whether you know what the terms of your agreement are? Do you know the interest rate? Do you know how long it will take you to pay off the debt you are reaffirming? Has the creditor filed suit against you to declare this debt non-dischargeable or has it threatened to file such a suit?

If you do not come to Court for the reaffirmation agreement hearing, I will deny the motion to reaffirm the debt. If I deny the motion to reaffirm the debt, you are under no legal responsibility to pay the creditor, but the creditor can seek to repossess the collateral (if there is any). However the creditor cannot obtain a judgment against you for the amount you owe on this debt.

NOTICE TO ALL DEBTORS APPEARING FOR REAFFIRMATION AGREEMENT HEARINGS

The Los Angeles County Bar Association has created a Debtor Assistance Program to provide free legal assistance to bankruptcy debtors who cannot afford an attorney. An attorney from this program will be available, free of charge, to answer questions which you may have regarding whether or not it is in your best interest to enter into the reaffirmation agreement. Please report to Courtroom 303 at 8:00 a.m. on the day of the scheduled reaffirmation agreement hearing.

C. *Submission of Orders for Signature*

SUBMISSION OF ORDERS FOR SIGNATURE

PLEASE REFER TO LOCAL RULE 116 PRIOR TO SUBMITTING YOUR ORDERS FOR SIGNATURE. ORDERS WILL BE HELD FOR AN OBJECTION PERIOD PURSUANT TO LOCAL RULE 116(1)(e). ORDER ON UNOPPOSED HEARINGS SHALL BE GOVERNED BY LOCAL RULE 116(1)(g).

IF YOUR PLEADING DOES NOT COMPLY WITH LOCAL RULES, IT WILL BE REJECTED. FOR YOUR REFERENCE AND ASSISTANCE THE FOLLOWING IS A LIST OF THE MORE COMMON REASONS AN ORDER IS REJECTED.

ORDER

1. Requires ORIGINAL plus ONE for Court, and ONE copy for each party in interest.

2. Requires self-addressed and stamped envelopes for each party in interest.

3. Requires proof of service.

4. Requires hearing date, time, and place under title of document.

5. Backing of all originals must have the short title of the document typed or printed in the LOWER RIGHT-HAND CORNER of backing.

6. Requires name, address and telephone number in the UPPER LEFT-HAND corner.

NOTICE OF ENTRY

7. Requires Notice of Entry of Judgment form.

8. Requires ORIGINAL plus ONE for Court, and ONE copy for each party in interest.

9 Requires listing to Notice of ALL persons who are to be mailed a copy of the Notice and the Order. (THE FIRM OR PERSON WHO PREPARES THE NOTICE MUST ALSO APPEAR ON THE LIST). Notice is to be stapled to back of Order as the last page.

10. Do not serve Notice of Entry or attach a proof of service to Notice of Entry.

MOTIONS UNDER RULE 111(7)(a) AND CHAPTER 7 MOTIONS FOR RELIEF FROM STAY, CASH COLLATERAL, ADEQUATE PROTECTION AND OBTAINING CREDIT

11. Proceed under Local Rule 111(7)(a) and/or National Bankruptcy Rule 4001(d).

12. FILE: Motion, Notice of Motion, Proof of Service on Motion.

13. Submit Declaration of Non-Opposition after expiration of the 20-day period. Attach copies of ALL SUPPORTING

14. DOCUMENTS TO ORIGINAL DECLARATION ONLY as exhibits. Do not attach to copies.

15. Submit Order after expiration of 20-day objection period as per above Rule together with Declaration.

16. Submit copies of Order and of Notice for parties per above Rule.

17. Requires service of Order on Trustee or the U.S. Trustee.

18. Requires listing of the following on Notice of Entry: Trustee, U.S. Trustee, debtor, debtor's attorney, creditors committee, parties who require special notice, or parties whose interest in real property is affected.

D. Telephonic Appearance Procedures

NOTICE RE TELEPHONIC APPEARANCE PROCEDURES FOR JUDGE GERALDINE MUND'S CASES

Effective September 1, 2007

I. POLICY GOVERNING TELEPHONIC APPEARANCES

Telephonic appearances are allowed in all matters before Judge Mund in Courtroom 303 except the following:

1. Trials and Evidentiary Hearings (all counsel and all witnesses must appear in person).

2. Chapter 11 Status Conferences (debtor and debtor's counsel must appear in person). Other parties in interest may appear telephonically.

3. Chapter 11 or Chapter 13 Confirmation Hearings (debtor, debtor's counsel, and all objecting creditors must appear in person).

4. Hearings on Reaffirmation Agreements (debtor must appear in person).

5. Any matter designated by the court as one requiring a personal appearance.

No telephonic appearance will be allowed unless it is made through Court Call, an independent conference call company, pursuant to the procedures set forth in Section II.

Before requesting a telephonic appearance, you should check Judge Mund's Calendar on the webPACER system and review any Tentative Ruling concerning the matter on calendar. If the court has issued a Tentative Ruling prior to the hearing, each individual who appears telephonically should have reviewed the Tentative Ruling prior to the hearing.

If movant's appearance has been waived, and a late objection or opposition is presented in writing or orally at the scheduled hearing, the Court may elect to call movant's attorney through Court Call in which case movant may be charged a telephonic appearance fee by Court Call.

If an individual schedules a telephonic appearance and then fails to respond to the call of a matter on calendar, the court may pass the matter or may treat the failure to respond as a failure to appear. Scheduling simultaneous telephonic appearances in multiple courts does not excuse a failure to appear when a matter is placed on calendar.

The 3:00 p.m. deadline for scheduling telephonic appearances noted below is independent of the Tentative Rulings process. Late scheduling of a telephonic appearance is not justified by the fact that Tentative Rulings have not been posted on the court's website by 3:00 p.m. the day before the hearing.

Individuals making use of the conference call service are cautioned that they do so at their own risk. Hearings generally will not be rescheduled due to missed connections.

II. SCHEDULING A TELEPHONIC APPEARANCE

By Telephone: Telephone appearances may be arranged by calling **Court Call at (866) 582-6878** not later than **3:00 p.m.** the day prior to the court hearing date. Any request for a telephonic appearance made after the 3:00 p.m. deadline must be court approved by contacting Judge Mund's Law Clerk, at (818) 587-2840.

By Facsimile: Use the court-approved "**Facsimile Request for Telephonic Appearance Form**" located under the *Procedures/Rules/Forms section, Judge's Forms & Instructions* subsection for Judge Mund, of the Court's website at www.cacb.uscourts.gov. Facsimile requests may only be used if the requested appearance is made at least 24 hours in advance of the court hearing date. The facsimile telephone number at Court Call is (866) 533-2946.

III. PROCEDURE FOR TELEPHONIC APPEARANCE

Court Call (866) 582-6878 will provide counsel with written confirmation of a telephonic appearance, and give counsel a number to call to make the telephonic appearance. It is counsel's responsibility to dial into the call not later than 10 minutes prior to the scheduled hearing. **Court Call does not place a call to counsel.** Court Call has advised that the initial charge per participant for a Court Call appearance is $50. The charge increases based upon the length of the call: (a) 0-90 minutes - $50; (b) 91-180 minutes - $80; (c) 181-270 minutes - $120; (d) 271-360 minutes - $160; (e) 360 and above - an additional $40 per each additional 90 minute increment. These charges are subject to change and you should confirm the schedule of fees directly with Court Call. If you do not timely call and connect with the Court Call operator, you will be billed for the call and the hearing may proceed in your absence.

Telephonic appearances are connected directly with the courtroom's public address system and electronic recording equipment so that a normal record is produced. To ensure the quality of the record, the use of car phones, cellular phones, speaker phones, public telephone booths, or phones in other public places is prohibited except in the most extreme emergencies. Participants should be able to hear all parties without difficulty or echo.

At the time of your hearing, you may initially be in the listening mode in which case you will be able to hear the case before yours just as if you were in the courtroom. After your call is connected to the courtroom, the Judge will call the case, request appearances, and direct the manner in which the hearing proceeds. Each time you speak, you should identify yourself for the record. The court's teleconferencing system allows more than one speaker to be heard, so the Judge can interrupt a speaker to ask a question or redirect the discussion. When the Judge informs the participants that the hearing is completed, you may disconnect and the next case will be called.

Telephonic appearances by multiple participants are only possible when there is compliance with every procedural requirement. Sanctions may be imposed when there is any deviation from the required procedures or the Court determines that a person's conduct makes telephonic appearances inappropriate. Sanctions may include dropping a matter from calendar, continuing the hearing, proceeding in the absence of an unavailable participant, a monetary sanction, and/or a permanent prohibition against a person appearing telephonically.

E. Trial Procedures

TRIAL PROCEDURES

EXHIBITS

1. Bring 4 copies of each exhibit to trial. Exhibits should be pre-marked and in notebooks in proper order.

2. Do not mark the same exhibit twice. If plaintiff is introducing it, do not mark it also for defendant.

WITNESSES

Declarants must be in court for cross-examination unless appearance is waived by the other side.

CONTINUANCE OF TRIAL DATE

Trials will not be continued unless very unusual circumstances exist.

PRE-TRIAL ORDERS

Pre-trial orders and declarations are as ordered by the Court at the final status conference/pre-trial conference.

Hon. Richard M. Neiter

Bankruptcy Judge

Contact Information

U.S. Bankruptcy Court, Central District of California
Courtroom 1645
255 E. Temple Street, Suite 1652
Los Angeles, CA 90012
Courtroom Deputy: (213) 894-5860

Biographical Information

Appointment(s):

- Appointed 02/18/06 by the United States Court of Appeals for the Ninth Circuit. (Current term expires 02/17/20.)

Education:

- University of California at Los Angeles, B.S., 1959 (with honors)
- University of Southern California Law Center, (J.D., 1962); Board of Editors of Law Review (1960-62)
- Pepperdine University School of Law, general and advanced courses in Mediation and Alternative Dispute Resolution.

Career Record:

- 1962-2006, Member of Stutman, Treister & Glatt Professional Corporation;
- 1995-2006, Mediator, U.S. Bankruptcy Court for the Central District of California

Awards: Numerous

Board of Directors: See Professional and Community Memberships

Teaching:

- University of San Fernando Valley Law School
- Lecturer/Presenter at numerous conferences, meetings and professional organizations

Professional and Community Memberships:

- Los Angeles County Bar Association (Commercial Law and Bankruptcy Section)
- American Bar Association (Business Law Section)
- The State Bar of California - Debtor/Creditor Relations and Bankruptcy Committee (Former Chairman Liaison: 1974-75, 1977-78; Liaison: 1979-80); Executive Committee, Business Law Section, 1979-81
- Board of Trustees, USC Law Center Alumni Association, 1986-87
- Fellows of Contemporary Art Board of Trustees
- Temple Judea (former President, member of Board of Trustees, etc.)
- National Conference of Soviet Jewry
- Community Relations Committee of Jewish Federation Counsel of San Fernando Valley and of the City of Los Angeles

I. Judge Neiter's Procedures and Practices

A. Instructions Regarding Chambers Copies of Pleadings Filed Electronically

INSTRUCTIONS RE CHAMBER COPIES OF PLEADINGS FILED ELECTRONICALLY

As a general rule, **chambers hard copies of all pleadings filed (electronically or otherwise) that are set for a hearing are prerequisites to having an application or motion heard.** No motion will be scheduled for a hearing unless a copy of all pleadings filed pertaining to the motion or application is submitted to the Court's chambers within 72 hours of the filing of the pleading and the motion or application is filed in accordance with the applicable Local Bankruptcy Rules.

With respect to pleadings on matters that are eligible for self-calendaring, the filing party **shall** deliver to the Intake Office of the Los Angeles division a hard copy of the pleading filed for the Judge Neiter's Courtroom Deputy. A second hard copy shall be delivered to the Judge Neiter's chambers located on the 16th Floor of the Roybal Federal Building, 255 East Temple Street, Suite 1652, Los Angeles, CA 90012.

Any chambers copy of a pleading filed electronically must be accompanied by an ECF receipt or a Notice of Electronic Filing stapled or fastened at the end of the pleading to show proof of filing the original document, and stamped **"Judge's Copy"** or **"Chambers Copy."** The chambers copy must also conform to the requirements of Local Bankruptcy Rule 1002-1, including the format and tabbing of exhibits. If a pleading contains **more than 5 exhibits**, exhibit tabs must be used for all chambers copies. E-filed responsive pleadings will not be considered unless a chambers copy is provided timely to the Court.

B. Procedures for Court Appearances

PROCEDURES FOR COURT APPEARANCES

Judge Neiter has adopted the following procedures for attorneys and parties appearing before him:

1. Judge Neiter posts his tentative rulings the day prior to the scheduled hearing on most matters. All parties appearing on a matter are required to review the Court's tentative rulings in preparation for their hearing.

2. Tentative rulings are usually NOT given for adversary status conferences, pretrial conferences, and chapter 11 (or 7) status conferences. However, parties must be prepared to discuss the status of each case or adversary proceeding and their plan for moving the case or adversary proceeding forward. Appearances are necessary unless expressly waived by the Court.

3. No appearance is required for unopposed motions that are granted by the Court. If an opponent appears at the hearing, the Court will either continue the matter to allow the Movant to respond to any opposition or disregard any late oppositions.

C. Procedures for Telephonic Appearances

PROCEDURES FOR TELEPHONIC APPEARANCES

I. GENERAL RULES REGARDING TELEPHONIC APPEARANCES.

Telephonic appearances may be made in all matters before Judge Neiter in Courtroom # 1645, except the following (unless excused by the Court):

1. Trials, Contested Matters, and evidentiary hearings (Counsel for all parties should appear in person. Witnesses should also appear in person where requested or if they are to be cross-examined).
2. Chapter 11 Status Conferences (debtor, debtor's counsel, and counsel for creditors' committee, if any, should appear in person). Other parties in interest may appear telephonically.
3. Adversary Proceeding Status Conferences (if an answer has been filed) and Pretrial Conferences.
4. Chapter 11, 12 & 13 plan confirmation hearings (debt or, debtor's counsel, and counsel for creditors' committee, if any, should appear in person).
5. Chapter 11 Disclosure Statement Hearings (debtor, debtor's counsel, and counsel for creditors' committee, if any, should appear in person).
6. Any matter designated by the court as requiring a personal appearance.

No telephonic appearance will be allowed unless it is made through *Court Call*, an independent conference call company, pursuant to the procedures set forth in **Section II**.

Before requesting a telephonic appearance, please check Judge Neiter's calendar to review any tentative ruling concerning the matter on calendar. Tentative rulings are normally issued no later than 3:00 p.m. on the day preceding the scheduled hearing. Absent opposition, either before or at the hearing, no appearance is required.

> If written opposition has been filed, the court may nevertheless issue a "Tentative Ruling." A final ruling is likely to be made at the hearing. **Individuals may appear in person or telephonically. All parties are encouraged to review and be familiar with the Tentative Ruling.**

If an individual schedules a telephonic appearance and fails to respond when th e matter is called on calendar, the court may pass the matter or may treat the failure to respond as a failure to appear. Scheduling simultaneous telephonic appearances in multiple courts does not excuse a failure to appear when a matter placed on the calendar is called.

Judge Neiter will not entertain any request for telephonic appearance after the deadline prescribed in **Section II** below except for cause. Late scheduling of a telephonic appearance is not justified by the fact that Tentative Rulings have not yet been posted on the court's website.

Individuals making use of the conference call service are cautioned that they do so at their own risk. Hearings generally will not be rescheduled due to missed connections.

II. SCHEDULING A TELEPHONIC APPEARANCE.

You must contact Court Call to arrange a telephonic appearance and inform Judge Neiter's Court Recorder, Tren Castro, at (213) 894-0804 of any arrangements to appear by telephone.

By Telephone: Telephone appearances may be arranged by calling *Court Call* at (866) 582-6878 no later than **twenty-four (24) hours** prior to the court hearing date. Any request for a telephonic appearance made after the 24-hour deadline must be court approved by contacting Judge Neiter's Courtroom Deputy, Phyllis Jones, at (213) 894-5860.

By Written Request: Written requests may only be done if the requested appearance is made at least **two (2) days** in advance of the court hearing date. The facsimile telephone number at *Court Call* is (866) 533-2946.

III. PROCEDURE FOR TELEPHONIC APPEARANCE.

Court Call will provide counsel with written confirmation of a telephonic appearance, and give counsel a number to call to make the telephonic appearance. It is counsel's responsibility to dial into the call not later than 10 minutes prior to the scheduled hearing. ***Court Call* does not place a call to counsel.** The initial charge per participant for a *Court Call* appearance is$30. The charge increases based upon the length of the call: (a) 0-45 minutes - $30 and $7 per 15 minute increments thereafter. If you do not call and connect with the *Court Call* operator timely, the hearing may proceed in your absence.

Telephonic appearances are con nected directly with the courtroom's public address system and electronic recording equipment so that a normal record is produced. To ensure the quality of the record, the use of car phones, cellular phones, speaker phones, public telephone booths, or phones in other public places is prohibited except in the most extreme emergencies. Participants should be able to hear all parties without difficulty or echo.

At the time of your hearing, you may be placed in a listening mode initially and will be able to hear the case before yours just as if you were in the courtroom. After your call is connected to the courtroom, the Judge will call the case, request appearances, and direct the manner in which the hearing proceeds. **Each time you speak, you should identify yourself for the record.** The court's teleconferencing system allows more than one speaker to be heard so the Judge can interrupt a speaker to ask a question or redirect the discussion. When the Judge informs the participants that the hearing is completed, you may disconnect and the next case will be called.

Telephonic appearances by multiple participants are only possible when there is compliance with every procedural requirement. Sanctions may be imposed upon any deviation from the required procedures or the court determines that a person's conduct makes telephonic appearances inappropriate. Sanctions may include dropping a matter from calendar, continuing the hearing, proceeding in the absence of an unavailable participant, a monetary sanction, and/or a permanent prohibition against a person appearing telephonically.

D. Status Conference Instructions

STATUS CONFERENCE INSTRUCTIONS OF BANKRUPTCY

1. A copy of these instructions must be attached to the copy of the complaint served upon each party, and the proof of service must state that these instructions, as well as a copy of the summons and complaint, was served.

2. If the proceeding involves money or property exceeding $10,000 or if the plaintiff believes trial time will be four (4) hours or more, plaintiff must serve, with the summons and complaint, a notice in compliance with Local Bankruptcy Rule 7026-1. Plaintiff must also file proof of service of the notice with proof of service of the summons and complaint.

3. If Local Bankruptcy Rule 7026-1 applies, counsel for the parties **MUST TIMELY MEET TO DISCUSS SETTLEMENT AND TO EXCHANGE DOCUMENTS, OTHER EVIDENCE AND LISTS OF WITNESSES AND PRELIMINARY DISCOVERY SCHEDULES AS PROVIDED IN THE RULE.**

4. Pursuant to Local Bankruptcy Rule 7016-1(a)(2), all parties must file a Joint Status Report at least fourteen (14) days before the date set for each status conference. The initial Joint Status Report should be in a form attached hereto as Exhibit A, *i.e.*, Local Form 7016-1.1.[*] Failure to file such a Joint Status Report may result in the imposition of monetary sanctions and/or the status conference being continued and parties being ordered to redo the status report to conform to Exhibit A. If cooperation in the filing of a Joint Status Report cannot reasonably be obtained, each appearing party must file a Unilateral Status Report and Declaration which complies with Local Bankruptcy Rule 7016-1(a)(2) and is filed within ten (10) days of the date set for each conference.

5. If a response to the complaint is not timely filed:

A. The plaintiff should promptly file a request for entry of default by the clerk. The plaintiff should also move for an entry of a default judgment by filing and serving (if necessary) an appropriate motion; *see* Fed. R. Bankr. P. 7055 and Local Bankruptcy Rule 9021-1(d); AND

B. No later than ten (10) days prior to the status conference, each appearing party must also file a Unilateral Status Report (completing Sections A–E of Exhibit A attached hereto) as required by Local Bankruptcy Rule 7016-1(a)(2).

6. If the parties dispute whether the adversary proceeding is "core" within the meaning of 28 U.S.C. § 157(b), they must file points and authorities in support of their positions. Any party who contends that the proceeding is "non-core" must file and serve a memorandum of points and authorities and evidence in support of his/her/its position no less than fourteen (14) days before the status conference. Any response must be filed at least seven (7) days before the status conference. **If a party does not timely file and serve his/her/its papers, that failure may be deemed a consent to whatever determination the Court makes.**

7. Any party claiming a right to trial by jury must make a timely demand as set forth in Local Bankruptcy Rule 9015-2. If the parties dispute whether a party has a right to a jury trial,

---

[*] [Editor's Note: Exhibit A (Local Form 7016-1.1) can be downloaded at the court's website at http://www.cacb.uscourts.gov.]

they must file points and authorities in support of their positions. Any party who contends that he/she/it has a right to a jury trial must file and serve a memorandum of points and authorities and evidence in support of his/her/its position no less than fourteen (14) days before the status conference . Any response must be filed at least seven (7) days before the status conference. **If a party does not timely file and serve his/her/its pleadings, that failure may be deemed a consent to whatever determination the Court makes.**

8. Counsel for each party and any party who does not have counsel must appear in person at the first status conference. With respect to subsequent status conferences, counsel for each party and any party who does not have counsel may appear by telephone if they make timely arrangements to do so in accordance with the Court's telephonic appearance procedures, which can be accessed by clicking "Information" on the upper left-hand corner of the Court's website at www.cacb.uscourts.gov. If a party has questions about these procedures or cannot locate them on the Court's website, the party may contact Phyllis Jones, the judge's Courtroom Deputy, at (213) 894-5860.

9. Unless otherwise ordered by the Court, within seven (7) court days after the initial status conference, the plaintiff must submit a Scheduling Order which complies with Local Bankruptcy Rule 7016-1(a)(3).

10. Failure to comply with these instructions may subject the responsible party to sanctions as may be warranted under the circumstances or allowed under Local Bankruptcy Rule 7016-1(f).

11. Failure of counsel for any party to appear at a status conference may be considered an abandonment or failure to prosecute or defend diligently and may result in dismissal of the proceeding or judgment entered against the defaulting party without further hearing, or such other sanctions as may be warranted under the circumstances or allowed under Local Bankruptcy Rule 7016-1(g).

E. Trial Procedures

TRIAL PROCEDURES SUPPLEMENTAL TO LOCAL RULES

1. **Trial Briefs: Unless otherwise ordered by the Court, plaintiff's trial brief shall be filed and served at least thirty (30) days before the trial date, defendant's trial brief shall be filed and served at least twenty-one (21) days before the trial date and any reply brief by plaintiff (which is not required) shall be filed and served at least fourteen (14) days before the trial date.** Courtesy copies of the briefs must be delivered to chambers, Suite 1652, on the same date as the brief is filed. The parties are encouraged to include a brief statement of the pertinent facts in their briefs, with citation to exhibits or anticipated testimony.

2. **Direct Testimony:** Unless otherwise permitted by the Court, trials will be conducted through oral testimony.

3. **Exhibits:** All trial exhibits shall be numbered and marked as required by Local Rule 9013-2(b). **At least seven (7) days before trial, each counsel shall deliver to chambers the original and one copy of a notebook containing all trial exhibits (the "Exhibit Book").** The original exhibits shall be tagged as required by Local Rule 9013-2(b). Counsel shall deliver to chambers an "exhibit register," on the form available from the Clerk's Office, at the same time as the Exhibit Book. Counsel shall exchange all exhibits on or before the date of the delivery to chambers. The Exhibit Books shall include all exhibits anticipated to be used at the trial, including all rebuttal exhibits. Exhibits to be used for impeachment only need not be included. At trial, counsel shall have sufficient conformed sets of exhibits for opposing counsel and for each party in the proceeding. Counsel shall also have sufficient copies of exhibits used for impeachment purposes or rebuttal for opposing counsel, the pertinent witness and, with respect to impeachment exhibits not included in the Exhibit Books delivered to chambers, the Court.

Any evidentiary objections to plaintiff's exhibits shall be filed and served at least twenty-one (21) days before the trial date. Any evidentiary objections to defendant's exhibits must be filed and served at least fourteen (14) days before the trial date.

Courtesy copies of evidentiary objections must be delivered to chambers, Suite 1652, on the same date the evidentiary objections are filed.

4. **Continuance/Postponement of Trial:** As a general rule, scheduled trials will not be continued prior to or at trial. Motions or Stipulations for continuance of trial must be submitted in writing at least two (2) court days prior to the scheduled trial date. The parties will be contacted by the judge's law clerk as to whether the continuance has been granted or denied.

5. **Settlement:** In the event of a settlement prior to trial, the parties shall immediately contact and advise the judge's law clerk.

6. **Service:** Service of briefs, declarations and evidentiary objections described herein shall be on counsel for the opposing party, or if the opposing party is appearing *pro se*, on the opposing party.

Hon. Charles E. Rendlen III

Bankruptcy Judge

Contact Information

U.S. Bankruptcy Court, Central District of California
Courtroom 1639
255 E. Temple Street, Suite 1634
Los Angeles, CA 90012
Courtroom Deputy: (213) 894-1485

Biographical Information

Appointments:

- Appointed by the Attorney General to serve as United StatesTrustee for Region 13, which comprised of Arkansas, Missouri and Nebraska, June 2003.
- Appointed to fourteen-year term as United States Bankruptcy Judge for the Eastern District of Missouri, May 23, 2006.
- Appointed as Pro Tem Member of the Bankruptcy Appellate Panel, August of 2010.

Education:

- William Jewell College, *magna cum laude*, 1972
- University of Missouri Columbia, J.D., 1976

Career Record:

- Private Practice for twenty-eight years; Managing Partner of the firm for thirteen years.

Hon. Robin L. Riblet

Bankruptcy Judge

Contact Information

U.S. Bankruptcy Court, Central District of California
Courtroom 201
1415 State Street
Santa Barbara, CA 93101
Courtroom Deputy: (805) 884-4873

Biographical Information

Appointment(s):

- Appointed 03/30/88 by the United States Court of Appeals for the Ninth Circuit;
- Reappointed 03/30/02 by the United States Court of Appeals for the Ninth Circuit. (Current term expires 03/29/16.)

Education:

- University of Florida, 1971, B.A. (*cum laude*);
- University of San Diego School of Law (California), 1975, J.D. (*cum laude*);
- New York University School of Law, 1979, LL.M.

Professional Memberships:

- Los Angeles County and Santa Barbara County Bar Associations;
- Financial Lawyers Conference;
- California Bankruptcy Forum;
- American College of Bankruptcy;
- Federal Bar Association (Central Coast Chapter)

I. Judge Riblet's Procedures and Practices

A. Guidelines for Submitting Exhibits

GUIDELINES FOR SUBMITTING EXHIBITS

1. Unless otherwise ordered by the court, an original and 1 copy of any trial/hearing exhibits and trial/hearing briefs must be submitted 1 week prior to the scheduled trial/hearing and served on opposing counsel. Both copies must be tabbed prior to submission for judicial review.

2. The exhibit title must state "Exhibit for Trial" or "Exhibit for Hearing" followed by any other description as warranted.

3. The exhibit register must be prepared in advance, and attached to exhibit upon submission to the Clerk's Office for lodging.

4. The exhibit must be bound, preferably on the left side, consistent with a 3-ring binder or reinforced cardboard covers on front and back.

5. Exhibits must be tagged prior to submission on the bottom left reverse side of the last page of each exhibit as follows:

Plaintiff = Yellow numeric tags **Defendant = Blue alphabetic tags**

6. All models, diagrams, documents or other exhibits lodged with the clerk that are admitted into evidence or marked at trial shall be retained by the clerk until expiration of the time for appeal without any appeal having been taken, entry of a stipulation waiving or abandoning the right to appeal, final disposition of any appeal, or order of the court, whichever occurs first. The clerk shall thereafter return such exhibit (except contraband) to the person or persons to whom it belongs. If any exhibit is not withdrawn from the Clerk's Office within 30 days after the person or persons to whom it belongs are given written notice to claim it, the clerk may destroy the exhibit or otherwise dispose of it as the court may approve (Local Rule 9070-1).

If you have any questions, please contact Kam Rust at (805) 884-4873.

Hon. Ernest M. Robles

Bankruptcy Judge

Contact Information

U.S. Bankruptcy Court, Central District of California
Courtroom 1568
255 E. Temple Street, Suite 1560
Los Angeles, CA 90012
Courtroom Deputy: (213) 894-4843

Biographical Information

Appointment(s):

- Appointed 06/12/93 by the United States Court of Appeals for the Ninth Circuit;
- Reappointed 06/12/07 by the United States Court of Appeals for the Ninth Circuit (Current term expires 06/11/21)

Education:

- University of California at Berkeley, 1974-78, B.A. in political science (with distinction);
- University of Michigan Law School, 1978-81, J.D.

Career Record:

- 1981-82, practicing attorney, Musick, Peeler and Garrett;
- 1982-87, Hancock, Rothert and Bunshoft, San Francisco, California;
- 1987-88, Kornblum and McBride, San Francisco, California;
- 1988-93, Assistant U. S. Trustee, Office of the U. S. Trustee, San Jose, California;
- Admitted to the California Bar, 1981; Ninth Circuit, 1984

Publications and Other Media:

- Co-author (with Linda Curtis), "United States Trustee's Role in Bankruptcy," Chapter 9 in *Business Lawyer's Bankruptcy Guide.*

I. Judge Robles' Procedures and Practices

A. *Instructions for Telephonic Appearance*

INSTRUCTIONS FOR TELEPHONIC APPEARANCES

Telephone appearances will be arranged through *Court Call, LLC*™. Court Call is an independent conference call company that arranges conference calls nationally for Courts.

It is counsel's responsibility to schedule their telephonic appearance at least 5 Court days prior to the hearing date by contacting CourtCall @ 866-582-6878 or via internet by registering at www.courtcall.com.

Participants automatically scheduled by the Court for the monthly *adversary status conference or pre-trial conference calendar* will receive a call from a CourtCall Representative to confirm their telephonic appearance prior to the date of their hearing.

Written Confirmation will be provided for each separate CourtCall Appearance. If you have not received a written Confirmation, prior to the hearing date, please contact CourtCall immediately or you may be precluded from the telephonic calendar.

It is the participant's responsibility to dial into to their conference by using the 800 number provided by CourtCall. **The CourtCall Operator will not dial out to connect a participant.**

Payment: CourtCall accepts 2 forms of payment:

1) Credit or Debit Card
2) CourtCall Debit Account

***Please contact CourtCall for more detailed information, not the Court.

Do not argue with Court Call or request special treatment. Court Call's function is no more than to offer you the opportunity to appear by telephone. Your election to appear by telephone constitutes your agreement for telephonic appearances.

At the time of the hearing, you will initially be placed in "Listen-only" mode and able to hear all proceedings just as if you were in the courtroom. Your line will be placed "Live" once the Judge calls your case. Each time a participant speaks to the Court, he or she must identify themself for the record. When the Judge informs the participants that the hearing is completed, the participants may disconnect and the next case will be called. Please remain on line if you are appearing on multiple cases on the same calendar.

Telephonic appearances are connected directly with the courtroom's public address system and electronic recording equipment so that a normal record is produced. To ensure a quality record, the use of car phones, public telephone booths, or phones in other public places is **prohibited** except in the most extreme emergencies. Participants should be able to hear all parties without difficulty or echo. The system also allows more than one speaker to be heard so that the Judge can interrupt a speaker to ask a question or redirect the discussion.

Telephonic appearances by multiple participants are only possible when there is compliance with every procedural requirement. Sanctions may be imposed when there is any deviation from the required procedures or the Court determines that a person's conduct makes telephonic appearances inappropriate. Sanctions may include dropping a matter from calendar, continuing the hearing, proceeding in the absence of an unavailable participant, a monetary sanction, or a permanent prohibition against a person appearing telephonically.

B. Mandatory Use of L.O.U. for All Orders

MANDATORY USE OF L.O.U. FOR ALL ORDERS

Effective June 10, 2010

These guidelines apply ***only*** *to parties represented by counsel. If you do not have an attorney you are allowed to lodge your order at the Intake window located at 255 East Temple Street, Room 940, Los Angeles, CA 90012.*

All proposed orders are to be lodged electronically on all cases and adversary proceedings using the court's Lodged Order Upload (LOU) program which is accessible via CM/ECF.

In order to file documents electronically for the United States Bankruptcy Court for the Central District of California, attorneys (and limited access filers) must register online at www.cacb.uscourts.gov and either provide proof of proficiency in ECF or complete an online training course. If you have further questions, please contact the ECF Help Desk by calling (213) 894-2365 or via email at ECF_Support@cacb.uscourts.gov. The ECF Help Desk is available Monday through Friday 9:00 a.m. - 4:00 p.m. (excluding Federal Holidays).

The guidelines will add certainty to the process and minimize costs/delay by:

1) Utilizing electronic processes of filing documents ("CM/ECF"), Lodged Order Upload ("LOU"), and service by Notice of Electronic Filing ("NEF");
2) Clarifying the "Service List for Entered Order"; and
3) Eliminating the need to provide envelopes and copies of orders.

A. Check Tentative Rulings

Judge Robles posts tentative rulings one court day prior to hearings.

Check to see if the motion will be granted without a hearing.

Go to www.cacb.uscourts.gov.

The Tentative Rulings link is on the bottom left-hand corner of page one.

B. Lodge Proposed Orders via LOU

All parties represented by counsel must lodge orders via LOU. NO exceptions.

C. When Should a Proposed Order be Lodged?

Lodged via LOU – Proposed orders must be lodged via LOU after tentative rulings are posted; if a tentative ruling is not posted, lodge the proposed order after the hearing.

Lodged at Intake Window – Only **pro per debtors** are allowed to lodge proposed orders after the hearing. **Paper orders lodged by non-pro per debtors will be returned unsigned.**

D. Preparing Proof of Service of Proposed Order

1. **Proposed Orders on Unopposed Motions** – There is no obligation to serve a

proposed form of order on any person, entity, or attorney ***who did not file an opposition to the motion. This includes a case trustee or the United States trustee.***

2. **Proposed Orders on Opposed Motions** – Pursuant to LBR 9021-1(b)(4) and 9021-1(b)(3)(A), a proposed order must be served only upon any person, entity, or attorney who filed an opposition to the motion. ***There is no obligation to serve the proposed order on any other person or entity.***

E. Prepare Service List for Entered Order

METHOD OF SERVICE

1. **Served Electronically by the Court** – List the names and email addresses *only* of attorneys who are listed in CM/ECF on the Electronic Mail Notice List to receive an email notice. ***The U.S. trustee and case trustee will always be in this category.*** (See the Court Manual for help in determining who receives electronic service.)
2. **Served via U.S. Mail by the Court** – list the names and mailing addresses of persons, entities, and/or attorneys listed in CM/ECF under Manual Notice List. ***The debtor will always be in this category.*** **DO NOT** list any of the same people being served electronically. **DO NOT** list anyone who is not one of the **Parties who will be served by the Court**. (See the Court Manual for help in determining who receives manual - U.S. Mail – service.)
3. **Service by Movant** – If Movant desires to serve a copy of the entered order on persons or entities not listed in **Parties who will be served by the Court**, Movant may do so. Movant must then file a Declaration re proof of service listing the parties' names addresses and method of service. Under this category, Movant can list other lien holders, co-borrowers, or persons/entities they want to serve.

F. Copies of Proposed Order; Envelopes

All Section 362 Orders are served electronically by the Court via NEF to case trustees, the United States trustee, and to attorneys who are on the Electronic Mail Notice List for the particular bankruptcy case.

- -

All Section 362 Orders are served by the Bankruptcy Noticing Center ("BNC") in Herndon, Virginia via U.S. Mail to debtor and to persons or entities that are on the Manual Notice List for the particular bankruptcy case.

- -

NOTICING. Orders that are uploaded via LOU, and then subsequently entered via the Court's Calendar and Order Generation program ("CIAO!"), will generate either an electronic or manual notice from the Bankruptcy Noticing Center (BNC) upon entry in the court's Case Management (CM) system. ***For more information on orders noticed through BNC, please refer to section 4-6 of the Court Manual.***

C. Revised Early Meeting of Counsel and Joint Status Conference Instructions

REVISED EARLY MEETING OF COUNSEL AND JOINT STATUS CONFERENCE INSTRUCTIONS

1. *A COPY OF THESE INSTRUCTIONS MUST BE ATTACHED TO THE COPY OF THE COMPLAINT SERVED UPON EACH PARTY, AND THE PROOF OF SERVICE OF THE SUMMONS AND COMPLAINT MUST INDICATE THAT SUCH COPY WAS SERVED THEREWITH.*

2. These instructions apply only to parties represented by counsel. If you do not have an attorney you must appear at the status conference in person.

3. This status conference will be conducted **by telephone** at the date and time shown on the summons.

Telephone appearances for status conference will be arranged through ***Court Call***™ pursuant to the attached Instructions for Telephonic Appearances. Court Call is an independent conference call company that arranges conference calls on a national and international basis for business. It has no business connection with this court.

4. If the proceeding involves money or property exceeding $10,000.00 or if the plaintiff believes trial time will be four hours or more, plaintiff must serve, with the summons and complaint, a notice that compliance with **Local Rule 7026-1** is required. Plaintiff must also file proof of service of the notice with proof of service of the summons and complaint.

5. If **Local Rule 7026-1** applies, counsel for the parties **MUST TIMELY MEET TO DISCUSS SETTLEMENT AND TO EXCHANGE DOCUMENTS, OTHER EVIDENCE, AND LISTS OF WITNESSES AND PRELIMINARY DISCOVERY SCHEDULES AS PROVIDED IN SAID RULE.**

6. Unless all defendants have defaulted, the parties shall file a Form F7016.1.1 Joint Status Report pursuant to **Local Rule 7016-1(a)(2)** at least 14 days before the date of the status conference. If **Local Rule 7026-1** applies, the parties must include in the Joint Status Report a statement that they have met to discuss settlement and have exchanged documents, other evidence, lists of witnesses and preliminary discovery schedules. If the parties request dates for discovery cut-off, pre-trial or trial other than those ordered herein, this request shall be made in the Joint Status Report.

7. If no response to the complaint is timely filed, plaintiff may request entry of default by the clerk or by the court. Plaintiff may also request entry of a default judgment by filing and serving an appropriate motion, *see* **FRBP Rule 7055** and **Local Rule 7055**.

8. If the parties dispute whether the adversary proceeding is **"core" or "non-core,"** they shall file points and authorities in support of their positions. Any party that contends the proceeding is "non-core" shall file and serve its points and authorities at least **14 days** before the status conference. Any response must be filed and served at least seven days before the status conference.

9. Failure to comply with these instructions including the failure to timely file a joint status report will subject the responsible party to monetary **sanctions**, without a further hearing.

10. Failure of counsel for any party to appear at a status conference or pre-trial conference may be considered an abandonment or failure to prosecute or defend diligently and the proceeding may be dismissed or judgment entered against the defaulting party without a further hearing.

11. Plaintiffs demanding trial by jury in the bankruptcy court shall file a demand with their complaint. All other parties stipulating to trial by jury in the bankruptcy court should file their stipulation not later than the date of the status conference.

II. Judge Robles' Case Management Orders

A. *Order Regarding Courtroom Procedures*

IN THE UNITED STATES BANKRUPTCY COURT
FOR THE CENTRAL DISTRICT OF CALIFORNIA

In re	)	Case No. LA ____________
	)	Adv. No. AD ____________
Debtor(s).	)	Chapter ____
________________________________	)	
	)	**ORDER RE: COURTROOM**
Plaintiff(s),	)	**PROCEDURES**
v.	)	
Defendant(s).	)	
________________________________	)	

This adversary proceeding or evidentiary matter having been set for trial or evidentiary hearing for the week of XXXXXXXXX it is hereby:

ORDERED that the following order shall apply to all matters set for trial or other proceeding in which evidence shall be taken:

1. Each party shall serve and exchange the following **not later than seven (7) court days prior to trial:** 1) a trial brief, 2) a set of proposed findings of fact and conclusions of law, 3) trial exhibits, 4) a list of trial exhibits and 5) a list of witnesses. Copies of the above must also be delivered **directly with Judge Robles' chambers not later than seven (7) court days prior to trial.** (*See also* paragraph 1(c)(ii) below).

a. Contents of trial brief

i. The trial brief shall contain all those items set forth in Local Bankruptcy Rule 9013-2;

ii. Unless otherwise ordered, the trial brief shall not exceed twenty (20) pages in length and shall be accompanied by a table of contents and table of authorities.

b. Contents of Proposed Findings of Fact and Conclusions of law

i. The contents of the proposed Findings of Fact and Conclusions of Law shall conform with Local Bankruptcy Rule 7052-1;

ii. The proposed Findings of Facts shall not contain argument or facts for which there was no evidence submitted. Each finding of fact shall be supported by a reference to an exhibit or to expected testimony.

c. Trial exhibits (the following procedures govern all exhibits except those used for purposes of impeachment):

i. There shall be sufficient copies of exhibits for the Court, all parties participating in the trial and the witness;

ii. Only the Judge's copies of the exhibits are required to be delivered seven (7) court days prior to trial. Copies for the witness and opposing counsel may be brought to court on the date set for trial.

iii. All copies of exhibits shall be premarked prior to lodging with the Judge's chambers and shall conform with the exhibit list. Exhibit tags are available from the courtroom deputy. The exhibit tag shall be placed on the document so that it does not obscure any portion of the document. Otherwise, it may be placed on the reverse of the document;

iv. Plaintiff's (or Movant's) exhibits shall be identified numerically commencing with "Exhibit 1." Defendant's (or Respondent's) exhibits shall be marked alphabetically commencing with "Exhibit A" through "Exhibit Z." Subsequent exhibits for the Defendant shall be marked "AA" through "AZ," "BA" through "BZ," *etc.* (*see* Local Bankruptcy Rule 9070-1); and

v. If a party has in excess of ten (10) exhibits, in addition to tagging the exhibit, that party's exhibits shall be placed in a three ring binder or binders. The exhibits shall be divided by a tab extending beyond the page on the right hand side and the tab shall bear the number or letter of the exhibit. If a party has less than ten (10) exhibits, each shall have an exhibit tag.

2. **Demonstrative Evidence:** The Court encourages the use of sketches, models, diagrams, pictures, summaries, charts, and other demonstrative evidence. Summaries may be required by the Court in actions on account, preferences, or other issues involving voluminous documentation of financial transactions.

3. **Courtroom Etiquette:** Opening statements, oral motions, questioning of witnesses and closing arguments are to be made from the podium. Permission must be obtained before approaching a witness. Counsel making an objection or addressing the court shall rise to be recognized. Following these procedures will ensure that the electronic recording equipment shall accurately record these proceedings.

4. **Counsel Tables:** Plaintiff or moving party should utilize the counsel table in front of and closest to, the witness stand. The defendant or responding party should utilize the counsel table furthest from the witness stand.

It is further ORDERED, that plaintiff (or moving party) is to serve this order on all parties appearing in the adversary or other evidentiary proceeding and must file with the court twenty days from the date of this order a proof of service demonstrating that service has been made.

It is further ORDERED, that failure to adhere to the above may result in those sanctions set forth in Local Bankruptcy Rule 9011-3, or such other sanctions as the Court deems appropriate.

Dated: _______________

____
ERNEST M. ROBLES
United States Bankruptcy Judge

B. *Status Report Order for Chapter 11 Cases*

IN THE UNITED STATES BANKRUPTCY COURT
FOR THE CENTRAL DISTRICT OF CALIFORNIA

In re	)	Case No. LA ____________-ER
	)	Chapter ____
Debtor(s).	)	DATE: __________
________________________________	)	TIME: ___________
		PLACE: 255 EAST TEMPLE STREET
		COURTROOM 1568
		LOS ANGELES, CA 90012

ORDER RE STATUS REPORT ON CHAPTER 11 CASE
AND HEARING THEREON

On XXXXXXXXXXXXX, the debtor(s) in possession filed the above-referenced chapter 11 petition. The Court's review of the file in this case has revealed little, if any, activity toward the confirmation of a plan of reorganization, therefore **GOOD CAUSE APPEARING IT IS HEREBY:**

ORDERED: Debtor will file with the Court and serve on the United States Trustee, and any committee of unsecured creditors, by XXXXXXXXXX, a report on the status of this reorganization case (Status Report). Said Status Report is to address the following issues specifically:

- Status of any contemplated disclosure statement and plan, and an estimate when these will be filed;
- Whether the Debtor has performed all of its duties under 11 U.S.C. §§ 521, 1106 and 1107;
- The post-petition operations of the Debtor and the status of reorganization efforts;
- Whether any professionals have been retained by the Debtor upon approval of the Court, and if no such approval was obtained, the reason why approval was not obtained; and it is further,

ORDERED: That on XXXXXXXXXXXX at XXXX, in Courtroom 1568 the Court will conduct a hearing on the Status Report; and it is further,

ORDERED: That, absent good cause, failure of the Debtor to file and serve the Status Report and appear at the hearing on the Status Report will be grounds sufficient to dismiss, convert or appoint a chapter 11 trustee in this case; and it is further,

ORDERED: That at the hearing on the Status Report, in addition to dismissing, converting or appointing a chapter 11 trustee, the Court may set deadlines for entry of an order approving a disclosure statement and entry of an order confirming a plan, or other orders which the Court deems appropriate under the circumstances.

DATED: _______________

____
ERNEST M. ROBLES
United States Bankruptcy Judge

Hon. Barry Russell

Bankruptcy Judge

Contact Information
U.S. Bankruptcy Court, Central District of California
Courtroom 1668
255 E. Temple Street, Suite 1660
Los Angeles, CA 90012
Courtroom Deputy: (213) 894-3687

Biographical Information

Appointment(s):

- Appointed to the Court in 1974 by the Judges of the District Court;
- Reappointed 08/27/86 and 08/27/00 by the United States Court of Appeals for the Ninth Circuit. (Current term expires 08/26/14.)
- Ninth Circuit Bankruptcy Appellate Panel, 03/88-12/01; Chief Judge, 09/99-12/01;
- Chief Judge, Bankruptcy Court, Central District of California, 2003-2006.

Education:

- University of California at Los Angeles, B.S., 1962 (engineering); J.D., 1966.

Other Government Service:

- 1966-67, U. S. Treasury Department;
- 1967-70, Los Angeles County Public Defender;
- 1970-74, Assistant U. S. Attorney, U. S. Department of Justice

Publications and Other Media:

- Bankruptcy Evidence Manual, West Publishing Co., since 1987, new edition published annually.

Awards:

- Franklin N. Flaschner Judicial Award, American Bar Association, 1987;
- First American invited by Supreme People's Court, People's Republic of China, to lecture on bankruptcy law, 1988;
- Judges' Award, Southern California Mediation Association, for distinguished service for promoting mediation in the courts;
- Emil Gumpert Judicial ADR Award, Los Angeles County Bar Association's Dispute Resolution Service
- "2004 Outstanding Jurist," Los Angeles County Bar Association

Teaching:

- 1977-present, Faculty Member, Federal Judicial Center, Washington, DC;
- 1975-present, Associate Clinical Professor of Psychiatry (Law), University of Southern California

Professional Memberships:

- Federal Bar Association, since 1971; National president, 1990-91;

- Los Angeles County Bar Association since 1967;
- Fellow of the American College of Bankruptcy, inducted 1992;
- Board of Directors for the Western Justice Center, 1996;
- Mensa, 1970

I. Judge Russell's Procedures and Practices

A. Telephonic Procedures

PROCEDURES REGARDING TELEPHONIC APPEARANCES

1. Telephonic appearances are permitted by Judge Russell on a case by case basis **for extreme emergencies only**. To request a telephonic appearance, contact Judge Russell's Courtroom Deputy, Stacey Fortier, as soon as possible at the following phone number: (213) 894-3687.

2. Provide the Courtroom Deputy with the following information:

(a) the name of the case and the bankruptcy case number or adversary proceeding number;

(b) the date and the time of the hearing;

(c) the reason for the telephonic appearance; and

(d) your telephone number.

3. If Judge Russell approves the request, the Courtroom Deputy will advise you of the telephone number to call for a telephone conference call.

4. If Judge Russell denies the request, the Courtroom Deputy will advise you.

Hon. Deborah J. Saltzman

Bankruptcy Judge

Contact Information
U.S. Bankruptcy Court, Central District of California
Courtroom 304
3420 Twelfth Street, Suite 385
Riverside, CA 92501
Courtroom Deputy: (951) 774-1075

Biographical Information

Appointment(s):

- Appointed 03/18/10 by the United States Court of Appeals for the Ninth Circuit. (Current term expires 03/18/24)

Education:

- Amherst College, B.A., 1991, Phi Beta Kappa
- University of Virginia School of Law, J.D., 1996

Career Record:

- 2008-2010: DLA Piper LLP (US)
- 2006-2008: Hennigan, Bennett & Dorman LLP
- 2001-2006; 1996-2000: O'Melveny & Myers LLP
- 2000-2001: Klee, Tuchin, Bogdanoff & Stern LLP
- Admitted to the California Bar, 1996

Professional Memberships:

- State Bar of California
- National Conference of Bankruptcy Judges
- Los Angeles County Bar Association
- American Bankruptcy Institute
- Financial Lawyers Conference

I. Judge Saltzman's Procedures and Practices

A. *Instructions Regarding Judge's Copies of Pleadings Filed Electronically*

INSTRUCTIONS REGARDING JUDGE'S COPIES OF PLEADINGS FILED ELECTRONICALLY FOR JUDGE DEBORAH J. SALTZMAN

As a general rule, hard copies of all pleadings filed (electronically or otherwise) must be delivered to chambers before an application or motion will be heard. No motion will be scheduled for a hearing unless the moving party submits a copy of all filed pleadings pertaining to the motion to the court's chambers within 72 hours of the filing of the pleading and the motion is filed in accordance with the applicable Federal Rules of Bankruptcy Procedure and Local Bankruptcy Rules.

With respect to pleadings on matters that are eligible for self-calendaring, the filing party shall mark a paper copy of the pleading "Judge's Copy" and serve it on the judge in chambers in the manner and not later than the deadline set forth in the Court Manual available from the clerk and on the court's website.

Any chambers copy of a pleading filed electronically must be accompanied by an ECF receipt or a Notice of Electronic Filing stapled or fastened at the end of the pleading to show proof of filing the original document and be marked "**Judge's Copy**." The chambers copy must also conform to the requirements of Local Bankruptcy Rule 5005-2(d), including the format and tabbing of exhibits. If a pleading contains more than 5 exhibits, exhibit tabs must be used for all chambers copies. E-filed responsive pleadings will not be considered unless a Judge's Copy is provided in a timely manner to the court.

B. Lodged Order Upload ("L.O.U.") Procedures

LODGED ORDER UPLOAD ("L.O.U.") ORDER PROCEDURES FOR JUDGE DEBORAH J. SALTZMAN

The Court is accepting electronic orders for all judges through the Lodged Order Upload ("L.O.U.") program. For more information on how to use this program and detailed L.O.U. instructions, please visit:
http://efile.cacb.uscourts.gov/CMECF/Home.nsf/Homepage?OpenForm

ALL L.O.U. ORDERS, AS WITH PAPER ORDERS, MUST COMPLY WITH LOCAL BANKRUPTCY RULE ("LBR") 9021-1.

Common Problems with L.O.U. Orders:
Below are some common problems with L.O.U. Orders. ***Orders with the following problems WILL NOT be processed or entered:***

- No proof of service of the proposed order attached reflecting notice to proper parties.
- Proof of service date programmed to reflect current date and not date of actual service. [It appears that certain word processing programs automatically updates the date when the document is viewed. Please disable this function so that the proof of service date will reflect the date of service and not the date chambers opens the document.]
- No or insufficient property description attached to Relief from Stay Orders (i.e., "Said County" language not sufficient)
- No "Notice of Entered Order and Service List." Please note that a notice of entry is NOT required.
- No stamped, pre-addressed envelopes for all parties not receiving electronic notice on the proposed order service list within 48 hours of electronic submission.
- **When formatting the order, please make sure there is no text or images in the last three inches of the last page of the order, i.e., you do *not* need to include a signature block, and there should be no text below line 23 if using pleading paper.**
- Pursuant to LBR 9021-1(b)(1)(B), **DO NOT** lodge orders until after the hearing or trial of the underlying matter.
- Pursuant to LBR 1017-1(a)(2) and (3), orders to convert a case must include ample notice and a declaration re no-objection.

Judge Saltzman's Procedures for Deficient Orders:
If a submitted L.O.U. order has any of the above problems or fails to comply with applicable bankruptcy rules, Judge Saltzman's chambers will send a notice (via phone, e-mail, or mail) to the party who submitted the order. No further notice will be given. The deficient order will be marked unused, being treated as if no order has been submitted.

Parties will still be responsible for complying with LBR 9021-1(a)(1) and for resubmitting a proper order within the time set forth in LBR 9021-1.

C. *Mandatory Use of Lodged Order Upload ("L.O.U.") for Section 362 Orders*

MANDATORY USE OF LODGED ORDER UPLOAD ("L.O.U.") FOR SECTION 362 ORDERS

These L.O.U. guidelines apply to orders on motions: (1) for relief from the automatic stay; (2) to impose the stay; or (3) to continue the stay (collectively, "Section 362 Orders").

The following guidelines will add certainty to the bankruptcy process and minimize costs/delay by:

1. Using electronic processes of filing documents ("CM/ECF"), L.O.U. and service by Notice of Electronic Filing ("NEF");
2. Clarifying the "Service List for Entered Order"; and
3. Eliminating the need to provide envelopes and copies of orders.

Judge Saltzman, like many other bankruptcy judges in the Central District of California, requires adherence to the following guidelines:

A. CHECK TENTATIVE RULINGS

Judge Saltzman posts tentative rulings at least one day before hearings. Check to see if relief will be granted without a hearing, and if so, exactly what relief.

Go to the Court's website at www.cacb.uscourts.gov. The "Tentative Rulings" link is on the bottom left-hand corner of the first page.

B. LODGE PROPOSED ORDERS VIA L.O.U.

All CM/ECF users **must** lodge Section 362 Orders via L.O.U. NO EXCEPTIONS.

C. WHEN TO LODGE A PROPOSED ORDER

Lodged via L.O.U. – Proposed orders may be lodged via L.O.U. **after the hearing has been held**. Judge Saltzman will not accept any orders prior to the actual hearing. If an order is lodged before the hearing, it will be rejected and will need to be re-lodged at the appropriate time.

Lodged at Intake Window – Non-CM/ECF users may lodge orders **after the hearing has been held**.

D. F 4001-1 FORM ORDERS ARE MANDATORY

Mandatory Forms – All Section 362 Orders must be prepared using a mandatory F 4001-1 order, available at the Court's website, www.cacb.uscourts.gov. Click on "Forms/Rules/General Orders" on the main page, and then "Local Bankruptcy Rules and Forms."

E. PREPARE PROOF OF SERVICE OF PROPOSED ORDER

Proposed Orders on Unopposed Motions – There is no obligation to serve a proposed form of order on any person, entity, or attorney **who did not file an opposition to the motion**. This includes a case trustee or the United States Trustee.

Proposed Orders on Opposed Motions – Pursuant to LBR 9021-1(b)(4) and 9021-1(b)(3)(A), a proposed order must be served only upon any person, entity, or attorney who filed an opposition to the motion. **There is no obligation to serve the proposed order on any other person or entity.**

F. PREPARE SERVICE LIST FOR ENTERED ORDER

Parties Who Will Be Served by the Court:

- Debtor
- Debtor's counsel (if any)
- Case trustee
- U.S. Trustee
- Movant
- Any person, entity, or attorney who filed an opposition to the motion.

Method of Service:

- **Served Electronically by the Court** – List the names and email addresses only of attorneys who are listed in the CM/ECF on the Electronic Mail Notice List to receive an e-mail notice. **The U.S. Trustee and case trustee will always be in this category.** (Please see the Court Manual for help determining who receives electronic service.)
- **Served via U.S. Mail by the Court** – List the names and mailing addresses of persons, entities, and/or attorneys listed in CM/ECF under Manual Notice List. **The debtor will always be in this category.** DO NOT list any of the same people being served electronically. DO NOT list anyone who is not one of the "**Parties who will be served by the Court**" listed above. (Please see the Court Manual for help determining who receives manual – U.S. Mail – service.)
- **Served by Movant** – If the Movant desires to serve a copy of the entered order on persons or entities NOT listed above in "**Parties who will be served by the Court**," the Movant may do so. The Movant must then file a Declaration re proof of service listing the parties' names, addresses and method of service. Under this category, the Movant can list other lien holders, co-borrowers, or other persons/entities they want to serve.

G. PROVIDE COPIES OF PROPOSED ORDERS AND ENVELOPES

All Section 362 Orders are served electronically by the Court via NEF to case trustees, the U.S. Trustee, and to attorneys who are on the Electronic Mail Notice List for the particular bankruptcy case.

All Section 362 Orders are served by the Bankruptcy Noticing Center ("BNC") in Herndon, Virginia via U.S. Mail to the debtor and to persons or entities that are on the Manual Notice List for the particular bankruptcy case.

Copies of all Proposed Orders, Regardless of How Lodged:

- **DO NOT** provide any copies of the proposed order for mailing because copies will be printed either by the BNC (for all relevant addresses on the Manual Notice List) or by the Court (in the rare, unique case).
- **ONLY SEND ONE COPY** to the Court along with the L.O.U. receipt per

the L.O.U. procedures (Judge Saltzman's L.O.U. procedures can be found on the Court's website, www.cacb.uscourts.gov, by clicking "Information" on the main page, and then "Saltzman, D." under "Individual Judges"), and do so the same day that the proposed order is lodged.

Stamped, Addressed Envelopes, Regardless of How Proposed Order Is Lodged:

- **DO NOT** provide envelopes for the debtor or other Manual Notice parties, as the BNC will prepare envelopes for them.
- **DO NOT** provide envelopes for case trustees, the U.S. Trustee or other Electronic Mail Notice parties, as they will be served electronically via NEF.
- **DO NOT** provide envelopes for any other person or entity as it is the responsibility of the Movant to serve the entered order and provide the Court with a Declaration re proof of service.

D. *Mandatory Use of Local Form 4003-2.4*

MANDATORY USE OF LOCAL FORM 4003-2.4 – MOTION, "DEBTOR'S NOTICE OF MOTION AND MOTION TO AVOID JUNIOR LIEN ON PRINCIPAL RESIDENCE [11 U.S.C. § 506(d)]," AND GUIDELINES FOR SERVICE AND EVIDENCE

Effective August 22, 2011, all motions filed by debtors in chapter 13 cases to avoid junior liens on the debtor's principal residence (commonly referred to as "lien strip motions," "motions to value," "Lam motions," etc.)[1] must be made on Local Form 4003-2.4-Motion, entitled "Debtor's Notice of Motion and Motion to Avoid Junior Lien on Principal Residence [11 U.S.C. § 506(d)]." The form may be found on the Court's website, www.cacb.uscourts.gov, by clicking on "Forms/Rules/General Orders," then "Local Bankruptcy Rules & Forms," and scrolling down to F 4003-2.4-MOTION under "Local Bankruptcy Rules & Forms."

All debtors filing a motion to avoid a junior lien on the debtor's principal residence must use Local Form 4003-2.4-Motion, including the proof of service. **If a motion to avoid a junior lien on the debtor's principal residence is not filed using Local Form 4003-2.4-Motion, including the proof of service, the motion will not be set for hearing. The motion will only be set for hearing after it is filed using Local Form 4003-2.4-Motion, and the hearing must be set to provide for the full notice period required under LBR 9013-1(d)(2) from the date the form motion is filed.**

Use of the form will streamline preparation of motions, lower costs for debtors, and result in motions being granted more quickly. To ensure that motions are granted, debtors and their counsel should fill out the form completely and accurately, including the proof of service, file and serve their papers in a timely manner in accordance with all applicable Federal Rules of Bankruptcy Procedure and Local Bankruptcy Rules, deliver a tabbed judge's copy to chambers, and follow the additional guidelines below.

Evidence

As the form indicates, all motions to avoid a junior lien must be supported by evidence regarding the amount and priority of the liens at issue, and the value of the property. Evidence must be admissible and persuasive.

Liens. Without evidence as to the validity and amount of the senior secured loan and the junior secured loan, the requested relief cannot be granted. The debtor's declaration, which contains the debtor's testimony regarding the liens and introduces the documents into evidence, along with a copy of the deed of trust, a loan statement, proof of claim or other statement from the current lender will establish the amount and validity of the lien. No documents will be considered as evidence unless they are accompanied by a declaration. The debtor's testimony alone, with no documentation, will not be sufficient to establish validity and amount (similarly, the debtor's schedules are not sufficient). The court also does not consider a credit report listing amounts owed to be admissible evidence of validity and amount; it is hearsay.

---

[1] The form is entitled "Debtor's Notice of Motion and Motion to Avoid Junior Lien on Principal Residence [11 U.S.C. § 506(d)]." More specifically, the relief sought is the valuation of a secured claim and determination of secured status pursuant to Fed. R. Bankr. P. 3012 and 11 U.S.C. § 506(d). This relief may be obtained through a noticed motion; an adversary proceeding is not necessary.

Value. The debtor may testify through a declaration regarding the value of the residence. The declaration should contain the basis for the testimony, which may include, among other factors, the debtor's familiarity with the residence, the neighborhood, and recent sales. It is insufficient for the declaration to state: "I believe that my residence is worth $xxx,xxx." Please note that the debtor may not rely solely on sources from the internet; this is hearsay. Therefore, a declaration stating "I believe my residence is worth $xxx,xxx based on the attached report from zillow.com [or cyberhomes.com or other similar website]" is not admissible evidence as to value.

While not always necessary, an appraisal can be persuasive evidence of value. To be admissible evidence, the appraisal must be accompanied by a declaration of the debtor or the appraiser.

The relief requested in these motions – extinguishing the lien of a creditor that extended a loan to the debtor based on the understanding that the loan would be secured – is extensive. The motion must be careful and complete, and must be supported by admissible and persuasive evidence. The failure to have adequate evidence in support of the motion will result in continuance or denial of the motion. Please be sure to review the court's tentative rulings (generally posted by Friday afternoon for hearings on the following Tuesday) to learn whether additional evidence is required before the motion will be granted. Unless specifically noted in the tentative, supplemental evidence will not be considered at the scheduled hearing; the matter will be continued to a date indicated in the tentative or set at the hearing.

Service

Use of the proof of service in Local Form 4003-2.4-Motion is mandatory. The proof of service must be completely filled out to indicate what parties were served, how they were served, and when they were served. Be sure to allow sufficient notice of the hearing to comply with LBR 9013-1(d) (notice to be served not later than 21 days before the hearing date). If a hearing date is chosen that is less than 21 days after service, the motion will be continued at least 21 additional days to allow the full notice period to pass.

Proper service of the motion – including compliance with Fed. R. Bankr. P. 7004 – is critical.

Which parties to serve. The chapter 13 trustee, the affected lienholder, and all other parties asserting a lien on the property must be served. If any party has made an appearance in the case, that party (and counsel, if applicable) must be served at the address used in its notice of appearance.

Compliance with F.R.B.P. 7004(b)(3). This rule applies to domestic and foreign corporations and provides that service may be made by first-class mail upon "an officer, a managing or general agent, or to any other agent authorized by appointment or by law to receive service of process." The address for the corporation and its agent, if any, can usually be found on the corporation's website or the California Secretary of State website.

Compliance with F.R.B.P. 7004(h). Rule 7004(b)(3), discussed above, is generally applicable to corporations, but its lead-in indicates that it applies "[e]xcept as provided in subsection (h)." Rule 7004(h) specifically applies to insured depository institutions (as defined in section 3 of the Federal Deposit Insurance Act). **Many lienholders are FDIC-insured institutions and must be served in accordance with Rule 7004(h).**

1. Is the lienholder an FDIC-insured institution? The FDIC website has a feature to search for institutions: http://www2.fdic.gov/idasp/main.asp. This feature will provide an address and list of officers for the institution. Please note that many institutions are subsidiaries of FDIC insured institutions (for example, Bank of America Home Loans is a subsidiary of Bank of America, N.A.). In these cases, the FDIC-insured parent must be served in accordance with Rule 7004(h).

2. How to accomplish service in accordance with Rule 7004(h)? Rule 7004(h) requires that service be made **by certified mail addressed to an officer of the institution**.

   a. Use Certified Mail. Regular first-class mail, overnight mail or courier, or any other delivery method does not comply with Rule 7004(h); certified mail must be used.

   b. Address service to an officer. Remember, an officer of the institution is not the registered agent for service of process, or the FDIC itself. The best sources for finding an officer of an FDIC-insured institution are the FDIC website noted above, and the institution's website. Many courts have held that addressing service to "Officer of the Institution," "Chief Executive Officer," or "President" complies with the rule. If the institution's address is correct, and it is not possible to locate an officer's name, the court will not find that the motion was served incorrectly (although as a practical matter, it would be rare that an officer's name could not be found).

As a general rule, if there is any doubt as to whether service needs to comply with Rule 7004(h), serve your motion (1) by U.S. mail, addressed to the agent for service of process and to any other address used for communication with the lienholder; **and** (2) by certified mail, addressed to an officer of the institution. Ultimately, it is to the debtor's benefit to ensure that service was correct. If, at the time of the debtor's discharge 3-5 years in the future, a junior lienholder objects to the extinguishment of its lien, the lienholder will have little basis to object if it is clear that service was made in accordance with all applicable rules. Therefore, a motion will not be granted without proper service and the filing of a proof of service clearly describing such service.

Order

When your motion is granted, submit an order within seven days after the hearing date. Use of Local Form 4003-2.4-Order is mandatory (the form replaces the form that was previously on the court's website under Judge Saltzman's forms and procedures).

E. Procedures for Telephonic Appearances

PROCEDURES FOR TELEPHONIC APPEARANCES

I. POLICIES GOVERNING TELEPHONIC APPEARANCES

Telephonic appearances are allowed in all matters before Judge Deborah J. Saltzman in Courtroom 304, except the following:

1. Trials and evidentiary hearings (all counsel and all witnesses must appear in person).
2. Chapter 11 status conferences (debtor's counsel must appear in person; other parties in interest may appear telephonically).
3. Adversary proceeding initial status conferences and pretrial conferences (all trial counsel must appear in person).
4. Chapter 11 and 13 confirmation hearings (debtor, debtor's counsel, and all objecting parties must appear in person).
5. Reaffirmation hearings (debtor and debtor's counsel must appear in person; other parties in interest may appear telephonically).
6. Any matter designated by the court as requiring a personal appearance.

All telephonic appearances must be arranged through Court Call, an independent conference call company, pursuant to the procedures set forth in Section II.

Before requesting a telephonic appearance, counsel should check Judge Saltzman'ss calendar on the court's website (www.cacb.uscourts.gov) to review any tentative ruling concerning the matter on calendar (to view the calendar click on ATentative Rulings@). Each party who appears telephonically will be expected to have reviewed and be familiar with the applicable tentative ruling. The 3:00 p.m. deadline for scheduling telephonic appearances noted below is independent of the tentative ruling process. Late scheduling of a telephonic appearance is not justified even if tentative rulings have not been posted on the court'ss website by 3:00 p.m. the day before the hearing.

Please be aware that individuals making telephonic appearances do so at their own risk. Absent extraordinary circumstances, hearings will not be rescheduled due to missed connections. If an individual schedules a telephonic appearance and then fails to respond to the call of a matter on calendar, the court may pass the matter, treat the failure to respond as an intent to accept the tentative ruling, or treat the failure to respond as a failure to appear. Scheduling simultaneous telephonic appearances in multiple courts does not excuse a failure to appear.

II. SCHEDULING A TELEPHONIC APPEARANCE

Standard Procedure

Counsel should arrange telephone appearances by calling Court Call at (866) 582-6878 **not later than 3:00 p.m. the day prior to the court hearing date**.

Emergency Procedure

If an unexpected emergency arises that prevents counsel from following the standard procedure above, counsel must telephone chambers and obtain a law clerk's approval to appear telephonically. A law clerk will only approve a late request for a legitimate and unanticipated emergency. Once your emergency request is approved, notify the courtroom deputy of the approved telephonic appearance. The courtroom deputy may be reached at (951) 774-1075. You must then contact Court Call at (866) 582-6878 to arrange a telephonic appearance. If Court Call is not able to accommodate counsel's late request or if a law clerk denies the request, counsel will not be permitted to appear telephonically and must make an appearance in court as usual.

III. PROCEDURE FOR TELEPHONIC APPEARANCE

Court Call will provide counsel with written confirmation of a telephonic appearance and will give counsel a number to call to make the telephonic appearance. It is counsel's responsibility to dial into the call not later than 10 minutes prior to the scheduled hearing. Court Call does not place a call to counsel. Court Call charges a fee for a telephonic appearance. If you do not call and connect with the Court Call operator in a timely manner, you will be billed for the call, the hearing may proceed in your absence, and the court may treat your absence as a failure to appear.

Telephonic appearances are connected directly with the courtroom's public address system and electronic recording equipment. Participants should be able to hear all parties without difficulty, echo or other interference. To ensure the quality of the record, the use of cellular phones is prohibited except in the most extreme emergencies. If an individual's cellular phone is causing any interference, the court may ask that individual to disconnect from the hearing, and that individual will be deemed to have waived his or her appearance in the matter. Similarly, if a cellular phone disconnects during a hearing, the party appearing on cellular phone will be deemed to have waived his or her appearance.

After you have placed your call to Court Call, at the time of your hearing, you may initially be in the listening mode, in which case you will be able to hear the matters before yours just as if you were in the courtroom. After your call is connected to the courtroom, the judge will call the case, request appearances, and direct the manner in which the hearing proceeds. Each time you speak, you should identify yourself for the record. The court's teleconferencing system allows more than one speaker to be heard, so the judge can interrupt a speaker to ask a question or redirect the discussion. When the judge informs the participants that the hearing is completed, you may disconnect and the next case will be called.

Telephonic appearances by multiple participants are only possible when there is compliance with every procedural requirement. Sanctions may be imposed when there is any deviation from the required procedures or the court determines that an individual's conduct makes telephonic appearances inappropriate. Sanctions may include dropping a matter from calendar, continuing the hearing, proceeding in the absence of an unavailable participant, a monetary sanction, and/or a permanent prohibition against an individual appearing telephonically.

F. Status Conference Procedures

STATUS CONFERENCE PROCEDURES

1. The Court will set an initial status conference in all adversary proceedings to be held approximately 60 days after the matter is filed and in all chapter 11 cases to be held approximately 30 – 40 days after the matter is filed. Trial counsel must appear at the initial adversary proceeding status conference in person, and debtor's counsel must appear at the initial chapter 11 status conference in person. Unless otherwise ordered by the court, parties and counsel may attend subsequent status conferences telephonically in accordance with Judge Saltzman's telephonic appearance procedures, which are available on the Court's website, www.cacb.uscourts.gov, by clicking on "Information," and then the judge's name.

2. A thorough, written status report, filed 14 days in advance, is required before each adversary proceeding and chapter 11 status conference. For adversary proceeding status conferences, the status report must be a Joint Status Report in a form substantially similar to the attached Exhibit A, i.e., Local Form 7016-1.1. Failure to file such a Joint Status Report may result in the imposition of monetary sanctions and/or the status conference being continued and parties being ordered to redo the status report to conform to Exhibit A.

3. Pursuant to Local Bankruptcy Rule 7016-1(a)(3), if a defendant has not responded to the complaint or fails to cooperate in the preparation of a joint status report, the plaintiff is required to file a unilateral status report not less than 10 days before the date scheduled for the status conference, which report should contain the information in Sections A-E of Exhibit A and include a declaration setting forth the attempts made by the plaintiff to contact or obtain the cooperation of the defendant in the preparation of a joint status report.

A status report is not required ***only*** in the following limited circumstances:

A. The matter is an adversary proceeding and, prior to the date scheduled for the status conference, the parties have filed and the court has entered an order approving a stipulation that resolves all issues raised by the adversary proceeding and provides either for dismissal of the action in its entirety or the entry of judgment in the action.

B. The matter is an adversary proceeding, defaults have been entered as against all defendants and the plaintiff has filed and served a motion for default judgment prior to the date scheduled for the status conference.

C. The parties have filed, and prior to the date scheduled for the status conference, the court has entered an order approving, a stipulation continuing the status conference to a later date (in which case a written status report must be filed not less than 14 days in advance of the continued status conference date).

D. The Court has expressly relieved the parties of the obligation to file a written status report.

4. Unless one of the four exceptions outlined above applies, status reports must be filed in a timely manner. Parties that fail to do so will be subject to a minimum sanction of $150, or such other sanctions as may be warranted under the circumstances or allowed under Local Bankruptcy Rule 7016-1(f).

5. Failure to appear for a status conference in an adversary proceeding may result in a

minimum sanction of $250, dismissal of the adversary proceeding for failure to prosecute or such other sanctions as may be warranted under the circumstances or allowed under Local Bankruptcy Rule 7016-1(f).

6. If a response to the complaint is not timely filed:

A. The plaintiff should file a request for entry of default by the clerk. The plaintiff also may request entry of a default judgment by filing and serving (if necessary) an appropriate motion; see Fed. R. Bankr. P. 7055 and Local Bankruptcy Rule 9021-1(d);

AND

B. No later than ten days prior to the status conference, each appearing party must file a Unilateral Status Report (containing the information set forth in Sections A-E of Exhibit A) as required by Local Bankruptcy Rule 7016-1(a)(2).

7. If the parties dispute whether the adversary proceeding is "core" within the meaning of 28 U.S.C. § 157(b), they must file points and authorities in support of their positions. Any party contending that the proceeding is "non-core" must file and serve a memorandum of points and authorities and evidence in support of its position no less than 14 days before the status conference. Any response must be filed at least seven days before the status conference. **If a party does not file and serve its papers in a timely manner, that failure may be deemed consent to whatever determination the Court makes.**

8. Any party claiming a right to trial by jury must make a timely demand as set forth in Local Bankruptcy Rule 9015-2. If the parties dispute whether a party has a right to a jury trial, they must file points and authorities in support of their positions. Any party asserting a right to a jury trial must file and serve a memorandum of points and authorities and evidence in support of its position no less than 14 days before the status conference. Any response must be filed at least seven days before the status conference. **If a party does not file and serve its papers in a timely manner, that failure may be deemed consent to whatever determination the Court makes.**

9. Unless otherwise ordered by the Court, within seven days after the status conference, the plaintiff must submit a Scheduling Order which complies with Local Bankruptcy Rule 7016-1(a)(3).

10. Extensions of time to respond to a pleading are ineffective by stipulation of the parties unless approved by the Court. The Court is likely to deny requests to extend the response deadline to a date within five days of the hearing date unless the hearing date is continued to a date which permits the Court adequate time to consider the pleadings.

11. A copy of these instructions, including Exhibit A, must be attached to every copy of the complaint served upon a party, and the affidavit of service must state that these instructions were served along with a copy of the summons and complaint.

G. *Trial Procedures Supplement to Local Rules*

TRIAL PROCEDURES SUPPLEMENT TO LOCAL RULES

I. TRIAL BRIEFS

Unless otherwise ordered by the court, trial briefs are required. Trial briefs must be filed at least seven (7) calendar days before trial. Judge's copies of the trial briefs should be delivered to Judge Saltzman's chambers on the same date.

The trial brief should contain (1) a concise statement of the facts of the case; (2) a short statement of any relevant procedural history; (3) a summary of the points of law involved with supporting authorities; (4) a summary of the disputed issues of fact and the testimony that such party plans to introduce in an effort to prove its version of the disputed facts, and (5) a brief discussion of any anticipated evidentiary issues or other problems that the party believes are likely to arise at trial. Unless specifically requested by the court, no additional trial briefs will be considered.

II. PRE-TRIAL ORDER

Unless otherwise ordered by the court, the parties must prepare and file a written joint pre-trial order pursuant to Local Bankruptcy Rule ("LBR") 7016-1(b) through (f) not later than seven (7) calendar days before trial. A judge's copy should be delivered to chambers the same day. The pre-trial order must contain the statements and information required by LBR 7016-1(b)(2).

In conjunction with the pre-trial order, the parties must meet and confer to attempt to stipulate to the authenticity and possible admissibility (without the necessity for live testimony) of the documents that have been exchanged. The court expects the parties to make good faith efforts to resolve all evidentiary issues.

III. PRESENTATION OF DIRECT TESTIMONY BY DECLARATION

The purpose of this procedure is to facilitate pretrial preparation and to streamline the adducement of direct testimony in trial so as to reduce trial time without sacrificing due process and a fair trial.

A. Except as provided herein, each party **must present the direct testimony of all of its witnesses, including expert witnesses, through the declarations of said witnesses**, under penalty of perjury, otherwise admissible under the Federal Rules of Evidence. See, e.g., Lee-Benner v. Gergely (In re Gergely), 110 F.3d 1448, 1452 (9th Cir. 1997); Adair v. Sunwest Bank (In re Adair), 965 F.2d 777, 779-80 (9th Cir. 1992). Each declaration must set forth the direct testimony that the witness would give as though questions were propounded in the usual fashion. Each statement of fact or opinion must be separately, sequentially numbered and must contain only matters that are admissible under the Federal Rules of Evidence (*e.g.*, avoiding redundancies, hearsay, and other objectionable statements).

B. All cross-examination, rebuttal, surrebuttal and appropriate impeachment evidence must be given by live testimony. The only oral testimony that may be offered at trial by a party through its own witnesses will be **STRICTLY** limited to rebuttal testimony or such additional testimony on matters relevant to the outcome of the proceeding as may be specifically requested by the court at the time of trial.

C. If a witness refers in the declaration to an exhibit to be admitted into evidence, the exhibit must be identified in the declaration by exhibit number or letter. The exhibit itself need not be attached to the witness's declaration, but must be included in the exhibit binder or notebook and properly marked for identification. Unless the parties stipulate to the admittance of an exhibit, the foundation for admittance of exhibits (other than for impeachment or rebuttal purposes) must be established in the declaration. Exhibits referenced in any declaration should be offered into evidence when the declaration is offered into evidence.

D. If a party is unable to obtain a declaration of a witness (such as, for example, in the case of a hostile witness), counsel for that party must file (by the applicable deadline for the filing of the witness' declaration) a declaration stating the name of the witness and a detailed summary of the expected testimony and why counsel was unable to obtain the witness' declaration. Failure to make every reasonable effort to obtain the declaration of any witness will result in the exclusion of any oral testimony of such witness by the party attempting to offer such testimony.

E. A party may present the direct testimony of a witness in the form of a transcript of a deposition of the witness, in which event the party must submit a declaration authenticating the excerpts from the transcript that contain the testimony that the party wishes to introduce (only the portions of the transcript that the party wishes to introduce should be attached to the declaration).

F. The declaration of a witness for a party will be admissible at trial, subject to timely objections, only if the declarant is present at trial and subject to cross-examination.

IV. EXHIBITS

A. All exhibits must be marked for identification prior to the commencement of the trial. Each exhibit must be marked for identification at the bottom (right) of the first page of the exhibit. Unless the parties agree upon a unified, joint set of exhibits, the plaintiff's exhibits must be marked in numerical order, and the defendant's exhibits must be marked in alphabetical order (e.g., Plaintiff's Exhibit 1, etc., Defendant's Exhibit A, etc.). If the parties agree on a unified, joint set of exhibits, the exhibits must be marked in numerical order.

B. All exhibits must be assembled in a binder or notebook. Each such binder or notebook must include as its first page an exhibit register. A sample exhibit register may be obtained from the court recorder or from the clerk's office and must be procured sufficiently in advance of the trial date to permit the completed register to be available at the commencement of trial.

C. At the commencement of trial, the parties must be prepared to stipulate into evidence all exhibits that are admissible for at least one purpose. Bona-fide objections may be reserved, with the issue of admissibility deferred, until the exhibit is offered into evidence.

V. DEADLINES FOR SUBMISSION OF DECLARATION, EXHIBITS AND OBJECTIONS

A. Plaintiff must submit to opposing counsel all declarations and exhibits comprising the plaintiff's case in chief not later than thirty (30) days before the trial date.

B. Defendant must submit to opposing counsel all declarations and exhibits comprising the defendant's case, together with any written objections to the admission of any of Plaintiff's exhibits or to the testimony contained in any of Plaintiff's witness declarations, not later than twenty-one (21) days before the trial date.

C. Plaintiff must submit to opposing counsel any written objections to the admission of any of Defendant's exhibits or to the testimony contained in any of Defendant's witness declarations not later than fourteen (14) days before the trial date.

D. All witness declarations and exhibits, together with any written objections to the admission of any of the exhibits or to any of the declarations or any portion thereof, must be lodged with the Courtroom Deputy at least seven (7) days before the trial date. Each party must lodge sufficient copies of its exhibit binder, containing the exhibit register and all exhibits, for all parties, the witness stand, the court recorder, and the judge.

E. At trial, each party must also have copies of any exhibits used for impeachment or rebuttal for the opposing party, witnesses and the court.

F. Evidentiary objections will be adjudicated at the time a witness declaration or exhibit is offered into evidence. Any evidentiary objections to testimony contained in a written declaration that is not raised in a written objection filed within the applicable time limit set forth above shall be deemed waived.

G. **NO OTHER DECLARATIONS WILL BE ALLOWED.** The only additional evidence that a party may offer at trial is true rebuttal evidence. If the court concludes that testimony that a party seeks to offer should more accurately be characterized as direct testimony that as rebuttal evidence, that testimony will be excluded or, if already provided, such testimony will be stricken, if it was not set forth in a timely-filed declaration submitted by such party.

VI. EXCERPTS FROM DISCOVERY DOCUMENTS

A. Deposition Transcripts. Each party intending to offer any evidence by way of deposition testimony pursuant to Fed. R. Civ. P. 32, other than for impeachment or rebuttal, must lodge with the clerk the original deposition transcript, together with a copy of the transcript or pages from the transcript to be offered, marked to reflect the portions to be offered, pursuant to LBR 7030-1(b) not later than the applicable deadline for submission of declarations, exhibits and objections set forth in Section V. Transcripts may be bound on the left side and do not have to be hole-punched or blue-backed.

B. Other Discovery Documents. Excerpts from interrogatories, requests for admissions, or other discovery documents to be offered at trial, other than those to be used for impeachment or rebuttal, must be filed pursuant to LBR 7026-2(c) not later than the applicable deadline for submission of declarations, exhibits and objections set forth in Section V.

VII. CONTINUANCE/POSTPONEMENT OF TRIAL DATE

Trials will be commenced promptly at the scheduled date and time. Trial dates are not continued or vacated absent good cause, on noticed motion, supported by competent evidence. The parties will be contacted by either of Judge Saltzman's law clerks as to whether the continuance has been granted or denied.

Parties are further advised that during the week prior to trial, the court may move the starting time or day. The Courtroom Deputy will advise the parties of any such change by telephone. All parties are cautioned to adjust their schedules accordingly. The court expects counsel and witnesses to be available on 2-3 hours telephone notice for the remainder of the week.

VIII. SETTLEMENT/COMPLIANCE

Not later than five (5) calendar days before the trial date, counsel for Plaintiff must telephone the Courtroom Deputy at (951) 774-1075 to report (a) whether the parties intend to go forward with trial as scheduled; (b) if settlement is likely; (c) whether the time reserved for trial is realistic; and (d) any other relevant information.

Stipulations for settlement must be in writing, executed by each party or their counsel, and delivered to chambers before the date of trial. If time constraints prevent reducing a settlement to writing prior to trial, all the parties, or their counsel, must (a) advise chambers of the settlement and (b) appear at the time set for trial to recite the stipulation on the record.

Failure to comply with this order may result in the imposition of sanctions, including but not limited to, removal from the trial calendar or the exclusion of evidence (i.e., witnesses who were not timely identified or exhibits which were not timely submitted).

II. Judge Saltzman's Case Management Orders

A. *Standing Order Regarding Time of Chapter 13 Confirmation Hearing*

IN THE UNITED STATES BANKRUPTCY COURT
FOR THE CENTRAL DISTRICT OF CALIFORNIA

	)	
RE TIME OF CHAPTER 13	)	**STANDING ORDER**
CONFIRMATION HEARING	)	
______________________________	)	

The undersigned Judge of the United States Bankruptcy Court, Central District of California, makes this standing order with respect to the time for the hearing on confirmation of Chapter 13 plans:

I hereby find and accordingly ORDER that it is in the best interests of the creditors and the estate to hold the hearing on the confirmation of the Chapter 13 plan on the same date as the meeting of creditors required under 11 U.S.C. § 341(a). **Any party in interest who objects to that timing of the confirmation hearing shall file a written objection thereto at least 20 calendar days before the scheduled confirmation hearing**; and it is

FURTHER ORDERED that the objecting party shall file the objection with the Court and serve it on the debtor, debtor's counsel, Chapter 13 trustee, and on any creditor who has filed an objection to confirmation, filed a request for special notice, or holds a security interest in the real property of the debtor. If a timely objection is received, the Court will reschedule the confirmation hearing.

DATED: March 24, 2010

____
DEBORAH J. SALTZMAN
United States Bankruptcy Judge

Hon. Erithe A. Smith

Bankruptcy Judge

Contact Information
U.S. Bankruptcy Court, Central District of California
Courtroom 5A
411 West Fourth Street, Suite 5041
Santa Ana, CA 92701
Courtroom Deputy: (714) 338-5360

Biographical Information

Appointment(s):

- Appointed by the Ninth Circuit Court of Appeals May 2, 1994;
- Ninth Circuit Bankruptcy Appellate Panel, 2004-2007;
- Reappointed by the United States Court of Appeals for the Ninth Circuit. May 2, 2008. Current term expires May 1, 2022.

Education:

- Loyola Marymount University, B.A., cum laud, Pi Gamma Mu, 1979;
- Boalt Hall School of Law, University of California at Berkeley, J.D., 1982

Career Record:

- Law Clerk to Hon. Marcus M. Kaufman, California Court of Appeal, 1982-1983;
- Law Clerk to Hon. Peter M. Elliott, U.S. Bankruptcy Court, 1983-1985;
- Associate, McKittrick, Jackson, DeMarco & Peckenpaugh, Newport Beach, CA 1985-1987;
- Associate/Partner, Lobel, Winthrop & Broker, Irvine, CA 1987-1994.

Professional Memberships:

- National Conference of Bankruptcy Judges, 1994 – present;
- Association of Business Trial Lawyers, Orange County Chapter; Judicial Advisory Council Memeber, 2007 – present;
- American Bankruptcy Institute; Associate Editor of ABI Law Journal, 2000 – present;
- Financial Lawyers Conference, Los Angeles, Board of Governors, 1995-1998;
- Turnaround Management Association, National Board of Directors, 1995-1998;
- Orange County Bankruptcy Forum, president, 1993-1994

I. Judge Smith's Procedures and Practices

A. Courtroom Policies and Procedures

COURTROOM POLICIES AND PROCEDURES

The following is a summary of general courtroom policies and procedures which will be observed by Judge Smith. Such policies and procedures are intended as a supplement to and not a replacement for the provisions of the Bankruptcy Code ("Code"), the Federal Rules of Bankruptcy Procedure ("Bankruptcy Rules"), the Federal Rules of Civil Procedure ("Federal Rules") and the Local Rules for the Central District of California ("Local Rules"), all of which are applicable to practice before this Court. The following summary is not intended to cover all circumstances of matters before the Court and certain policies and procedures may be adjusted in certain cases where appropriate.

I. MOTIONS IN GENERAL

A. Evidentiary Requirements:

All motions and applications must be supported by declaration(s). Pleadings submitted without supporting declarations will likely be denied, even if no opposition is filed. In matters where an appraisal is submitted in support of a pleading, e.g., relief from stay matters, the appraisal must be authenticated by a declaration of the appraiser or the appraisal will not be considered.

B. Motions without Hearings:

With respect to all motions filed pursuant to Local Rule 9013-1(g) or otherwise not requiring a hearing absent an objection and request for a hearing, the moving party must file a declaration stating that no opposition to the motion has been served within the objection period. The order will not be signed absent such a declaration.

II. RELIEF FROM STAY MOTIONS

A. Evidentiary Requirements:

Moving parties asserting a security interest in property of the debtor must attach evidence of such recorded security interest to the motion. In cases where the original note/deed of trust as been assigned, copies of all recorded assignments must be attached to the motion. Stated otherwise, no orders granting relief from the stay will be signed absent properly authenticated documentary evidence of the movant's beneficial interest in the debtor's property.

With respect to unlawful detainer motions, such motions must be supported by a declaration of the owner or property manager and a properly authenticated copy of the unlawful detainer complaint (with state court's stamp) and/or the state court judgment. Failure to provide such evidence may result in denial of the motion even if the debtor fails to respond or appear.

B. Extraordinary Relief:

1. Prospective Relief as to Debtor (i.e., relief from the stay effective in any subsequent bankruptcy filed by the debtor within a 180-day period):

Granted only upon good cause shown, e.g., multiple filings.

2. "In Rem" Relief (i.e., relief from the stay effective in any subsequent bankruptcies -- even non-debtors -- involving the subject property): Granted only in the most egregious bad faith cases, usually involving multiple transfers of property.

III. ADVERSARY PROCEEDINGS

A. Motions for Entry of Default Judgment

A prove-up hearing is required. The motion must be served upon the defendant in accordance with Local Rule 9013-1 and must be supported by declaration and appropriate documentary evidence, e.g., invoices, statements, contracts, etc. Absent exigent circumstances (as shown by declaration of the moving party's attorney), a motion for entry of default judgment will not be continued more than once.

B. Joint Status Report/Joint Pretrial Order:

Joint Status Reports and Joint Pretrial Orders must be timely filed in accordance with Local Rule 7016-1. Parties failing to do so will be subject to a minimum sanction of $100.00 or other sanctions as allowed under Local Rule 7016-1. Failure to appear for a status conference or pretrial conference may result in a minimum sanction of $150.00 or other sanctions as allowed under Local Rule 7016-1. The attorney responsible for litigating the trial MUST appear at the pretrial conference. Failure to appear may result in the imposition of sanctions.

IV. SELF-CALENDARING

Judge Smith is currently utilizing the self-calendaring system for all hearings, with exceptions as noted in the self-calendaring instructions. Please go to the Court's website at www.cacb.uscourts.gov for self-calendaring instructions and/or to select a self-calendaring hearing date before Judge Smith. If you should experience a problem, please contact Tina Duarte, Courtroom Deputy, directly at (714) 338-5360.

V. TENTATIVE RULINGS

Judge Smith generally issues tentative rulings regarding law and motion matters by 5 p.m. of the day prior to the beginning of the hearing day. Tentative rulings are posted on the bulletin board outside the courtroom, at the attorney tables in the courtroom, and on Web PACER. Tentative rulings may not be rendered on every matter. If a tentative ruling has been issued and the moving party wishes to accept the tentative ruling, and 1) no opposition has been filed and, 2) the tentative ruling does not specifically require an appearance, the moving party need not check in or make an appearance. Proposed orders may be left in the order box at the Court Recorder's desk or lodged in the Clerk's Office.

If the moving party chooses to rest on the tentative ruling and an opposing party appears to argue against the ruling, the Court will determine if a continuance of the hearing is warranted and will notify the moving party of the continued hearing date. The court will not reverse a tentative ruling without a continued hearing.

VI. HEARINGS BY TELEPHONIC CONFERENCE CALL

Parties wishing to appear telephonically must coordinate directly with Court Call (the court's selected conference call coordinator) at (888) 882-6878. Court Call appearances can be scheduled, without prior approval from Judge Smith's chambers, until the start time of the scheduled hearing.

VII. PROFESSIONAL EMPLOYMENT APPLICATIONS

In order to expedite the processing of professional employment orders, applicants should file a declaration attesting that no opposition to the application was received during the response period if in fact no such opposition was received. Otherwise, the execution of the employment order will be delayed pending the Court's determination that no opposition was filed.

VIII. SERVICE OF PLEADINGS

Failure to properly serve pleadings in accordance with applicable rules will result in either a continuance of the hearing or denial of the relief requested. Under Bankruptcy Rule 9014, certain contested matters must be served in accordance with Bankruptcy Rule 7004. For example, Rule 7004(b)(3) requires that service upon a corporation or partnership be made to the attention of an officer, managing or general agent or any other person authorized by appointment or by law to receive service.

IX. COURTROOM ETIQUETTE

Unless court is in session, please check in with the Court Recorder prior to your scheduled hearing. Do not approach or speak with the Court Recorder while a hearing is in progress except to leave a proposed order in the order box. When leaving orders for the court's signature, write the calendar number of the case in the upper left-hand corner of the order.

The use of electronic devices (e.g., pagers, cellular phones, and other devices subject to ring or buzz) in the courtroom are **strictly** prohibited.

"Second Call" - If you have a conflict which needs to be placed on "second call," please contact Judge Smith's Chambers at (714) 338-5440. If you are not present when your matter is called, and no communication has been received, your motion may be denied for failure to appear.

COURT STAFF:

David Wood, Law Clerk	(714) 338-5441
Melissa Prochilo, Law Clerk	(714) 338-5443
Tina Duarte, Courtroom Deputy	(714) 338-5360
Rick Reid, Court Recorder	(714) 338-5361
Glenda DeRamus, Courtroom Services Specialist	(714) 338-5304

B. Mandatory Use of L.O.U. for Section 362 Orders

MANDATORY USE OF L.O.U. FOR SECTION 362 ORDERS

Effective January 1, 2009

These guidelines apply to orders on motions: (1) for relief from the automatic stay; (2) to impose the stay; or (3) to continue the stay (collectively "Section 362 Orders").

The guidelines will add certainty to the process and minimize costs/delay by:

1) Utilizing electronic processes of filing documents ("CM/ECF"), Lodged Order Upload ("LOU"), and service by Notice of Electronic Filing ("NEF");

2) Clarifying the "Service List for Entered Order"; and

3) Eliminating the need to provide envelopes and copies of orders.

A. Check Tentative Rulings

Judge Smith posts tentative rulings one court day prior to hearings. Check to see if relief will be granted without a hearing, and if so, what relief. Go to www.cacb.uscourts.gov. The Tentative Rulings link is on the bottom left-hand corner of page one.

B. Lodge Proposed Orders via LOU

All CM/ECF users must lodge Section 362 Orders via LOU. NO exceptions.

C. When Should a Proposed Order be Lodged?

Lodged via LOU – Proposed orders may be lodged via LOU after tentative rulings are posted; if a tentative ruling is not posted, lodge the proposed order after the hearing.

Lodged at Intake Window – Non CM/ECF users may only lodge proposed orders after the hearing.

D. Are F 4001-1 Form Orders Mandatory?

MANDATORY FORMS – All Section 362 Orders must be prepared using a mandatory F 4001-1 order available at www.cacb.uscourts.gov under Local Bankruptcy Rules ("LBR") and Forms.

E. Preparing Proof of Service of Proposed Order

1. Proposed Orders on Unopposed Motions – There is no obligation to serve a proposed form of order on any person, entity, or attorney ***who did not file an opposition to the motion. This includes a case trustee or the United States trustee***.

2. Proposed Orders on Opposed Motions – Pursuant to LBR 9021-1(b)(4) and 9021-1(b)(3)(A), a proposed order must be served only upon any person, entity, or attorney who filed an opposition to the motion. ***There is no obligation to serve the proposed order on any other person or entity.***

F. Prepare Service List for Entered Order

Parties who will be served by the Court:

- Debtor
- Debtor's Counsel (if any)

- Case Trustee
- U.S. Trustee
- Movant
- Any person, entity, or attorney who filed an opposition to the motion

METHOD OF SERVICE

1. **Served Electronically by the Court** – List the names and email addresses *only* of attorneys who are listed in CM/ECF on the Electronic Mail Notice List to receive an email notice. ***The U.S. trustee and case trustee will always be in this category.*** (*See* the Court Manual for help in determining who receives electronic service.)

2. **Served via U.S. Mail by the Court** – list the names and mailing addresses of persons, entities, and/or attorneys listed in CM/ECF under Manual Notice List. ***The debtor will always be in this category.*** **DO NOT** list any of the same people being served electronically. **DO NOT** list anyone who is not one of the **Parties who will be served by the Court**. (*See* the Court Manual for help in determining who receives manual – U.S. Mail – service.)

3. **Service by Movant** – If Movant desires to serve a copy of the entered order on persons or entities not listed in **Parties who will be served by the Court**, movant may do so. Movant must then file a Declaration re proof of service listing the parties' names addresses and method of service. Under this category, Movant can list other lien holders, co-borrowers, or persons/entities they want to serve.

G. Copies of Proposed Order; Envelopes

All Section 362 Orders are served electronically by the Court via NEF to case trustees, the United States trustee, and to attorneys who are on the Electronic Mail Notice List for the particular bankruptcy case.

All Section 362 Orders are served by the Bankruptcy Noticing Center ("BNC") in Herndon, Virginia via U.S. Mail to debtor and to persons or entities that are on the Manual Notice List for the particular bankruptcy case.

1. Copies of All Proposed Orders, Regardless of How Lodged

DO NOT provide any copies of the proposed order for mailing, because copies will be printed either by the BNC (for all relevant addresses on the Manual Notice List) or by the court (in the rare, unique case).

ONLY SEND ONE COPY to the court along with the LOU receipt per the LOU procedures, and do so the same day that the proposed order is lodged.

2. Stamped, Addressed Envelopes, Regardless of How Proposed Order is Lodged

DO NOT provide envelopes for the debtor or other Manual Notice parties, as the BNC will prepare envelopes for them.

DO NOT provide envelopes for the case trustee or U.S. trustee or other Electronic Mail Notice parties, as they will be served electronically via NEF.

DO NOT provide envelopes for any other person or entity as it is the responsibility of the Movant to serve the entered order and provide the Court with a Declaration re proof of service.

C. *Notice to Practitioners Regarding LBR 7016-1(a)(2)*

NOTICE TO PRACTITIONERS – SANTA ANA DIVISION REGARDING REQUIREMENT FOR TIMELY FILING OF STATUS CONFERENCE REPORTS IN ADVERSARY PROCEEDINGS AND IMPOSITION OF SANCTIONS

The Judges of the Santa Ana Division have noticed a steady increase in the number of parties failing to file either timely or at all the status conference reports required under Local Bankruptcy Rule 7016-1(a)(2). The Rule requires a filing of the status conference report *at least 14 days* before the status conference and provides for imposition of sanctions under Local Rule 7016-1(f) for noncompliance. Until now the Judges have merely exhorted practitioners to remember the Rule and have threatened imposition of sanctions for noncompliance, but have rarely actually imposed sanctions. However, these measures appear to have been ineffective. Failure to abide by the Rule severely interferes with the processes of the Court and last-minute filing of status conference reports imposes an undue burden on the Court and its staff. **Therefore, please take notice that commencing January 2009 sanctions will be imposed** as the rule rather than the exception for failure to comply with Local Rule 7016-1.

D. Telephonic Appearance Procedures

TELEPHONIC APPEARANCE PROCEDURES

I. POLICY GOVERNING TELEPHONIC APPEARANCES

Telephonic appearances are allowed in all matters before Judge Smith in Courtroom 5A except the following:

1. Trials and Evidentiary hearings (all counsel and all witnesses must appear in person).
2. Contested Chapter 11 Confirmation Hearings (debtor, debtor's counsel, and all objecting creditors must appear in person). All other parties in interest may appear telephonically.
3. Hearings on Reaffirmation Agreements (debtor must appear in person).
4. Any matter designated by the Court as one requiring a personal appearance.

No telephonic appearance will be allowed unless it is made through **CourtCall**, an independent conference call company, pursuant to the procedures set forth in Section II.

Before requesting a telephonic appearance, you should check Judge Smith's Calendar on the Court's website (www.cacb.uscourts.gov) and review any Tentative Ruling concerning the matter on calendar. (Click on Tentative Ruling Box on bottom left corner of homepage). If the court has issued a Tentative Ruling prior to the hearing, each individual who appears telephonically should have reviewed the Tentative Ruling prior to the hearing.

If an individual schedules a telephonic appearance and then fails to respond to the call of a matter on calendar, the court may pass the matter, treat the failure to respond as an intent to accept the tentative ruling, or treat the failure to respond as a failure to appear. Scheduling simultaneous telephonic appearances in multiple courts does not excuse a failure to appear.

Individuals making use of the conference call service are cautioned that they do so at their own risk. Hearings generally will not be rescheduled due to missed connections.

Parties are also cautioned to consider whether their cases are ones suitable to telephonic appearance. On closer, contested matters, there is no doubt that personal presence adds weight to the presentation of the case.

II. SCHEDULING A TELEPHONIC APPEARANCE

By telephone: Telephone appearances may be arranged by calling **CourtCall at (866) 582-6878** until the start of the scheduled hearing.

III. PROCEDURE FOR TELEPHONIC APPEARANCE

CourtCall will provide counsel with written confirmation of a telephonic appearance and give counsel a number to call to make the telephonic appearance. It is counsel's responsibility to dial into the call not later than 10 minutes prior to the scheduled hearing. **CourtCall does not place a call to counsel.** The initial charge per participant for a CourtCall appearance is \$25 for the first 45 minutes, \$6.50 for each additional 15 minutes.

These rates are subject to change without prior notice; please confirm current rates with CourtCall.

Telephonic appearances are connected directly with the courtroom's public address system and electronic recording equipment so that a normal record is produced. To ensure the quality of the record:

- No car phones
- No cellular phones
- No speaker phones
- No public telephone booths, or phones in other public places

Exceptions to these restrictions may be permitted only in the most extreme circumstances.

At the time of your hearing you may initially be in the listening mode, in which case you will be able to hear the case before yours, just as if you were in the courtroom. After your call is connected to the courtroom, the Judge will call the case, request appearances, and direct the manner in which the hearing proceeds. Each time you speak you should identify yourself for the record. The court's teleconferencing system allows more than one speaker to be heard, so the Judge can interrupt a speaker to ask a question or redirect the discussion. When the Judge informs the participants that the hearing is completed, you may disconnect and the next case will be called.

Telephonic appearances by multiple participants are only possible when there is compliance with every procedural requirement. Sanctions may be imposed when there is any deviation from the required procedures or the Court determines that a person's conduct makes telephonic appearances inappropriate. Sanctions may include dropping a matter from calendar, continuing the hearing, proceeding in the absence of an unavailable participant, a monetary sanction, and/or a permanent prohibition against a person appearing telephonically.

E. Trial Procedures Supplemental to Local Rules

TRIAL PROCEDURES SUPPLEMENTAL TO LOCAL RULES
Effective as to all adversary proceedings

Trial Briefs: Unless otherwise ordered by the Court, trial briefs are required. Pursuant to Local Bankruptcy Rule 9013-2(a), trial briefs shall be filed seven (7) calendar days prior to trial. Courtesy copies of the trial briefs should be delivered to Judge Smith's Chambers on the same date.

Testimony: Based on Local Rule 43-1 of the District Court for the Central District of California, attorneys are **required** to submit all direct testimony **by declaration** unless:

i) the witness is adverse or refuses to give testimony by declaration; or

ii) the testimony is offered to impeach or rebut.

The parties may request permission to offer oral testimony supplementing matters covered in the declarations or present portions of the testimony in the declaration orally and the court may grant such a request in the interest of justice.

Witnesses whose declarations are offered shall be present for cross-examination when the declarations are offered into evidence (unless the parties agree otherwise).

Plaintiff shall file and serve its declarations on counsel for the defendant thirty (30) days before the trial date. Defendant shall serve its declarations on counsel for the plaintiff twenty-one (21) days before the trial date.

Evidentiary objections to any declaration must be served and filed at least seven (7) calendar days before the trial date.

Unless the parties stipulate in the pre-trial order to the admittance of an exhibit, foundation for admittance of exhibits (other than for impeachment or rebuttal purposes) shall be established in the declarations, although the court may allow oral testimony for this purpose. Exhibits referenced in any declaration shall be offered into evidence when the declaration is offered into evidence.

Exhibits: Pursuant to Local Bankruptcy Rule 9070-1(a), the Court shall be given a bench copy of exhibits to be offered into evidence (other than exhibits offered for impeachment or rebuttal purposes) on or before trial. Counsel shall have a conformed set of exhibits for opposing counsels', witnesses. Counsel shall also have copies of exhibits used for impeachment or rebuttal for opposing counsel, witnesses and the court. If the number of exhibits exceeds ten (10), they shall be placed in a binder properly indexed, numbered and tabbed. An exhibit register shall be provided with each set of exhibits.

Continuance/Postponement of Trial: As a general rule, scheduled trials will NOT be continued prior to or at trial, except in extraordinary circumstances and in the interest of justice. Motions/Stipulations for continuance of the trial must be submitted in writing at least two (2) court days prior to the scheduled trial date. The parties will be contacted by the Judge's law clerk as to whether the continuance has been granted or denied.

Settlement: In the event that the adversary matter is settled prior to trial, the parties shall immediately contact and advise the Judge's law clerk.

Hon. Maureen A. Tighe

Bankruptcy Judge

Contact Information

U.S. Bankruptcy Court, Central District of California
Courtroom 302
21041 Burbank Boulevard, Suite 324
Woodland Hills, CA 91367
Courtroom Deputy: (818) 587-2815

Biographical Information

Appointment(s):

- Appointed 11/24/03 by the United States Court of Appeals for the Ninth Circuit. (Current term expires 11/23/17.)

Education:

- Douglass College of Rutgers University, B.A., 1979;
- Rutgers Law School, 1984, J.D.; Editor-in-Chief of the Rutgers Law Review, 1983-84

Career Record:

- 1998-2003, U. S. Trustee, Office of the U. S. Trustee for the Central District of California, Los Angeles California;
- 2002-2003, U. S. Trustee for the Districts of Southern California, Hawaii, Guam, and the Northern Mariana Islands;
- 1999-2000, U. S. Trustee for the Districts of Eastern and Northern California and Nevada;
- 1988-1998, Assistant U. S. Attorney, Office of the U. S. Attorney, Los Angeles, California; Deputy Chief, Major Frauds Section; and chairperson, Bankruptcy Fraud Task Force;
- 1986-1988, private practice, Sullivan and Cromwell, New York, New York;
- 1984-1986, Law Clerk, U. S. District Judge Harold Ackerman, District of New Jersey;
- Admitted to the New Jersey Bar, 1985; New York Bar, 1988; California Bar, 1988

Professional Memberships:

- American Bankruptcy Institute
- Los Angeles Bankruptcy Forum

I. Judge Tighe's Procedures and Practices

A. Emergency Motions Procedures

EMERGENCY MOTIONS PROCEDURES

To obtain a hearing date for a motion on an emergency basis, the movant must file the following documents with the Clerk's Office:

1. Application for an order setting the hearing date for a motion on an emergency basis and a proposed order thereon;

2. Supporting declaration(s) justifying the setting of a hearing on an emergency basis; and

3. Motion, including all supporting papers, for which the movant seeks an emergency hearing.

Initial Motions in new Chapter 11 cases may contact chambers for possible hearing times, but no hearing will be calendared until copies of the actual motions have been filed. The written application for order shortening time may be waived telephonically if adequate cause is clear from the phone call.

To expedite the process of obtaining an emergency motion hearing date, when the movant files the documents with the Bankruptcy Court Clerk's Office, they should also place courtesy copies of all the pleadings in the courtesy copy box adjacent to the elevators on the third floor of the San Fernando Divisional Office, 21041 Burbank Boulevard, Woodland Hills, CA 91367.

Judge Tighe's law clerk will call the movant within 24 hours of the documents being filed. If the movant is not contacted by Judge Tighe's law clerk within 24 hours of filing the emergency motion, the movant may call Judge Tighe's law clerk at (818) 587-2806.

B. *Instructions Regarding Proceeding to Avoid a Lien on Real Property (Chapter 13)*

INSTRUCTIONS RE: PROCEEDING TO AVOID A LIEN ON REAL PROPERTY (CHAPTER 13) FOR JUDGE MAUREEN TIGHE'S CASES

Pursuant to LBR 1001-1(d), by Order of the Bankruptcy Judges in the San Fernando Valley Division for bankruptcy cases filed or pending in the San Fernando Valley Division, until further notice, LBR 4003-2(a)(2) is hereby modified so that a proceeding to avoid a lien on real property under Chapter 13, often referred to as a Lam motion, may be brought by motion under the requirements of LBR 9013-1 through LBR 9013-4.

C. L.O.U. Order Procedures

L.O.U. ORDER PROCEDURES FOR JUDGE TIGHE

The court is accepting electronic orders for all judges through the court's Lodged Order Upload (L.O.U.) program. For more information on how to use this program and detailed L.O.U. instructions, please visit: http://efile.cacb.uscourts.gov/CMECF/Home.nsf/Homepage?OpenForm

All L.O.U. orders, as with paper orders, must comply with L.B.R. 9021-1.

Common Problems with L.O.U. Orders:

Below are some common problems that we have seen with L.O.U. orders. ***Orders with the following problems WILL NOT be processed or entered:***

- No proof of service of the proposed order attached reflecting notice to proper parties.
- No or insufficient property description attached to Relief from Stay Orders (i.e. "Said county" language not sufficient).
- No service list for entered order.
- No stamped, pre-addressed envelopes for all parties not receiving electronic notice on the proposed order service list within 48 hours of electronic submission
- Proof of service date programmed to reflect current date and not date of actual service. [It appears that certain word programs automatically updates the date when the document is viewed. Please disable this function so that the proof of service date will reflect the date of service and not the date chambers opens the document.]
- Please note that a notice of entry is NOT required.

Judge Tighe's Procedures for Deficient Orders:

If a submitted L.O.U. order has any of the following problems above or fails to comply with applicable bankruptcy rules, Judge Tighe's chambers will send a notice (via phone, email, or mail) to the party who submitted the order. No further notice will be given. The deficient order will be marked unused, being treated as if no order has been submitted.

Parties will still be responsible for complying with L.B.R. 9021-1(a)(1) and for resubmitting a proper order within the time set forth in L.B.R. 9021-1.

D. *Procedures for Motions Setting Value – "LAM Motions"*

PROCEDURES FOR MOTIONS SETTING VALUE – "LAM MOTIONS"

Pursuant to L.B.R. 1001-1(d), for bankruptcy cases filed or pending before Judge Tighe, until further notice, L.B.R. 4003-2(a)(2) is hereby modified so that a proceeding to avoid a lien on real property under Chapter 13, often referred to as a Lam motion, may be brought by motion under the requirements of L.B.R. 9013-1 through L.B.R. 9013-4.

E-FILING DOCKETING:

Please note that the correct event code when e-filing a "LAM Motion" is the following: Bankruptcy > Motions/Applications > Setting Property Value (motion)

SERVING LAM MOTIONS:

Please note that Judge Tighe's procedure re serving LAM Motions is the following:

- If the entity is an insured depository institution, then Fed. R. Bankr. P. 7004(h) applies. Service "shall be made by certified mail addressed to an officer of the institution." Fed.R. Bankr. P. 7004(h). However, if this entity has filed a proof of claim in the instant bankruptcy case, then service may be made to the address on the proof of claim listed as the address where notices should be sent.
- If the entity being served is not covered by Fed. R. Bankr. P. 7004(h), then service shall be provided pursuant to: 1) a proof of claim filed in the instant bankruptcy case, on the address listed as the address where notices should be sent; 2) the California Secretary of State's website (http://kepler.sos.ca.gov/); or 3) Fed. R. Civ. P. 4(h).

EVIDENCE OF VALUATION:

Motions must include the following evidence:

- Evidence establishing the value of the subject property;
- Evidence establishing priority; and
- Evidence establishing the creditor's interest in the subject property

TENTATIVES:

On the day before the hearing, the parties should check the Tentative Rulings. If there is no opposition and the motion meets all requirements, then appearances will be waived. YOU MUST APPEAR AT THE 9:00 A.M. CALENDAR IF APPEARANCES ARE NOT WAIVED.

ORDERS:

The prevailing party should submit the form order, a blank copy of which may be downloaded from Judge Tighe's forms section on the court's website.

E. Procedures Regarding Telephonic Appearances

PROCEDURES REGARDING TELEPHONIC APPEARANCES

Effective January 1, 2009

Telephonic appearances before Judge Maureen A. Tighe in Courtroom 302 are generally allowed. **No telephone appearances are allowed for the Chapter 13 calendar or any evidentiary hearings.** However, in order to appear telephonically, counsel must adhere to the following procedure:

Standard Procedure

1. At least 48 hours prior to the hearing, counsel must call Court Call, an independent conference call company, to arrange their telephonic appearance. Counsel may reach Court Call at (888) 882-6878.

2. After Court Call has confirmed a telephonic appearance, counsel must immediately notify the courtroom deputy of counsel' approved telephonic appearance. The courtroom deputy may be reached at (818) 587-2815.

Emergency Procedure (Approval requested without 48 hours notice)

If an unexpected emergency arises that prevents counsel from following the standard procedure detailed above, counsel must telephone chambers and obtain a law clerk's approval to appear telephonically. A law clerk will only approve late requests for legitimate and unanticipated emergencies. Once approved, counsel must contact Court Call to arrange a telephonic appearance.

If Court Call is not able to accommodate counsel's late request or if the Judge's law clerk denies the request, counsel will not be permitted to appear telephonically and counsel must make an appearance in court, as usual.

Individuals choosing to appear telephonically do so at their own risk. Hearings generally will not be rescheduled due to missed connections. Furthermore, in deciding to appear telephonically, counsel is agreeing to waive any prejudice attributable to quality deficiencies or irregularities of the record that may result.

Please be advised that poor reception will cause counsel's appearance to be disconnected. Repeated poor connections may cause counsel to be banned from future telephonic appearances.

If an individual schedules a telephonic appearance and then fails to respond to the call of a matter on calendar, the court may pass the matter or may treat the failure to respond as a failure to appear. Scheduling simultaneous telephonic appearances in multiple courts does not excuse a failure to appear when a matter is placed on calendar.

Before appearing, check Judge Tighe's calendar and review any tentative ruling on WebPACER.

Hon. Mark S. Wallace

Bankruptcy Judge

Contact Information

U.S. Bankruptcy Court, Central District of California
Courtroom 6C
411 West Fourth Street, Suite 6135
Santa Ana, CA 92701
Courtroom Deputy: (951) 774-1097

Please note: Judge Wallace is hearing both Riveside and Santa Ana cases.

Biographical Information

Appointment(s):

- Appointed January 20, 2011 by the United States Court of Appeals for the Ninth Circuit (current term expires January 20, 2025)

Education:

- Princeton University, A.B. 1976 (summa cum laude) in History, Phi Beta Kappa
- Columbia University School of Law, J.D. 1977
    - Notes and Comments Editor, Columbia Law Review
    - Harlan Fiske Stone Scholar
    - Judge Wallace participated in the joint Princeton-Columbia Accelerated Interdisciplinary Legal Education Program. He is a member of the Princeton University Class of 1975.

Career Record:

- 1991-2011 Stutman, Treister & Glatt Professional Corporation
- 1979-1991 Meyer Hendricks Victor Osborn & Maledon
- 1977-1979 Judicial Law Clerk to the Honorable William B. Enright, United States District Judge, Southern District of California

Professional Memberships:

- State Bar of California
- American Bankruptcy Institute
- American Bar Association

I. Judge Wallace's Procedures and Practices

A. General Policies and Procedures

GENERAL POLICIES AND PROCEDURES

Updated 2/4/2011

Judge Wallace permanently sits in Santa Ana, but is assigned both Riverside division and Santa Ana division cases. Please note that unless ordered otherwise, counsel and parties may appear at either Judge Wallace's courtroom in Santa Ana, or his video courtroom in Riverside:

Santa Ana	**Riverside**
United States Bankruptcy Court	United States Bankruptcy Court
Central District of California	Central District of California
411 West Fourth Street	3420 Twelfth Street
Courtroom 6C	Video Courtroom 225
Santa Ana, CA 92701-4593	Riverside, CA 92501-3819

All hearings for Judge Wallace's Santa Ana division cases must be noticed with the Santa Ana address; and all hearings for Judge Wallace's Riverside division cases must be noticed with the Riverside address.

SANTA ANA DIVISION CASES

Absent unusual circumstances, court will start on time. Counsel should make every effort to arrive in the courtroom no later than 30 minutes prior to the scheduled time of the hearing and should provide the Courtroom Deputy or the DECRO with the calendar number of the matter on which he or she is appearing, the name of the person, company or organization on whose behalf the appearance is made and a business card on which counsel's name is imprinted. The Courtroom Deputy and DECRO have been instructed to cut off the taking of business cards 10 minutes prior to the scheduled time of the hearing in order to permit sufficient time for such information to be provided to Judge Wallace in a usable format.

Counsel who are not present at the time their matter is called risk having the matter heard and determined in their absence. If opposing counsel is present and consents, the matter will be transferred to second call.

Self-represented persons (also called "pro se litigants" or "persons who have chosen to represent themselves without an attorney") are subject to the same rules applicable to counsel. A self-represented person who does not have a card with his or her name imprinted on it should simply provide the Courtroom Deputy or DECRO with the correct spelling of his or her first and last names and the matter number on which he or she is appearing. When the matter number is called, please step forward, stand before the lectern and state your name so the Court knows you would like to be heard in the matter. (If you do not do this, the Court may not be aware that you are in the courtroom or would like to be heard).

If an attorney or self-represented person is unavoidably detained for reasons beyond his or her control (for example, a flat tire or accident), please call Claudia Lee (Judge Wallace's law clerk) at (714) 338-5471 to explain the circumstances and provide an estimated time of arrival.

RIVERSIDE DIVISION PROCEDURES

Hearings on Riverside Division cases usually will occur by video. The court will make every effort to start on time, but occasionally technical difficulties relating to the video technology will make this impossible. Nevertheless, every effort will be made to commence proceedings as soon as the technical problems have been resolved. Please be aware of this possible contingency in making your plans for the day.

Subject to the preceding paragraph, court will start on time. Counsel should make every effort to arrive in the courtroom no later than 30 minutes prior to the scheduled time of the hearing and should provide the Courtroom Deputy or the DECRO with the calendar number of the matter on which he or she is appearing, the name of the person, company or organization on whose behalf the appearance is made and a business card on which counsel's name is imprinted. The Courtroom Deputy and DECRO have been instructed to cut off the taking of business cards 10 minutes prior to the scheduled time of the hearing in order to permit sufficient time for such information to be provided to Judge Wallace in a usable format.

Counsel who are not present at the time their matter is called risk having the matter heard and determined in their absence. If opposing counsel is present and consents, the matter will be transferred to second call.

Self-represented persons (also called "pro se litigants" or "persons who have chosen to represent themselves without an attorney") are subject to the same rules applicable to counsel. A self-represented person who does not have a card with his or her name imprinted on it should simply provide the Courtroom Deputy or DECRO with the correct spelling of his or her first and last names and the matter number on which he or she is appearing. When the matter number is called, please step forward, stand before the lectern and state your name so the Court knows you would like to be heard in the matter. (If you do not do this, the Court may not be aware that you are in the courtroom or would like to be heard).

If an attorney or self-represented person is unavoidably detained for reasons beyond his or her control (for example, a flat tire or accident), please call Claudia Lee (Judge Wallace's law clerk) at (714) 338-5471 to explain the circumstances and provide an estimated time of arrival.

B. Procedures for Disclosure Statement and Confirmation Hearings

PROCEDURES FOR DISCLOSURE STATEMENT AND CONFIRMATION HEARINGS

This outline of procedures is intended to assist counsel in preparing for Chapter 11 disclosure statement hearings and confirmation hearings before Judge Mark S. Wallace. These procedures are not inflexible. The Court may modify them to accommodate the needs of counsel and any particular Chapter 11 case.

1. Disclosure Statement Hearings

A plan should be filed separately from the disclosure statement. In addition, a copy of the plan should be attached to the disclosure statement as an exhibit.

Prior to the disclosure statement hearing the Court reviews each proposed disclosure statement (whether or not objections have been filed). Accordingly, counsel are requested to notify chambers by calling 714.338.5470 no later than 7 days prior to the scheduled hearing if the disclosure statement hearing will be continued.

The Court may present a checklist of deficiencies in the proposed disclosure statement at the disclosure statement hearing. Assuming no other objections have been filed and depending on the extent of the revisions required, the Court will either continue the disclosure statement hearing or allow conditional approval of the disclosure statement. When the Court has conditionally approved the disclosure statement, the plan proponent will need to file and serve an amended disclosure statement together with a proposed order approving the amended disclosure statement that conforms to Official Form 13.

If the plan proponent amends its proposed disclosure statement to correct for deficiencies noted by the Court or in response to objections that have been filed, a "red-lined" version and a clean, non-red-lined version of the amended disclosure statement both should be filed with the Court and served on opposing counsel no later than 7 days prior to the scheduled disclosure statement hearing. If the plan proponent will require a continuance to prepare the amended disclosure statement, it should notify opposing counsel and the Court not later than 7 days prior to the scheduled disclosure statement hearing. If objections cannot be resolved by stipulation and/or amendment of the proposed disclosure statement, the Court will consider any unresolved objections at the disclosure statement hearing.

Once a disclosure statement has been approved, the Court will schedule the confirmation hearing at the conclusion of the disclosure statement hearing. The plan proponent should prepare a proposed order approving the disclosure statement that conforms to Official Form 13 with the dates supplied by the Court at the disclosure statement hearing.

If any objections to a disclosure statement are filed, the Court *may* require counsel to appear in Santa Ana if the case in question is a Riverside Division case.

2. Confirmation Hearings

Prior to confirming any proposed plan of reorganization, the Court will require evidence of compliance with each requirement of 11 U.S.C. § 1129(a) and, when applicable, § 1129(b). Counsel are cautioned that the failure of a class to vote does not constitute acceptance of the plan. Bell Road Inv. Co. v. M. Long Arabians (In re M. Long Arabians), 103

B.R. 211, 215-16 (B.A.P. 9th Cir. 1989). A class must vote affirmatively to accept the plan. *See* In re Townco Realty, Inc., 81 B.R. 707, 708 (Bankr. S.D. Fla. 1987).

A completed tabulation of ballots should be filed by the plan proponent not later than 7 days prior to the confirmation hearing. If no objections to confirmation have been filed, the plan proponent should also file declarations in support of confirmation that address the elements of § 1129.

If objections to confirmation have been filed, the Court will either rule on the objections or treat the confirmation hearing as a scheduling conference. In the event the confirmation hearing is treated as a scheduling conference, the Court will establish a briefing schedule, if appropriate, and set a further evidentiary hearing during which live testimony may be presented.

If the objecting parties and the plan proponent so stipulate, the objections may be resolved based on written evidence and briefs filed with the Court prior to the confirmation hearing. The Court may also allow live testimony and cross-examination, time permitting, at the initial confirmation hearing upon stipulation of the parties.

If the case is a Riverside Division case, counsel and witnesses will be required to appear in Santa Ana and will not be permitted to appear telephonically or in Riverside by video.

C. Procedures Regarding Telephonic Appearances

PROCEDURES REGARDING TELEPHONIC APPEARANCES

Updated 1/31/2012

I. Prior Court Approval Required

A. Prior court approval of telephonic appearances is required for the following matters:

1) Sale Motion;
2) Cash Collateral Motion;
3) Chapter 11 Plan confirmation or Disclosure Statement approval or Chapter 13 Plan confirmation;
4) Motion for approval of Debtor-in-Possession Financing;
5) Evidentiary Hearings and Trials;
6) Status Conference;
7) Reaffirmation hearings; or
8) Any matter designated by the Court as requiring a personal appearance.

B. To obtain Court approval in order to appear telephonically, **no later than 3 court days prior** to the hearing send to Claudia_Lee@cacb.uscourts.gov an email entitled (subject line) "Telephonic Appearance Request" and containing all of the following:

1) Case name and bankruptcy case number (and adversary case number, if any);
2) Date and time of hearing;
3) Calendar number (or statement that such has not yet been assigned);
4) Reason telephonic appearance is sought; and
5) Contact information, including email address and telephone number.

The Law Clerk will advise whether your request has been approved. If your request is approved, you will be responsible for making the arrangements for the conference call using CourtCall (toll-free 888-882-6878; or 310-342-0888).

II. Prior Court Approval Not Required

A. Prior Court approval is not required for telephonic appearances in all matters other than those listed in Part I.A. Additionally, prior Court approval is not required if you will solely be monitoring a proceeding and do not intend to advance a position in a matter listed in Part I.A.

B. You must still notify the Court of your telephonic appearance, **no later than 3 court days prior to the hearing**, by sending to Claudia_Lee@cacb.uscourts.gov an email entitled "Telephonic Appearance Notification" and containing all of the following:

1) Case name and bankruptcy case number (and adversary case number, if any);
2) Date and time of hearing;
3) Calendar number (or statement that such has not yet been assigned);

4) Reason telephonic appearance is sought; and

5) Contact information, including email address and telephone number.

After you have received confirmation that the Court has noted your telephonic appearance, you must arrange for the conference call using CourtCall (toll-free 888-882-6878; or 310-342-0888).

III. Conduct During Telephonic Appearances

When appearing by phone, utilize your mute button to avoid interfering with other hearings in progress. Speaker phones are never allowed. No cell phones are allowed without a very good reason. **By appearing telephonically, you assume the risks of any and all technical problems that may occur during the call.**

D. Status Conference Procedures

STATUS CONFERENCE PROCEDURES

Updated 2/4/2011

A thorough, written status report, filed 14 days in advance, is required before each chapter 11 status conference and adversary status conference, unless one of the following is true:

1. The matter is an adversary proceeding and, prior to the date scheduled for the status conference, the parties have filed and the Court has entered an order approving a stipulation that resolves all issues raised by the adversary proceeding and provides either for dismissal of the action in its entirety or the entry of judgment in the action;

2. The matter is an adversary proceeding, defaults have been entered as against all defendants, and the plaintiff has filed and served a motion for default judgment prior to the date scheduled for the status conference;

3. The parties have filed and, prior to the date scheduled for the status conference, the Court has entered an order approving, a stipulation continuing the status conference to a later date (in which case a written status report must be filed not less than 10 court days in advance of the continued status conference date); or

4. The Court has expressly relieved the parties of the obligation to file a written status report.

In adversary proceedings, use of the court-approved forms is strongly recommended.

Please note also that, pursuant to Local Bankruptcy rule 7016-1(a)(3), if a defendant has not responded to the complaint or fails to cooperate in the preparation of a joint status report, the plaintiff is required to file a unilateral status report not less than 7 days before the date scheduled for the status conference, which report should include a declaration setting forth the attempts made by the plaintiff to contact or obtain the cooperation of the defendant in the preparation of a joint status report.

Unless one of the four exceptions outlined above applies, Judge Wallace expects parties to file full and complete status reports in a timely manner. Parties that fail to do so may be subject to sanction as may be warranted under the circumstances or allowed under Local Bankruptcy Rule 7016-1(f). Failure to appear for a status conference in an adversary proceeding may result in dismissal of the adversary proceeding for failure to prosecute, entry of judgment against the defaulting party either with respect to a specific issue or as to the entire proceeding, or such other sanctions as may be warranted under the circumstances or allowed under Local Bankruptcy Rule 7016-1(f).

Failure to Timely File Required Status Reports – Counsel/Parties Must Appear in Santa Ana

All required status reports in adversary proceedings and chapter 11 cases must be filed timely. Please carefully review all Central District Local Bankruptcy rules and all orders arising in adversary proceedings and chapter 11 cases for the timing, content and service of such status reports.

Any counsel or party required to file and serve a status report by a date certain pursuant to the Local Bankruptcy rules or by order of the Court, but fails to do so, must physically appear for hearing in Courtroom 6C at the United States Bankruptcy Court – Ronald Reagan Federal Building and Courthouse, 411 West Fourth Street, Santa Ana, CA 92701.

NOTE: Attorneys who timely file such a status report have the option to appear in either

(a) Courtroom 6C at the United States Bankruptcy Court, Central district of California – Ronald Reagan Federal Building and Courthouse, 411 West Fourth Street, Santa Ana 92701, or

(b) Video Courtroom 225 at the United States Bankruptcy Court, Central District of California – 3420 – 12th Street, Riverside, CA 92501.

E. Tentative Ruling Procedures

TENTATIVE RULING PROCEDURES

In most cases, Judge Wallace issues tentative rulings 24 to 48 hours prior to the date scheduled for a hearing. These rulings are generally available via the Court's webPACER service and appear on the calendars posted outside the courtroom and placed on counsel tables inside the courtroom.

Please note, however, that, notwithstanding the issuance of a tentative ruling, unless (1) Judge Wallace's chambers or calendar clerk has confirmed that no appearance is necessary or (2) the tentative ruling itself states that no appearance is necessary, **appearances are required**. A moving party's failure to attend the hearing on its motion will result in denial of the motion for failure to prosecute and may result in the issuance of an order to show cause re sanctions. An opposing party that fails to attend the hearing on a motion that it has opposed will be deemed to have withdrawn its opposition to the relief requested in the motion.

F. *Trial Procedures – Supplement to Local Rules*

TRIAL PROCEDURES OF JUDGE MARK S. WALLACE SUPPLEMENT TO LOCAL RULES

A. PRETRIAL CONFERENCE

The Court expects the parties to fully comply with LBR 7016-1(b), (c), (d) and (e).

The joint pretrial order must be lodged and served not less than 14 days before the date set for the pretrial conference. All parties must meet and confer at least 28 days before the date set for the pretrial conference for the purpose of preparing the joint pretrial order. If one party refuses to join in the preparation of a joint pretrial order, the other party may file a unilateral pretrial order as set forth in LBR 7016-1(e). (Such non-cooperation is highly discouraged and may lead to the Court dismissing the case for want of prosecution or striking the answer and entering a default). The contents of the pretrial order shall be as set forth in LBR 7016-1(b)(2).

At the pretrial conference the Court will set the trial date(s) and establish a schedule for the filing of trial briefs and the date for delivering a courtesy copy of exhibits to chambers.

B. TRIAL BRIEFS

Unless otherwise ordered by the Court, trial briefs are required and must be filed and served at least fourteen (14) calendar days before the first day of trial. A courtesy copy of the trial brief must be delivered to Judge Wallace' chambers on the same day the briefs are filed.

The trial briefs **must** contain:

(1) a concise statement of the facts of the case;

(2) a short statement of any relevant procedural history, including the resolution of all motions;

(3) a summary of the relevant law involved with supporting authorities;

(4) a summary of the disputed issues of fact and the testimony that such party plans to introduce in an effort to prove its version of the disputed facts; and

(5) a brief discussion of any anticipated evidentiary or other issues that the party believes are likely to arise at trial.

Unless specifically requested by the Court, no additional trial briefs will be considered.

C. EXHIBITS

It is critically important for trial exhibits to be precisely identified. Inevitably, this will require separate tagging of documents, and numbering of pages. In the absence of tagging and numbering, it may be difficult or impossible to determine where one exhibit ends and another begins. Additionally, it will often be necessary to address a witness's attention to a particular page of a particular exhibit (and hence the need for the consecutive numbering of pages).

For these reasons, parties are required to strictly comply with LBR 9070-1. Any failure to do so may result in an exhibit being excluded from evidence.

All parties presenting exhibits have the responsibility to tag their own exhibits well in advance of trial. Evidence tags may be obtained from the clerk's office or the courtroom deputy. The plaintiff's exhibits must be marked with numbers in increasing order. The defendant's exhibits must be marked with letters in alphabetical order.

At trial, each party must bring one original set of exhibits and at least four sets of copies: one for each counsel, one for the judge and one for the witness. All parties presenting exhibits must prepare an exhibit register on Form B 3024 "EXHIBIT REGISTER AND NOTICE RE DISPOSITION OF EXHIBITS" available at the Court's website, www.cacb.uscourts.gov under "Court Forms." Exhibits to be used for impeachment only need not be included.

A tabbed set of all exhibits must be delivered to Judge Wallace's chambers and to opposing counsel no later than fourteen (14) days prior to the first day of trial.

D. AUTHENTICATION OF TRIAL EXHIBITS

Each trial exhibit shall be authenticated by declaration, under penalty of perjury. Each such declaration shall be filed and served on opposing counsel (with a courtesy copy delivered to chambers) no later than fourteen (14) days prior to the first day of trial. Objections to the authentication of any exhibit shall be by a timely-filed motion in limine, as described below.

E. MOTIONS IN LIMINE

Any motion in limine shall be filed and served no later than seven (7) days prior to the first day of trial. Any party desiring to object on any ground to any trial exhibit must do so through motion in limine. Any objection to any trial exhibit not made by motion in limine shall be deemed waived (absent extraordinary circumstances). If an objection is made by motion in limine to a trial exhibit, the opposing party must make available for cross-examination at trial the declarant who authenticated such exhibit. A failure to do so is likely to result in the exhibit being excluded from evidence.

F. DIRECT TESTIMONY, CROSS-EXAMINATION, RE-DIRECT, ETC.

Direct testimony, cross-examination, re-direct, etc. shall be by live testimony. Any objection to a question or other matter must state the precise ground or grounds for the objection.

Hon. Gregg W. Zive

Bankruptcy Judge

Contact Information

U.S. Bankruptcy Court, Central District of California
Courtroom 1445
255 E. Temple Street, Suite 1452
Los Angeles, CA 90012
Courtroom Deputy: (213) 894-1485

Biographical Information

Appointments:

- Appointed U.S. Bankruptcy Judge for the District of Nevada, January 23, 1995; reappointed in 2009
- Chief Judge, U.S. Bankruptcy Judge for the District of Nevada, October 1, 1999 to September 30, 2008
- Chair of the Ninth Circuit Conference of Chief Bankruptcy Judges, October 2005 to September 2006

Education:

- University of Nevada, B.A., 1967
- University of Notre Dame Law School, magna cum laude, 1973

Career Record:

- Practiced as a general civil litigator, concentrating in the areas of commercial, contract, real property, and employment relations law

Professional Memberships:

- President of the National Conference of Bankruptcy Judges
- Fellow of The American College of Bankruptcy (inducted in 2005)
- Director of the American Bankruptcy Institute, since 2008
- Member of the Washoe County Bar Association (president, 1992-1993)
- Member of Nevada State-Federal Judicial Council
- Member of State Bar of Nevada Advisory Commission on Law Related Education
- Master Emeritus of the Bruce R. Thompson Chapter of the American Inns of Court
- Member of the Ninth Circuit Public Information & Community Outreach Committee and the Ninth Circuit Standing Committee on ADR

I. Judge Zive's Procedures and Practices

A. *Trial and Evidentiary Hearing Procedures*

TRIAL AND EVIDENTIARY HEARING PROCEDURES

During the week prior to a trial or evidentiary hearing, Judge Zive may move the starting date and time of a particular matter. Judge Zive's Courtroom Deputy, Sonny Milano, will advise parties of any such change by telephone. Parties are cautioned to be prepared to adjust their schedules accordingly. The first trial or evidentiary hearing of the week will begin promptly on Monday morning. Judge Zive will expect counsel and witnesses to be available on 2-3 hours telephonic notice for the remainder of the week.

BRIEFS

LBR Reference: Please comply with LBR 9013-2

Judge's Copy: Please comply with LBR 5005-2(d)
Please comply with Court Manual Sections 2-5(d), 3-5(b) and Appendix F

EXHIBITS

LBR Reference: Please comply with LBR 9070-1

Identification: Per LBR 9070-1(a)(2): Planitiff/movant and Defendant/respondent must submit a joint set of exhibits marked in numerical order.

Tags All parties presenting exhibits are responsible for tagging their own exhibits prior to the start of trial. Exhibit tags may be obtained from the Courtroom Deputy, Sonny Milano, in Room 940 or the court recorder prior to the trial.

# of Copies Please bring one original set for the court recorder and 4 sets of copies (1/each counsel, 1/judge, 1/witness)

Exhibit Register All parties presenting exhibits must prepare an exhibit register on Form B 3024 "EXHIBIT REGISTER AND NOTICE RE DISPOSITION OF EXHIBITS" available on the court's website at www.cacb.uscourts.gov., under "Court Forms."

Orders Orders that are capable of being lodged electronically shall be lodged with the original assigned judge via the Court's electronic Lodge Order Upload (LOU) system.

If you have further questions regarding Judge Zive's procedures please contact Sonny Milano @ 213.894.1485.

Hon. Vincent P. Zurzolo

Bankruptcy Judge

Contact Information

U.S. Bankruptcy Court, Central District of California
Courtroom 1368
255 E. Temple Street, Suite 1360
Los Angeles, CA 90012
Courtroom Deputy: (213) 894-5855

Biographical Information

Appointment(s):

- Appointed 04/18/88 by the United States Court of Appeals for the Ninth Circuit;
- Reappointed 04/18/02 by the United States Court of Appeals for the Ninth Circuit. (Current term expires 04/17/16.);
- Chief Judge, Bankruptcy Court, Central District of California, 2007-present.

Education:

- University of California, San Diego, 1978, B.A.;
- University of California, Davis, School of Law, 1982, J.D.

Professional Memberships:

- Los Angeles County Bar Association;
- National Conference of Bankruptcy Judges;
- State Bar of California.

I. Judge Zurzolo's Procedures and Practices

A. *How to Get Section 362 Orders Entered and Served Correctly and Quickly*

HOW TO GET SECTION 362 ORDERS ENTERED AND SERVED CORRECTLY AND QUICKLY

Effective July 1, 2008

These guidelines apply to orders on motions: (1) for relief from the automatic stay; (2) to impose the stay; or (3) to continue the stay ("Section 362 Orders"). The guidelines will add certainty to the process and minimize costs/delay by:

1) fully utilizing electronic processes of filing documents ("CM/ECF"), Lodged Order Upload ("LOU"), and service by Notice of Electronic Filing ("NEF");

2) eliminating or minimizing the need to provide envelopes and copies of orders;

3) establishing a process for resolving Section 362 motions by stipulation;

4) clarifying the court's duty to serve copies of orders; and

5) giving movant control of the timing of preparing proposed orders.

Complying with these guidelines will result in Section 362 Orders being entered and served correctly and quickly.

A. Check Tentative Rulings

Judge Zurzolo posts tentative rulings two court days prior to hearings. Check to see if relief will be granted without a hearing, and if so, what relief. Go to www.cacb.uscourts.gov. The Tentative Rulings link is on page one.

B. Lodge Proposed Orders via LOU

All CM/ECF users must lodge Section 362 Orders via LOU. No exceptions.

C. When Should a Proposed Order be Lodged?

Lodged via LOU – Proposed orders may be lodged via LOU after tentative rulings are posted; if a tentative ruling is not posted, lodge the proposed order after the hearing.

Lodged at Intake Window – Proposed orders may only be lodged after the hearing.

D. Are F 4001-1 Form Orders Mandatory?

MANDATORY – All Section 362 Orders must be prepared using a F 4001-1 order available at www.cacb.uscourts.gov under Local Bankruptcy Rules ("LBR") and Forms.

NOT MANDATORY – If LBR allow for a stipulation regarding the Section 362 Stay without filing a motion, a F 4001-1 order is not required. The stipulation must first be signed and filed via CM/ECF. Next, lodge a separate proposed order approving the stipulation.

E. What if the Motion is Settled by Stipulation?

Motions "Settled by Stipulation" require approval from counsel for debtor and movant. **NOTE: "/s/ followed by attorney's name"** ***may only be used by the attorney who lodges the proposed order.*** **DO NOT lodge orders with multiple "/s/ followed by attorney's name."** Therefore, before lodging a F 4001-1 order in which the "Settled by Stipulation" box on page one is checked, movant must first file via CM/ECF the signed Adequate Protection Attachment pages of the proposed order: (A) granting relief from the automatic stay (F 4001-10.PP or F 4001-10.RP); (B) imposing or continuing the stay (F 4001-10.IS); or (C) continuing the stay (F 4001-10.TCS). The process is:

1) obtain all necessary signatures on the Adequate Protection Attachment pages of the appropriate F 4001-1 form order;

2) file via CM/ECF the Adequate Protection Attachment pages **with signatures**, accompanied by a pleading cover sheet titled: "Stipulation for Adequate Protection re Section 362 Stay";

3) lodge the entire F 4001-1 order, **including the unsigned** Adequate Protection Attachment pages; and

4) when lodging the proposed order via LOU, link the proposed order to the motion, not to the stipulation.

F. How Soon Will the Order be Entered?

1. Orders on Unopposed Motions – Orders on unopposed motions will be entered as soon as the court reviews and approves the terms of the proposed order. Pursuant to LBR 9021-1(a)(6), there is no mandatory waiting period.

2. Orders on Opposed Motions – If all parties who filed an opposition to the motion sign off on the form of the proposed order, the order will be entered as soon as the court reviews and approves the terms of the proposed order. If all parties who filed an opposition to the motion do not sign off on the form of the proposed order, the court will wait seven court days for objections to be filed before reviewing and approving the terms of the order. *See* LBR 9021-1(a)(4)-(5).

G. Preparing Proof of Service of Proposed Order

**** SEE SAMPLE "PROOF OF SERVICE" -- MS WORD FORMAT ****

1. Proposed Orders on Unopposed Motions – There is no obligation to serve a proposed form of order on any person, entity, or attorney who did not file an opposition to the motion. This includes a case trustee or the United States trustee.

2. Proposed Orders on Opposed Motions – Pursuant to LBR 9021-1(a)(3), a proposed order must be served only upon any person, entity, or attorney who filed an opposition to the motion. There is no obligation to serve the proposed order on any other person or entity.

H. Prepare Service List for Notice of Entry of Order

**** SEE SAMPLE "SERVICE LIST FOR ENTERED ORDER" – MS WORD FORMAT ****

Categories for Service List: Pursuant to Fed. R. Bankr. Proc. 9022, the court has the duty to transmit a copy of an order only to the U.S. trustee, and to deliver notice of entry of an order only to contesting parties or as the court directs. Allowable service methods are in

Fed. R. Civ. Proc. Rule 5(b), and include service via NEF. Recognizing that a movant may wish for additional persons or entities to receive a copy of an entered order, and balancing this with limiting the court's duty to serve notice of entry of an order, please organize all service lists for notice of entry of orders using the ***three underlined categories*** identified below:

1. ***Court Service*** – At most include the debtor (and counsel, if any), U.S. Trustee (except Ch 13 cases), case trustee, and persons or entities (or their counsel, if any) who filed an opposition to the motion. **DO NOT** list any other person/entity, ***including other lien holders, co-borrowers, or persons/entities who merely filed a request for special notice.***

Served Electronically by the Court – List the names and email addresses of attorneys (*including movant's counsel*) who qualify under "Court Service" and are listed in CM/ECF on the Electronic Mail Notice List to receive NEF transmission. ***The U.S. Trustee and case trustee will always be in this category.***

Served via U.S. Mail by the Court – ***The debtor will always be in this category.*** Also list the names and mailing addresses of persons, entities, and/or attorneys (*including movant's counsel*) who qualify under "Court Service" but are not listed in CM/ECF on the Electronic Mail Notice List to receive NEF transmission. **DO NOT** list names that are served via NEF.

2. ***Movant Service*** – If Movant desires to serve a copy of the entered order on persons or entities not listed above, movant may do so. Movant must then file a proof of service.

To be Served by Movant After Order is Entered - List the names and service method for persons, entities, and/or attorneys who qualify under "Movant Service."

I. Copies of Proposed Order; Envelopes

All Section 362 Orders are served electronically by the court via NEF to trustees, the United States trustee, and to attorneys who are on the Electronic Mail Notice List for the particular bankruptcy case.

All Section 362 Orders are served by U.S. Mail via the Bankruptcy Noticing Center ("BNC") to debtor (and debtor's attorney, if any), and to persons or entities who are on the Manual Notice List for the particular bankruptcy case.

By using LOU and complying with these guidelines, it will rarely be necessary to send the court copies and envelopes for Section 362 Orders.

1. Copies of All Proposed Orders, Regardless of How Lodged

DO NOT provide any copies of the proposed order for mailing, because copies will be printed either by the BNC (for all relevant addresses on the Manual Notice List) or by the court (in the rare case when a contesting party's address is missing from the Manual Notice List).

ONLY SEND ONE COPY to the court along with the LOU receipt per the LOU procedures, and do so the same day that the proposed order is lodged.

2. *Stamped, Addressed Envelopes, Regardless of How Proposed Order is Lodged*

DO NOT provide envelopes for the debtor and debtor's attorney, because the BNC will prepare envelopes for them.

DO NOT provide envelopes for the case trustee or U.S. trustee, because they will be served electronically via NEF.

DO NOT provide envelopes for any other person or entity unless that person or entity filed an opposition to the motion and qualifies under "***Served via U.S. Mail by the Court.***"

B. Instructions for Filing First Status Report Regarding Consummation of Confirmed Plan

INSTRUCTIONS FOR FILING FIRST STATUS REPORT REGARDING CONSUMMATION OF CONFIRMED PLAN

Pursuant to 11 U.S.C. § 1142(a), I may require the Reorganized debtor to file with this court and serve upon the U.S. Trustee a FIRST STATUS REPORT REGARDING CONSUMMATION OF PLAN (the "Report"), supported by a declaration describing the actions taken by the reorganized Debtor advancing the consummation of the Plan. The Report shall include, as a minimum, the following information:

(1) A schedule of any real property, and its cost, acquired since confirmation of the Plan, and a schedule of each item of personal property acquired at a cost of more than $5,000.00 since confirmation of the Plan.

(2) A schedule of each debt and each class, listing the total amount the Plan required to be paid, the amount required to be paid to date, the amount actually paid to date, and the amount unpaid.

(3) A schedule of executory contracts entered into or assumed after plan confirmation.

(4) A statement indicating that post-petition taxes of every kind have been paid current, identifying each type of tax which has been paid and is current (*i.e.*, income, payroll, property, sales, etc.), or a detailed explanation of any and all delinquencies, by type of tax, and dollar amount.

(5) An estimate of the time for plan consummation and application for final decree.

(6) Any other pertinent information needed to explain the progress toward completion of the Plan.

If the Plan is fully consummated, the reorganized debtor, in lieu of filing and serving the Report, shall file and serve on United States Trustee and all creditors and parties in interest a MOTION FOR FINAL ORDER CLOSING THE CHAPTER 11 CASE, supported by a declaration, containing all actions taken to consummate the Plan including such things as claims paid, cash or property distributed or sold and the dates these actions were taken.

C. *Instructions for Pre-Trial Stipulation*

INSTRUCTIONS FOR PRE-TRIAL STIPULATIONS

When searching for items on the court's website, visit www.cacb.uscourts.gov.

Preface

The parties to an adversary proceeding must carefully read and comply with the following instructions ("PTS Instructions") for preparing a Pre-Trial Stipulation and an Order Approving Pre-Trial Stipulation. The PTS Instructions are intended to supplement, not supplant, the requirements contained in Local Bankruptcy Rule ("LBR") 7016-1(b). The Parties must also read LBR 7016-1 pertaining to pre-trial and trial procedures, 7030-1 pertaining to depositions, 9013-2 pertaining to trial briefs, 9070-1(a) pertaining to trial exhibits, and 5005-2(d) and Court Manual Appendix F re serving a Judge's Copy.

NOTICE TO PARTIES: Any Party that fails to explicitly follow the PTS Instructions may be subject to sanctions pursuant to LBR 1001-1(f) and 7016-1(f), and 11 U.S.C. § 105(a).

Required Papers to File or Lodge

1) A model Pre-Trial Stipulation ("Model Pretrial Stipulation") is separately posted on Judge Zurzolo's section of the court's website, and all Pre-Trial Stipulations filed with this Court must comport to the Model Pretrial Stipulation.

2) A model Order re: Pretrial Stipulation ("Model Order re: Pretrial Stipulation") is separately posted on on Judge Zurzolo's section of the court's website, and all such orders must comport to the Model Order re: Pretrial Stipulation.

Required Contents for the Pre-Trial Stipulation

3) Each Pre-Trial Stipulation must contain the following:

a) **Section I** – Underlying Issues of Fact Common to multiple Claims for Relief:

i) Only facts <u>fundamental</u> to the adversary proceeding should be included.

ii) Each fact should be stated in a separate paragraph.

iii) State whether each fact is contested or not contested. Please carefully consider whether facts identified as contested are truly contested. The Court carefully reviews whether the Parties' argument(s) and supporting evidence directly controvert the asserted fact.

iv) For each fact that is not contested, stating "not contested" is adequate. For each contested fact, in separate paragraphs provide a brief statement of each party's argument and supporting evidence including any admissions and proposed witnesses and exhibits.

v) No legal issues/assertions should be listed in this section.

b) **Section II** – Claims for Relief:

i) Elucidate each claim for relief and specify the elements which establish the claim.

ii) State whether each element of the claim for relief is contested or not contested. Please carefully consider whether an element identified as contested is truly contested. The Court carefully reviews whether the Parties' argument(s) and supporting evidence are relevant to the element being contested.

iii) For each element that is not contested, stating "not contested" is adequate.

iv) For each contested element, in separate paragraphs, provide a brief statement of each party's argument (including a brief citation of authority supporting the position) and supporting evidence including any admissions and proposed witnesses and exhibits.

c) **Section III** – Damages:

i) Plaintiff should specifically state damages claimed and how the damages are calculated.

ii) State whether the claim of damages is contested or not contested. Please consider that contesting liability does not require contesting damages, and vice versa.

iii) If damages are not contested, stating "not contested" is adequate.

iv) If contested, in separate paragraphs provide a brief statement of each party's argument and supporting evidence including any admissions and proposed witnesses and exhibits.

d) **Section IV** – Affirmative Defenses:

i) Elucidate each affirmative defense and specify the elements which establish the defense.

ii) State whether each element of the affirmative defense is contested or not contested.

iii) For each contested element, in separate paragraphs provide a brief statement of each party's argument (including a brief citation of authority supporting the position) and supporting evidence including any admissions and proposed witnesses and exhibits.

e) **Section V** – Exhibits:

i) The Parties must attach and state that their exhibits are listed and attached to the Pre-Trial Stipulation in the appropriate Appendix. Plaintiff's exhibits are to be indexed and attached in Appendix 1. Defendant's exhibits are to be indexed and attached in Appendix 2.

ii) Each Party must identify which exhibits are stipulated to be admitted at trial and which are subject to objection. The failure to object to the admission of exhibits listed on Appendices 1 and 2 shall be deemed a waiver of any objection.

iii) If there is a dispute as to the admissibility of either party's exhibits for any purpose which cannot be remedied, NOT an evidentiary objection which may be remedied at trial (such as lack of foundation) or which may only be determined at trial (such as relevance or hearsay where there may be a non-hearsay purpose for offering the evidence), the objecting party must file and serve a Motion to Exclude concurrently with the Pre-Trial Stipulation. See Section 3 below.

iv) Legible copies of each exhibit a party intends to use at trial must be attached to the Pre-Trial Stipulation unless the exhibit is to be used for impeachment purposes only.

v) If any party is attaching deposition transcripts as an exhibit, please be aware that the Court requires strict compliance with Local Bankruptcy Rule 7030-1(b).

f) **Section VI** – Witnesses to Be Offered by Each Party:

i) The Parties must use the language in Section VI of the Model Pretrial Stipulation.

ii) In the appropriate appendix, each party must list the witnesses which the party intends to call to testify at trial.

iii) For each witness listed, summarize the witness' anticipated testimony and estimate the time needed for the direct and cross examination of the witness. It is important to be as accurate as possible in estimating the time needed as that is what the Court uses to allocate the appropriate amount of trial time.

g) **Section VII** – Rebuttal Testimony and Stipulation:

i) The Parties must use the language in Section VII of the Model Pretrial Stipulation.

4) **Motions to Exclude**

a) As a general rule, motions to exclude evidence are only appropriate to object to patently inadmissible or prejudicial evidence.

b) If there is any dispute as to the admissibility of either party's evidence, the objecting party must file and serve concurrently with the Pre-Trial Stipulation a motion to exclude the subject evidence with a supporting memorandum of points and authorities.

c) Any response to the motion must be filed and served two court days prior to the pre-trial conference. All objections to admission of exhibits must be resolved at the pre-trial conference.

Settlement Instructions

5) If the Parties are considering settling or are in the process of settling, the following

instructions must be followed:

a) Unless a settlement is reached prior to the pre-trial conference date, a pre-trial stipulation must be timely filed and served. Failure to timely comply may result in sanctions.

b) A stipulation to continue of the pre-trial conference will rarely be granted if the reason for the continuance is that the parties are "discussing settlement" or "in the process of settling."

6) If the Parties have reached a settlement:

a) The pre-trial conference may be continued to allow for execution and filing the written settlement if the stipulation to continue contains a copy of the settlement or a substantial recitation of its terms.

b) The stipulation to continue must be filed at least two (2) court days prior to the pre-trial conference and a judge's copy delivered so that it arrives at the judge's chambers at least two (2) court days prior to the pre-trial conference.

7) If the adversary is based on 11 U.S.C. §523(c), then the settlement or stipulated judgment must contain an admission of liability under §523(a)(2), (4) or (6) on behalf of Defendant for it not to be treated as a reaffirmation agreement controlled by §524. If no admission is present, then the requirements of §524(c) and (d) must be followed.

Trial Instructions

8) Trial dates are firm and continuances at the parties' request are rarely granted.

9) The Court generally will contact counsel the week before the scheduled trial date to determine any revised trial estimate times. If the parties reach a settlement prior to trial, they must inform the Court promptly at (213) 894-3635. A written stipulation must be filed and a proposed order must be lodged at least two (2) court days prior to the trial date. A written settlement may be subject to review as discussed above in Paragraphs 4 and 5.

10) The Parties must comply with Local Bankruptcy Rule 9070-1(a) with respect to identifying and marking trial exhibits, preparing an exhibit register on the form available on the court's website under "Court Forms," and preparing and bringing to the trial adequate exhibit sets for all counsel and the witness. In most instances, the required number is three (3). As a complete copy of the exhibits is to be attached to the Pre-Trial Stipulation, no additional copy of the exhibits need be brought to trial for the Judge. If the exhibits are longer than ten (10) pages, they should be assembled in binders and tabbed (with exhibit numbers for the plaintiff and letters for the defendant). Exhibit tags may be obtained from either the calendar clerk in Room 941 of the Roybal Buidling (213-894-5855) or the court recorder prior to the trial.

11) All trial briefs must be filed and served not less than seven (7) days in advance of the trial date, with a Judge's Copy served by personal delivery or overnight mail to chambers to arrive not less than seven (7) days prior to the trial date.

12) Opening statements are permissible (but not required). Counsel should be prepared to complete closing arguments as soon as the parties have rested. Post-trial briefs are appropriate only if ordered by the Court.

13) Counsel are to instruct their witnesses to pause briefly before answering the question asked of them, to allow opposing counsel to object. Objections are signaled to the Court by standing prior to the witness' answer. In the event the witness begins the answer prior to counsel raising an objection, opposing counsel must wait until the witness is finished answering the question before standing and raising the objection.

D. Instructions for Telephoning Chambers

INSTRUCTIONS FOR TELEPHONING CHAMBERS

December 2010

The court is experiencing an unprecedented number of bankruptcy filings. Consequently it is not possible to answer every phone call, as this takes time away from processing orders and preparing for hearings. We are doing everything possible to process your orders and prepare for hearings in a timely manner. Delay is caused by us answering and returning phone calls regarding information (1) which may be readily obtained elsewhere or (2) which is inappropriate for the court to provide, such as what documents to file, when to file them, which rules apply, etc. Please do not place any calls asking for such information. It is inappropriate for the court to assist a party in obtaining relief against another party.

In light of the above, and in addition to the limitations imposed by Federal Rules of Bankruptcy Procedure Rule 9003, Judge Zurzolo has instructed his law clerks to limit telephone communications with the public. Please read these instructions carefully before you place a call to chambers, as we designed them to help you quickly obtain information you seek without waiting on a law clerk to call you back.

Thank you for your cooperation.

A. PHONE CALLS THAT WILL NOT BE RETURNED

Do not leave messages about any of the following items.

1) Status of Case or Result of Hearing: Judge Zurzolo has instructed us not to return calls asking about the status of a case or the result of a hearing. It is inappropriate for the court to provide explanations over the phone about what is going in a case or what happened at a hearing. Consult the CM/ECF docket, contact a party who participated in the case or hearing, or obtain an audio or written transcript of a proceeding. Instructions are posted on the court's website on the "Court Forms" page under the links "Audio Recording of Court Proceedings Order Form" or "Transcripts Order Form and Instructions."

2) Asking For Advice: Judge Zurzolo has instructed us not to return calls asking how to file or respond to pleadings, which procedures to follow, which rules apply, etc. The court cannot act as your attorney or co-counsel. Federal Rules and Code of Ethics/Conduct preclude us from answering such questions.

3) Inquiring if Hearing was Continued or to Avoid an Appearance: Do not call to see if a hearing was "taken off calendar." All hearings remain on the calendar, but some are vacated or continued.

A. Motion or Stipulation to Continue Hearing: Judge Zurzolo follows LBR 9013-1(m) which requires a stipulation or motion to continue a hearing to be filed (and a proposed ordered lodged) at least 3 days prior to a hearing. Attorneys who file electronically will receive email notification (NEF) of entry of the order. You may also wish to check the Tentative Rulings link 2 court days prior to a hearing to see if the hearing was vacated or continued, and if an appearance has been waived.

B. Stipulation Resolving a Motion or Adversary Proceeding: Judge Zurzolo requires compliance with LBR 9071-1, LBR 9013-1(k) and FRBP 7041, if applicable. On your stipulation and on your proposed order, PLEASE put the date of the next hearing or status conference that has been scheduled so that the court may prioritize review of your stipulation and post a tentative ruling or that your matter has been vacated. Proposed orders lacking a hearing date will be marked unused.

C. Serving a Judge's Copy of a Stipulation/Motion and Order Resolving a Hearing: The best way to insure your stipulation/motion is promptly ruled upon is to deliver a judge's copy to chambers. Please comply with LBR 5005-2(d) by using tabs for all exhibits and declarations, and stapling/binding the copy. Court Manual Appendix F indicates how to list the judge on the Proof of Service, and identifies delivery addresses for all judges in the Central District of California.

4) **Special Procedures and Required Forms for Judge Zurzolo:** If you are looking for any special procedures or required forms for Judge Zurzolo, such as a Joint Status Report or Pre-Trial Stipulation and Order, they are posted on his section of the website at www.cacb.uscourts.gov. If a special procedure is not provided, Judge Zurzolo requires compliance with applicable Local Bankruptcy Rules.

5) **LBR Forms, Avoiding Junior Lien:** See LBR forms for adversary proceedings to avoid a junior lien on debtor's residence (F4003-2.5. COMPLAINT, F 4003-2.5. DEFAULT. MOTION, and F4003-2.5.DEFAULT.JUDGMENT. When the adv. proc. is settled by stipulation, ***DO NOT USE*** F4003-2.4.ORDER. That form is used when a judge allows lien avoidance by motion instead of by adv. proc.

6) **Problems Filing or Lodging Documents:** If you have an issue with electronically filing or lodging a document, please call the CM/ECF Help desk at 213-894-2365. If you received an email about making an error on a docket, please contact Judge Zurzolo's courtroom deputy (Mrs. Johnson) at 213-894-5855.

B. PHONE CALLS THAT MUST BE MADE BY AN ATTORNEY WHO IS KNOWLEDGEABLE ABOUT THE CASE OR PROCEEDING, UNLESS SOMEONE IS NOT REPRESENTED BY AN ATTORNEY

1) **Status of Order:** Only a party who is not represented by an attorney, or an attorney who is knowledge about the bankruptcy case or adversary proceeding, may call about the status of an order. First, verify you have not received an email indicating the order was marked unused. Do not leave a message if you received an email. Court Manual Section 4 provides instructions on lodging proposed orders. If no rejection email was received, and at least 10 court days have elapsed since the order was lodged, you may leave a message stating the date the order was lodged, case or adversary proceeding number, name of the debtor, and a direct phone number at which you may be reached.

2) **Requesting Emergency or Shortened Notice Hearing:** Comply with LBR 9075-1, which provides:

A. Emergency Hearing: If you have a true emergency requiring a hearing on less than 48 hours notice under LBR 9075-1(a), please leave a message and a law clerk will call back to discuss the situation and determine if the court will set a hearing without the emergency motion being filed first.

B. Application for Order Setting Hearing on Shortened Notice: If you seek a hearing on shortened notice under LBR 9075-1(b), do not leave a message, as the papers must be filed first. This entails (1) filing the underlying motion, (2) filing LBR form F 9075-1.1.APPLICATION, and (3) lodging LBR form F 9075-1.2.ORDER. The Court will not act on the application until a judge's copy of all documents is delivered to chambers. Do not put a hearing date on the application or underlying motion. If the application is granted, the court will notify you of the hearing date and time and deliver to you a copy of the entered order containing deadlines to provide telephonic and written notice of the hearing.

C. PHONE CALLS THAT MAY BE MADE BY A NON-ATTORNEY

1) Placing Hearing on Second Call: If you are calling to place a matter on second call, please identify the calendar number of your matter by checking the tentative ruling calendar on the main page of the court's website, www.cacb.uscourts.gov. Please indicate how late the attorney will arrive, the reason for being late, and whether you've notified other attorneys who are appearing on the same matter.

2) Requesting Telephonic Appearance: If you are calling to request an appearance by telephone, Judge Zurzolo requires advance approval. Please read the judge's instructions on his section of the court's website, www.cacb.uscourts.gov.

E. Instructions for the Professional Compensation and Fee Budget

INSTRUCTIONS FOR THE PROFESSIONAL COMPENSATION AND FEE BUDGET

Professional providing services to a Chapter 11 debtor must comply with the following instructions in completing the Professional Compensation and Fee Budget.

1. A model budget is attached. All budgets submitted must contain the categories denoted in the model, but are not required to be in this model form. However, any other format used must be clear, concise, and adequately labeled. Although it is obviously difficult to predict and quantify every action taken in administration of a bankruptcy case, carefully contemplated estimates should be provided along with sufficient detail with respect to the activity code categories.

2. The information required to complete each category should be in compliance with the Office of the United States Trustee for the Central District of California's "Guide to Applications for Professional Compensation," December 2002 revision. Judge Zurzolo has supplemented those guidelines with regard to the following expenses:

a. In-house photocopying charges are limited to a maximum of $0.10/page.

b. Charges for transmitting facsimiles are not allowed. Only the actual long-distance telephone charge may be charged.

c. Charges for receipt of facsimile copies may not exceed $0.10/page.

3. A copy of the complete budget must be served attached to the status report as required by this Status Conference Order. In addition, a copy of the budget must be served upon the debtor prior to the status conference hearing date.

PROFESSIONAL COMPENSATION & REIMBURSEMENT BUDGET
for Chapter 11

Case Number: LA-99999-VZ
Case Name: Widget Manufacturing and Supply Company
Date Commenced: 11/01/95

Applicant Name: Mary O. Lawyer
Applicant firm: Lawyer, Lawyer & Lawyer (if applicable)
Location: Los Angeles, California

Type of Services to be Rendered: Bankruptcy Counsel for all matters except real estate transactions. Asset analysis/Recovery/Disposition; Case Administration; Claims; Litigation; Plan & Disclosure Statement; Financing.

Category: **Asset Recovery/Analysis/Disposition**

Professional

Name and/or Type	Hourly Rate ($/hr)	Total ($)
Mary Lawyer/Partner (P)	$200 (@ 15 hrs)	$3,000.00
John James/Paralegal (PL)	$75 (@ 30 hrs)	$2,250.00

Expenses & Costs: **Title Searches/UCC Reports $500**

Total for Category: **$5,750**

Category: **Litigation**

Professional

Name and/or Type	Hourly Rate ($/hr)	Total ($)
Mary Lawyer/P	$200 (@ 20 hrs)	$4,000.00
Stephen Associate/A	$125 (@ 80 hrs)	$10,000.00
Susan Professional/PL	$90 (@ 60 hrs)	$5,400.00

Expenses & Costs: **Anticipated Litigation Costs (filing/summons) - $2,500**

Trial preparation Costs (if not settled) - $8,000

Total for Category: **$29,900**

F. *Notice of Amended Standards to be Employed in the Review of Applications for Authorization of Employment of Professionals*

NOTICE OF AMENDED STANDARDS TO BE EMPLOYED IN THE REVIEW OF APPLICATIONS FOR AUTHORIZATION OF EMPLOYMENT OF PROFESSIONALS

In addition to the requirements of 11 U.S.C. Section 327 and Bankruptcy Rule 2014, and the standards set forth in the United States Trustee Guides, I shall apply the following standards in reviewing all applications for authorization of employment of professionals in bankruptcy cases over which I preside. Applications filed after June 1, 1990 must comply with these standards.

1. Contents of Application. The application must state:

a. the necessity for employment of the professional;

b. the reason for the selection of this particular professional. A copy of the resume of each professional who will provide services to the estate must accompany the application;

c. the specific description of services to be rendered by the professional;

d. the proposed arrangement for compensation of the professional; and

e. whether the professional has any connection with the debtor, debtor-in-possession, creditors of the estate, or any other party in interest.

I emphasize that specificity of description is necessary.

2. Fee and Expense Schedule. An exhibit to the application shall set forth:

a. the rates of compensation charged by the professional;

b. to the extent that the professional has established a rate of reimbursement for expenses, these rates shall also be disclosed.

Approval of the employment of the professional does not mean I approve the rates of compensation or reimbursement disclosed in the application. If you seek advance approval of these rates, you must state so in the application and include appropriate language in your proposed order.

3. Disclosure of Employment Agreement. A true and correct copy of any written agreement concerning the terms of employment and/or compensation between the professional and the applicant shall be attached to the application. If any oral or written modification of this agreement is made, it must be disclosed by the professional to the court and the United States Trustee. If you believe the employment agreement contains privileged material, you may by separate motion request an order allowing an *in camera* inspection of the agreement by the court.

4. Disclosure of Source of Payments. The applicant must disclose the identity of the source of payments to the professional, whether it be the debtor, the estate, or a third party.

5. Disclosure of Retainer. If the professional has received or is seeking to obtain a retainer or an advance fee payment, the applicant must disclose in the application the nature of the retainer or advance fee payment, e.g. an "earned upon receipt" retainer. You are referred to *In re Hathaway Ranch Partnership*, 116 B.R. 208 (Bkrtcy. C.D. Cal. 1990).

If you seek approval of an earned upon receipt retainer, you must provide evidence and argument sufficient to persuade the court that such approval is warranted.

If you have received an advance fee payment that must be maintained in a segregated trust account and you wish to draw upon that trust fund more frequently than every 120 days, you must request that relief in your employment application, support that request with evidence establishing that it is necessary and appropriate, and include pertinent language in your proposed order. Upon a proper showing, I will allow monthly draws on advance fee payments pursuant to Local Bankruptcy Rule 9013-1(g)(1)(N) with ten days notice.

If you seek to use the "Professional Fee Statement" procedure described in U.S. Trustee's Guides, you must meet the standards set forth in *In re Knudsen Corp.*, 84 B.R. 668 (9th Cir. BAP 1988).

The applicant must disclose whether the professional has received or will receive any lien or other interest in property of the debtor or of a third party to secure payment of the professional's fees.

6. **Conflicts of Interest.** The professional's declaration accompanying the application must expressly and specifically disclose:

a. Whether or not the applicant has a pre-petition claim against the estate and, if so, the amount of the claim;

b. Whether or not the professional has or had any connection with any insider of the debtor or any insider of an insider of the debtor; and

c. Whether or not the professional has represented, is representing, or intends to represent any related debtor in a bankruptcy case in this or any other court.

7. **Awareness of and Compliance With Applicable Law.** The professional must declare in the declaration accompanying the application that he, she, or it is familiar with the Bankruptcy Code, the Bankruptcy Rules, and the Local Bankruptcy Rules and shall comply with them.

8. **Trustee Employing Own Firm.** If a trustee seeks approval of the employment of his own law firm or accounting firm, the applicant must demonstrate with argument, supported by admissible evidence, that there is cause under 11 U.S.C. § 327(d).

9. **Real Estate Brokers and Salespersons.** Before compensation can be paid to a real estate broker or salesperson, court approval must be obtained pursuant to 11 U.S.C. § 330 or § 331.

Such approval may be obtained concurrently with approval of the broker's or salesperson's employment if: (1) the request is stated in the application and appropriate language is included in the proposed order; (2) the application is served upon any appointed committee, or if no committee has been appointed, upon all creditors with an interest in the subject property and the twenty largest unsecured creditors, exclusive of insiders as defined in 11 U.S.C. § 101(30); and it is demonstrated that the commission sought is reasonable.

G. *Notice of Standards to be Employed in the Review of Applications for the Allowance of Compensation and the Reimbursement of Expenses*

NOTICE OF STANDARDS TO BE EMPLOYED IN THE REVIEW OF APPLICATIONS FOR THE ALLOWANCE OF COMPENSATION AND THE REIMBURSEMENT OF EXPENSES

All applications for compensation and reimbursement must comply with 11 U.S.C. §§ 330 and 331, Bankruptcy Rules 2002(a)(6) and 2016, Local Bankruptcy Rules 9013-1(a) and 2016-1, and U.S. Trustee Guides.

These statutes, rules, and guides do not provide applicants with guidance on many issues. In fairness to applicants, I have prepared these standards so they may have adequate notice of my concerns. Please be aware of these standards in preparing your applications for compensation and reimbursement.

IF AN APPLICANT FAILS TO COMPLY WITH THESE STANDARDS, COMPENSATION AND/OR REIMBURSEMENT MAY BE DENIED UNTIL THERE IS COMPLIANCE.

The following standards shall apply to all applications filed after June 1, 1990.

USUALLY REIMBURSABLE EXPENSES

1. Postage;
2. Long distance telephone charges;
3. The cost of using messenger services;
4. Filing fees;
5. The actual cost of recurring telecopies of documents.

Each application should set forth the number of pages that were received by telecopier. I will not allow a reimbursement of more than ten cents per pages unless a declaration under penalty of perjury accompanies the application and demonstrates that the actual costs of receiving one page of a telecopied document exceeds ten cents. I will not allow reimbursement for the cost of transmitting a document by telecopier except for any long-distance phone charges. These phone charges should be described and listed with other long distance phone charges;

6. The actual cost of computer research services. The applicant should describe specifically what service was used, the per unit cost of the service, the number of time units used by applicant, and the total cost;

7. The actual cost of photocopying documents.

Each application should set forth the number of pages that were copies and the charge per page. I will not allow a reimbursement of more than ten cents per page unless a declaration under penalty of perjury accompanies the application and sets forth specific and convincing justification for a higher per page rate.

If an applicant requests a disproportionately large reimbursement for any of the forgoing items of expense, a specific and convincing explanation should be set forth in an accompanying declaration. If the applicant receives volume discounts or rebates on any costs for which applicant seeks reimbursement these discounts or rebates must be disclosed in the application.

EXPENSES USUALLY NOT REIMBURSABLE

1. Word processing.

2. Secretarial overtime.

3. Travel expenses for "first class" or other luxury transportation, unless an accompanying declaration states that:

   (a) an emergency existed;

   (b) what the emergency was; and

   (c) a lower fare was not available.

ALLOWANCE OF FEES

1. Fee rates must be comparable to those charged by similarly experienced and skilled professionals, with bankruptcy and non-bankruptcy practices, in the Central District of California. Upon review of any application for allowance of fees, the court may require the applicant to provide evidence that its rates are comparable to prevailing rates in the Central District of California.

2. Whenever an applicant's rates are changed while the case is pending, it is the applicant's duty to apprise the court of the change in the first fee application submitted after the change occurs. Compensation shall be allowed at the rate in effect when the services in question were provided.

FORM OF APPLICATIONS

A. The following information must be included at the beginning of each fee application before the narrative description of services:

(1) Name and location of applicant.

(2) Types of services rendered, i.e., general bankruptcy counsel, special litigation counsel, accountant for Chapter 7 trustee, etc..

(3) The date upon and the chapter in which the case was commenced and, if applicable, the date the case was converted to a different chapter.

(4) The date of entry of the order approving the applicant's employment and the date upon which the applicant's employment commenced.

(5) The date applicant filed his, her, or its last fee application.

(6) A summary of fees paid and costs reimbursed including the following:

   a. Amount of advance fee payment received.

   b. Amount of advance fee payment remaining.

c. Total amount actually paid pursuant to prior applications.

d. Total amount remaining to be paid pursuant to prior applications.

e. Total amount allowed yet reserved pending final fee application.

B. The narrative portion of the application must include the following:

(1) A description of the history and progress of the bankruptcy case in general. The amount of funds in the estate available to pay the fees and expenses. When seeking interim compensation in a Chapter 11 case, counsel for the debtor in possession should discuss prospects for reorganization and provide a specific time estimate for submission of the disclosure statement and plan. When seeking interim compensation in a Chapter 7 case, the trustee or counsel for the trustee must provide an estimate as to when the final report will be filed.

(2) The narrative portion of the application should also provide a description of services by subject matter, i.e., "obtaining approval of cash collateral," "fraudulent transfer litigation," etc. This portion of the narrative should concisely describe the different aspects of the services provided, the results achieved, the number of hours spent, and the amount of compensation being sought for the particular type of services.

(3) Each application should set forth the "blended rate" of the applicant. This is the average hourly rate for all of applicant's personnel who performed services described in the fee application.

H. Pre-Status Conference Instructions and Status Report Format

PRE-STATUS CONFERENCE INSTRUCTIONS

1. Pursuant to Local Bankruptcy Rule 7016-1(a)(2), all parties shall file a Joint Status Report at least fourteen (14) days before the date set for each Status Conference. The Joint Status Report shall conform to **Exhibit "A"** attached to these instructions. Use of the form attached as **Exhibit "A"** is mandatory. Failure to use the form in **Exhibit "A"** may result in the imposition of monetary sanctions and/or the status conference being continued and parties being ordered to redo the status report to conform to **Exhibit "A."**

2. A copy of these instructions shall be attached to every copy of the complaint served upon a party, and the affidavit of service must state that these instructions as well as a copy of the summons and complaint and, if applicable, a copy of the Debtor Assistance Program Notice was served.

3. If no response to the complaint is timely filed, (1) plaintiff should file a request for entry of default by the clerk and a default judgment hearing date will be set at the Status Conference (the party should be prepared to propose an appropriate date to Judge Zurzolo based on Judge Zurzolo's self-calendaring procedure) and (2) no later than ten (10) days prior to the Status Conference plaintiff must file a Unilateral Status Report (completing Sections A, B and C of **Exhibit "A"**) and a declaration setting forth the attempts made by plaintiff to contact or obtain the cooperation of the defendant as required by LBR7016 1(a). For self calendaring dates, visit the Court's website at www.cacb.uscourts.gov :

- Click "**Information**"
- Under "**Judges**," click "**Zurzolo, V.**"
- Click "**Forms/Instructions/Procedures/Self-Calendaring**"
- Under "**Self Calendaring**," click "**Hearing Calendar for 2006"** and/or "**Instructions and Key for Self-Calendar**"

4. During the Status Conference, it will be decided whether a pre-trial order should be required or a pre-trial conference should be set.

5. During the Status Conference, the Court shall set a trial or a pre-trial conference. The parties should be prepared to state whether they will agree to try the adversary proceeding by declaration in lieu of oral testimony.

6. If one or more parties dispute whether the adversary proceeding is core within the meaning of 28 U.S.C. § 157(b), the party/parties disputing that the proceeding is core shall file and serve a memorandum of points and authorities and evidence in support of their positions fourteen (14) court days before the Status Conference. Any reply must be filed at least seven (7) court days before the Status Conference.

The Court will resolve this dispute at the Status Conference. If any party fails to comply timely with these instructions, that failure shall be deemed a consent to a determination that the proceeding is core within the meaning of 28 U.S.C. § 157(b).

7. If one or more parties dispute the jurisdiction of this Court, the party/parties disputing jurisdiction shall file and serve a memorandum of points and authorities and evidence in support of their positions at least fourteen (14) court days prior to the Status

Conference. Any response shall be filed and served no later than seven (7) court days prior to the Status Conference. The Court will resolve this dispute at the Status Conference. If the objecting party does not timely file and serve its papers, that failure shall be deemed a consent to whatever determination the Court makes.

8. If one or more parties dispute whether a party has a right to a jury trial, the disputing party/parties shall file and serve a memorandum of points and authorities and evidence in support of their positions at least fourteen (14) court days prior to the Status Conference. Any response shall be filed and served no later than seven (7) court days prior to the Status Conference. The Court will resolve this dispute at the Status Conference. If the objecting party does not timely file and serve its papers, that failure shall be deemed a consent to whatever determination the Court makes.

9. Please take note that extensions of time to respond to a pleading are ineffective by stipulation of the parties absent court approval. Requests to extend the response deadline to a date within five (5) days of the hearing date will likely be denied unless the hearing date is continued to a date which permits the Court adequate time to review and consider the pleadings.

10. Please also take note that requests to continue a hearing will not be granted unless adequate cause for the continuance is stated in the request. Merely discussing settlement is inadequate cause and unless a settlement is reached prior to the hearing date, the parties must comply with all applicable filing deadlines. If the parties have settled, a hearing may be continued to allow for execution and filing of the written settlement if (1) the request for continuance contains a copy of the settlement or a substantial recitation of its terms and (2) the request for a continuance is filed at least two (2) court days prior to the hearing date. Generally, if a Respondent/Defendant is not represented by an attorney, an appearance by the Respondent/Defendant will be required.

EXHIBIT "A"

IN THE UNITED STATES BANKRUPTCY COURT
FOR THE CENTRAL DISTRICT OF CALIFORNIA

In re	)	BK. No. LA ___________
	)	Adv. No. LA ___________
Debtor(s).	)	Chapter ____
______________________________	)	
	)	□ **JOINT STATUS REPORT**
Plaintiff(s),	)	□ **UNILATERAL STATUS REPORT FOR**
v.	)	**ADVERSARY PROCEEDING**
Defendant(s).	)	**LOCAL BANKRUPTCY RULE 7016-1(a)(2)**
______________________________	)	
		DATE: ___________
		TIME: ___________
		PLACE: ___________

TO THE HONORABLE UNITED STATES BANKRUPTCY JUDGE _________________. In accordance with Local Bankruptcy Rule ("LBR") 7016-1(a)(2), the party/parties submit the following G JOINT STATUS REPORT or G UNILATERAL STATUS REPORT:

A. SERVICE/SUMMONS

1. Have all parties been served? □ YES □ NO

2. Has Plaintiff filed a declaration of service stating that the Pre-Status Conference Instructions, summons, complaint and, if applicable, Debtor Assistance Program Notice was served? □ YES □ NO

If yes, go on. If no, why not? Please explain: _________________________.

B. RESPONSIVE PLEADINGS

1. Did all defendants timely file a plain answer (i.e. no counterclaims) to the complaint? □ YES □ NO

If yes, go to Section D. If no responsive pleading was filed proceed to Section C, otherwise continue.

2. If any defendant's answer includes counterclaims, are any parties other than Plaintiff included as defendants to the claims? □ YES □ NO

3. If counterclaims have been filed, have all counter-defendants responded to the counterclaims? □ YES □ NO

If no, what is the response deadline to the counter-complaint?

4. Did any defendant filed a 12(b) motion or other such responsive pleading?

□ YES □ NO

If yes, please identify the responsive pleading(s) filed and the date(s) of the hearing(s) on the responsive pleading(s): ______________________________.

C. DEFAULT

1. If any defendant has not responded timely, has plaintiff requested entry of default? □ YES □ NO

If no, why not? Please explain: ___________________.

2. If default has been requested, has it been entered? □ YES □ NO

If no, why not? Please explain: ___________________________.

3. If default has been entered has plaintiff scheduled a motion for default judgment? □ YES □ NO

If no, please explain why not and state a proposed date for a hearing on a motion for default judgment: ________________________________.

D. FEDERAL RULE OF CIVIL PROCEDURE ("FRCP") 26(A), (F) AND LBR 7016-1(A)(2) COMPLIANCE

1. The parties certify that they met and discussed the nature and basis of the claims and defenses.

Plaintiff: □ YES □ NO

Defendant: □ YES □ NO

2. The parties certify that they have exchanged documents.

Plaintiff: □ YES □ NO

Defendant: □ YES □ NO

3. The parties certify that they have exchanged witness lists.

Plaintiff: □ YES □ NO

Defendant: □ YES □ NO

4. The parties certify that they have exchanged other evidence as required by Rule 26(a)(1).

Plaintiff: □ YES □ NO

Defendant: □ YES □ NO

5. The parties certify that they have made the disclosures required by Rule 26(a)(1)(C) and (D) where applicable.

Plaintiff: □ YES □ NO

Defendant: □ YES □ NO

6. The parties certify that they have discussed settlement.

Plaintiff: □ YES □ NO

Defendant: □ YES □ NO

7. The parties certify that they have proposed a joint discovery plan.

Plaintiff: □ YES □ NO

Defendant: □ YES □ NO

8. If any party answered no to any of the prior six (6) questions, please explain the reason(s): ________________________________.

E. DISCOVERY (FRCP 26(f))

A Discovery Plan should be prepared and attached to this status report if it cannot be described below.

1. Do the parties believe that changes should be made in the timing, form or requirement for disclosures under Rule 26(a)?

Plaintiff: □ YES □ NO

Defendant: □ YES □ NO

If any party answered yes, please explain the reason(s): ____________________.

2. List the form(s) of discovery each party will propound.

Plaintiff: ________________________.

Defendant: ________________________.

3. Do the parties anticipate any unusual discovery issues?

Plaintiff: □ YES □ NO

Defendant: □ YES □ NO

If any party answered yes, please identify the issues and explain the reason(s) for them: ____________________________.

4. Date by which each party expects to complete their discovery efforts:

Plaintiff: ___________.

Defendant: ____________.

F. SETTLEMENT

1. Do all parties request a judge to aid in settlement? If either party indicates "no," go to question 3.

Plaintiff: □ YES □ NO

Defendant: □ YES □ NO

2. Do all parties request the trial judge to aid in settlement? If yes and if applicable, please name the judge(s) of this Court that the parties would like to participate in settlement efforts:

PLAINTIFF □ YES □ NO	**DEFENDANT** □ YES □ NO
(1)	(1)
(2)	(2)
(3)	(3)

3. Do all parties seek any other type of mediation, arbitration, etc.? If both

indicate yes, list the types.

PLAINTIFF □ YES □ NO	**DEFENDANT** □ YES □ NO
(1)	(1)
(2)	(2)

G. PRE-TRIAL

In most adversary proceedings, it is necessary to prepare a joint pre-trial stipulation and appear at a pre-trial conference.

1. Date after which the pre-trial conference should be set:

   Plaintiff: _________.

   Defendant: ___________.

2. Do you believe you can go directly to trial without a pre-trial stipulation and/or conference?

   Plaintiff: □ YES □ NO

   Defendant: □ YES □ NO

If either party answered yes, please state why: _________________.

H. OTHER PROPOSED DEADLINES

1. Proposed date by which all motions except motions to exclude evidence or approve a settlement must be filed, set and heard:

   Plaintiff: ______________.

   Defendant: _______________.

2. Proposed deadline for amendment of pleadings and/or joinder of parties (any order permitting amendment or joinder must be entered by this date):

   Plaintiff: __________.

   Defendant: ___________.

3. Are there any other deadlines which the parties wish the Court to set:

   Plaintiff: □ YES □ NO

   Defendant: □ YES □ NO

If either party states yes, please identify the proposed subject and timing of the deadline: _____________________________.

I. MISCELLANEOUS

1. Do you dispute the jurisdiction of this Court?

   Plaintiff: □ YES □ NO

   Defendant: □ YES □ NO

2. Do you dispute any party's allegation regarding the core/non-core nature of the adversary proceeding?

Plaintiff: □ YES □ NO

Defendant: □ YES □ NO

3. Do you dispute the asserted claim of any party to the right to a jury trial?

Plaintiff: □ YES □ NO

Defendant: □ YES □ NO

4. If a party answered yes to any of the above three (3) questions, has the party answering yes prepared a memorandum of points and authorities and supporting evidence detailing their position, which memorandum is to be filed fourteen (14) days prior to the Status Conference? □ YES □ NO

5. Are there any other unusual issues of which the Court should be aware? □ YES □ NO

If yes, please explain: ___________________________.

Respectfully submitted,

DATED: _______________

FIRM NAME:_________________
NAME: ______________________
ATTORNEY FOR:_____________

DATED: _______________

FIRM NAME:_________________
NAME: ______________________
ATTORNEY FOR:_____________

I. *Procedure for Authorizing Repossession of Residential Premises Without a Hearing*

PROCEDURE FOR AUTHORIZING REPOSSESSION OF RESIDENTIAL PREMISES WITHOUT A HEARING IS *NO LONGER AVAILABLE*

(Effective September 1, 2011)

Effective **September 1, 2011**, Judge Zurzolo's procedure for obtaining an order authorizing repossession of residential premises without a hearing is no longer available.

Please schedule these types of motions on a Tuesday @ 9:30 a.m. A calendar of available Tuesdays is posted on Judge Zurzolo's section of the court's website@ www.cacb.uscourts.gov.

Please use LBR form motion F 4001-1M.UD and LBR form order F 4001-1O.UD.

If a creditor seeks to obtain a hearing on shortened notice for a relief from stay motion to pursue an unlawful detainer action, the creditor must use the procedure set forth in Local Bankruptcy Rule 9075-1(b). **Please note that cause for setting a hearing on shortened notice does not exist merely because the creditor has a pending unlawful detainer action in state court.**

J. Procedure for Requesting and Making Telephonic Appearance

PROCEDURE FOR REQUESTING AND MAKING TELEPHONIC APPEARANCE

Updated 7-9-2009

Judge Zurzolo approves some requests for telephonic appearances at hearings and status conferences. He **does not approve** telephonic appearances for: (1) pre-trial conferences; (2) chapter 13 plan confirmation hearings; (3) chapter 13 miscellaneous hearings; or (4) attorneys who have not filed papers in connection with the hearing/status conference. Please follow the guidelines below:

I. Check Tentative Rulings

It is possible that a matter has been posted "no appearance required." Please check the "**Tentative Rulings**" link on the main page of the court's website at www.cacb.uscourts.gov.

Monday Chapter 13 Confirmation & Miscellaneous matters – no tentative rulings.

Tuesday hearings – tentative rulings are posted the prior Thursday or Friday.

Thursday hearings/status conferences – tentative rulings are posted the prior Tuesday.

II. Advance Request

At least 2 full court days prior to a hearing or status conference, contact Judge Zurzolo's law clerk (213-894-3721 or 213-894-3755). Please provide the following information:

- Confirm that you have read all of these procedures
- Identify type of paper filed for this matter (e.g. motion, opposition, joint status report, etc.)
- Date and time of hearing/status conference
- Name & BK case number of Debtor, and Adversary Proceeding number (if applicable)
- Name & phone # of attorney requesting appearance.
- Confirmation that the attorney is either admitted to practice in the Central District of California or has received court approval to appear *pro hac vice.*
- Name of client
- Specific reason(s) for request (location, unavoidable scheduling, emergency, etc.)

A clerk will promptly call back to provide notice of Judge Zurzolo's decision.

III. Conditions for Approval

If **only one attorney is approved** for a specific time, that attorney has the choice to call the chambers line directly or via Court Call on the day of the hearing/status conference.

If **more than one attorney** is approved for a specific time, all approved attorneys must call together on one line, as there is only one phone line available in the courtroom. The first attorney approved has the choice of calling chambers directly via conference call, or having all approved attorneys use a pay service. All attorneys approved must cooperate to place the call.

IV. Making the Telephonic Appearance on the Day of the Hearing/Status Conference

TIME – Call 10 minutes prior to the hearing/status conference (213-894-3755).

METHOD – Call on a regular land-line. Absolutely no cell phones or speaker phones.

K. Procedures Regarding Trials and Evidentiary Hearings

TRIALS AND EVIDENTIARY HEARINGS

If these instructions are not followed explicitly, sanctions may be imposed.

A. BRIEFS

LBR Reference

- Please comply with LBR **9013-2**

Judge's Copy

- Please comply with LBR 5005-2(d)
- Please comply with Court Manual Sections 2-5(d), 3-5(b) and Appendix F

B. EXHIBITS

LBR Reference

- Please comply with LBR **9070-1**

Identification

- Per LBR 9070-1(a)(2):
  - Numbers: plaintiff/movant's exhibits must be marked with numbers in increasing order
  - Letters: defendant/respondent's exhibits must be marked with letters in alphabetical order.

Tags

- All parties presenting exhibits have the responsibility to tag their own exhibits prior to the start of trial. Exhibit tags may be obtained from the courtroom deputy in Room 941 or the court recorder prior to the trial.

 # Copies

- Please bring **one original set** (court recorder)
- Please bring **at least 4 sets of copies** (1/each counsel, 1/judge, 1/witness)

Exhibit Register

- All parties presenting exhibits must prepare an exhibit register on Form B-3024 "EXHIBIT REGISTER AND NOTICE RE DISPOSITION OF EXHIBITS" available on the court's website, www.cacb.uscourts.gov, under "Court Forms."

L. Requirement of Individual Chapter 11 Debtors to Use Local Bankruptcy Rules Forms

REQUIREMENT OF INDIVIDUAL CHAPTER 11 DEBTORS TO USE LOCAL BANKRUPTCY RULES FORMS

Effective **August 1, 2011**, use of the following LBR Forms in individual chapter 11 cases is **mandatory**:

- F 2081-1.DISCLSR.STMT - Individual Debtor's Disclosure Statement in Support of Plan of Reorganization;
- F 2081-1.PLAN - Individual Debtor's Chapter 11 Plan of Reorganization;
- F 2081-1.1.MOTION.CASH.COLLATERAL - Notice of Motion and Motion in Individual Chapter 11 Case for Order Authorizing Interim Use of Cash Collateral [11 U.S.C. § 363];
- F 2081-1.1.ORDER.CASH.COLLATERAL - Order Re: Notice of Motion and Motion in Individual Chapter 11 Case for Order Authorizing Interim Use of Cash Collateral [11 U.S.C. § 363];
- F 2081-1.2.MOTION.BUDGET - Notice of Motion and Motion in Individual Chapter 11 Case for Order Setting Budget for Interim Use of Estate Property as Defined in 11 U.S.C. § 1115;
- F 2081-1.2.ORDER.BUDGET - Order Re: Notice of Motion and Motion in Individual Chapter 11 Case for Order Pursuant to 11 U.S.C. § 363(b) Setting Budget for Interim Use of Estate Property as Defined in 11 U.S.C. § 1115;
- F 2081-1.3.MOTION.PAYROLL - Notice of Motion and Motion in Individual Chapter 11 Case for Order Authorizing Payment of Prepetition Payroll and to Honor Prepetition Employment Procedures: LBR 2081-1(a)(6); and
- F 2081-1.3.ORDER.PAYROLL - Order Authorizing Payment of Prepetition Payroll and to Honor Prepetition Employment Procedures: LBR 2081-1(a)(6).

These forms may be found on the Court's website, www.cacb.uscourts.gov, by clicking on "Forms/Rules/General Orders," then "Local Bankruptcy Rules & Forms" and scrolling down to the appropriate form.

After August 1, 2011, if an individual chapter 11 debtor does not use these forms, the matter will not be set for hearing and/or the order will not be signed.